LATYMER

Prize for Excellence

awarded to

Duncan Littlejohns

_____ Head

TOP 10
OF EVERYTHING
2004

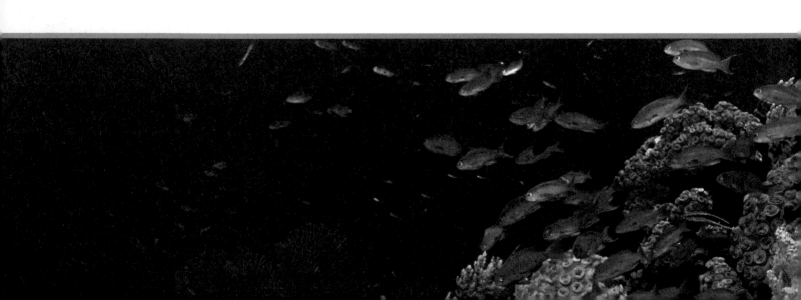

TOP 10

OF EVERYTHING
2004
RUSSELL ASH

Contents

LONDON, NEW YORK, MUNICH, MELBOURNE, DELHI
A PENGUIN COMPANY

Senior Editor Nicki Lampon
Senior Art Editor Kevin Ryan
DTP Designer Rajen Shah
Production Controller Heather Hughes

Managing Editor Adèle Hayward
Managing Art Editor Karen Self
Category Publisher Stephanie Jackson

Produced for Dorling Kindersley by
The Bridgewater Book Company,
The Old Candlemakers, West Street,
Lewes, East Sussex BN7 2NZ

Editor Hazel Songhurst
Designer Lisa McCormick

Author's Project Manager Aylla Macphail

Published in Great Britain in 2003 by
Dorling Kindersley Limited, 80 Strand,
London WC2R 0RL

2 4 6 8 10 9 7 5 3 1

A CIP catalogue record of this book is available from
the British Library.

ISBN 14053 0052 3

Reproduction by Colourscan, Singapore
Printed and bound by GGP Media GmbH, Germany

See our complete catalogue at
www.dk.com

Contents

Introduction

ACCORDING TO HISTORIAN Edward Creasy, there were Fifteen Decisive Battles of the World. The planet Uranus has 15 moons, while in *Treasure Island* there are "15 Men on a Dead Man's Chest". Now, with the publication of this book, there have been 15 editions of *The Top 10 of Everything*. It's all too easy to slip into this list-geared mode, since we are constantly assailed with lists: from the 100 Greatest Film Stars and the FBI's 10 Most Wanted to the bestselling DVDs and the most-visited Internet sites, lists have become a part of our world view.

A SENSE OF PERSPECTIVE

One function of *The Top 10 of Everything* is to distil down a wealth of data by drawing together a diversity of quantitative superlatives. They are not anyone's "10 bests" (which are qualitative judgements), but there are some "10 worsts" in the case of accidents and disasters, since, sadly, these can be gauged by numbers of victims. The only "bests" are bestsellers, because sales can be measured. There are the results of major polls and also some "firsts" and "latests", which recognize pioneers, most recent achievers, and award-winners.

SOURCE MATERIAL

My data sources include "official" and government departments, from the United Nations and sports governing bodies to commercial organizations and research groups, every one of whom has granted me privileged access to their databases. Among the most rewarding sources of all are the private individuals who are specialists in everything from poisonous creatures to the world's tallest buildings, and who have been generous enough to share with me the results of their researches.

AS TIME GOES BY...

Entry-levels for Top 10 lists have changed, often dramatically, over the 15 annual publications of *The Top 10 of Everything*: the richest American of 15 years ago had a mere $6.7 billion, while Bill Gates is today more than six times wealthier. We have ever-bigger cruise liners, spiralling transfer fees for sporting superstars, and increasing levels of worldwide box office income – the criterion on which the film lists are mostly based – which means that *Star Wars*, the highest-earning film in 1990, is now ranked tenth.

A COMEDY OF ERRORS

I endeavour to ensure that the information in *The Top 10 of Everything* is as up to date and as accurate as possible, but arguments continue to rage over the precise lengths of rivers, how many copies of the Bible have ever been sold, how fast a bee flies, and so on, and just as other sources disagree with each other, some may disagree with me. But then at least I don't claim – as certain respected reference books have – that Mt. Pico in the Azores is 20,639 m (67,713 ft) high (more than twice the height of Everest), that Iceland has 1,754 tractors per hectare (hence a total of 180 billion tractors), or that Manila has a population of 21 people per square foot…

KEEP IN CONTACT

Do please send me your comments and any corrections or ideas for new lists by writing to me c/o the publishers or by e-mailing me direct at ash@pavilion.co.uk

Other Dorling Kindersley books by Russell Ash:
The Factastic Book of 1,001 Lists
The Factastic Book of Comparisons
Great Wonders of the World
The Top 10 of Sport (with Ian Morrison)
The Top 10 of Film

SPECIAL FEATURES

- Over 700 lists on everything under – and beyond – the Sun

- Completely updated with many innovative lists, from pop star film debuts and films from song titles, to the strongest men and the most valuable comics

- "First Fact" features throughout on such diverse subjects as the first in-flight wedding and the first million-selling soundtrack album to the first computer games and the first 200 mph car

- Further Information – a valuable guide to the Top 10 websites to explore for each of the principal themes in *The Top 10 of Everything*

THE UNIVERSE
& THE EARTH

Heavenly Bodies

TOP 10 COMETS COMING CLOSEST TO THE EARTH

	COMET	DATE*	(AU)#	DISTANCE (KM)	(MILES)
1	Comet of 1491	20 Feb 1491	0.0094	1,406,220	873,784
2	Lexell	1 July 1770	0.0151	2,258,928	1,403,633
3	Tempel-Tuttle	26 Oct 1366	0.0229	3,425,791	2,128,688
4	IRAS-Araki-Alcock	11 May 1983	0.0313	4,682,413	2,909,516
5	Halley	10 Apr 837	0.0334	4,996,569	3,104,724
6	Biela	9 Dec 1805	0.0366	5,475,282	3,402,182
7	Grischow	8 Feb 1743	0.0390	5,834,317	3,625,276
8	Pons-Winnecke	26 June 1927	0.0394	5,894,156	3,662,458
9	Comet of 1014	24 Feb 1014	0.0407	6,088,633	3,783,301
10	La Hire	20 Apr 1702	0.0437	6,537,427	4,062,168

* Of closest approach to the Earth

Astronomical Units: 1 AU = mean distance from the Earth to the Sun
(149,597,870 km/92,955,793 miles)

TOP 10 LARGEST METEORITES EVER FOUND

	LOCATION	ESTIMATED WEIGHT (TONNES)
1	Hoba West, Grootfontein, Namibia	more than 60.0
2	Ahnighito ("The Tent"), Cape York, West Greenland	57.3
3	Campo del Cielo, Argentina	41.4
4	Canyon Diablo*, Arizona, USA	30.0
5	Sikhote-Alin, Russia	27.0
6	Chupaderos, Mexico	24.2
7	Bacuberito, Mexico	22.0
8	Armanty, Western Mongolia	20.0
9	Mundrabilla#, Western Australia	17.0
10	Mbosi, Tanzania	16.0

* Formed meteor crater; fragmented; total in public collections is around 11.5 tonnes

In two parts

ASTEROID DISCOVERED!

FIRST FACT

ON NEW YEAR'S DAY, 1801, at the observatory at Palermo, Sicily, Giuseppe Piazzi (1746–1826), a monk, astronomer, and professor of mathematics, was working on what was later published as a catalogue of 7,646 stars when he observed an object in the constellation of Taurus. Having recorded its location, he noted over the next six weeks that it had moved, thus demonstrating the existence of asteroids – rocks orbiting between Mars and Jupiter. Named Ceres, the asteroid has been examined by the Hubble Space Telescope, and NASA's *Dawn* mission, scheduled launch in 2006, will make a close study of Ceres in 2014.

TOP 10 LARGEST ASTEROIDS

	ASTEROID	YEAR DISCOVERED	DIAMETER (KM)	(MILES)
1	Ceres	1801	936	582
2	Pallas	1802	607	377
3	Vesta	1807	519	322
4	Hygeia	1849	450	279
5	Euphrosyne	1854	370	229
6	Interamnia	1910	349	217
7	Davida	1903	322	200
8	Cybele	1861	308	192
9	Europa	1858	288	179
10	Patientia	1899	275	171

NASA's NEO (Near Earth Object) programme monitors close approaches of asteroids and other space objects to the Earth. "Near" in this context means within 45 million km (28 million miles) of the Earth's orbit.

TOP 10 LARGEST PLANETARY MOONS

	MOON	PLANET	DIAMETER (KM)	(MILES)
1	Ganymede	Jupiter	5,269	3,274
2	Titan	Saturn	5,150	3,200
3	Callisto	Jupiter	4,806	2,986
4	Io	Jupiter	3,642	2,263
5	Moon	Earth	3,475	2,159
6	Europa	Jupiter	3,130	1,945
7	Triton	Neptune	2,704	1,680
8	Titania	Uranus	1,578	980
9	Rhea	Saturn	1,528	949
10	Oberon	Uranus	1,522	946

▶ **Galileo and Ganymede**
The cratered surface of Ganymede, seventh largest of Jupiter's moons and larger than the planet Mercury. It was discovered by Italian astronomer Galileo on 7 January 1610, and investigated by NASA's aptly named *Galileo* probe, which reached it in 1996.

GALAXIES NEAREST TO THE EARTH

	GALAXY	DISTANCE (LIGHT YEARS)
1	Large Cloud of Magellan	169,000
2	Small Cloud of Magellan	190,000
3	Ursa Minor dwarf	250,000
4	Draco dwarf	260,000
5	Sculptor dwarf	280,000
6	Fornax dwarf	420,000
7	= Leo I dwarf	750,000
	= Leo II dwarf	750,000
9	Barnard's Galaxy	1,700,000
10	Andromeda Spiral	2,200,000

These, and other galaxies, are members of the so-called "Local Group", although with vast distances such as these, "local" is clearly a relative term.

▶ **By Jupiter!**
The Solar System's largest planet is more massive than all the other eight planets combined. The prominent Great Red Spot, seen here on the right, rotates anticlockwise and is easily large enough to swallow Earth.

LARGEST BODIES IN THE SOLAR SYSTEM

	BODY	MAXIMUM DIAMETER (KM)	(MILES)
1	Sun	1,392,140	865,036
2	Jupiter	142,984	88,846
3	Saturn	120,536	74,898
4	Uranus	51,118	31,763
5	Neptune	49,532	30,778
6	Earth	12,756	7,926
7	Venus	12,103	7,520
8	Mars	6,794	4,222
9	Ganymede	5,269	3,274
10	Titan	5,150	3,200

Most of the planets are visible to the naked eye and have been the object of systematic study since ancient times. The planets that are too small to be seen unaided are Uranus, discovered on 13 March 1781 by the British astronomer Sir William Herschel; Neptune, found by German astronomer Johann Galle, who announced his discovery on 23 September 1846; and, outside the Top 10, Pluto, located by US astronomer Clyde Tombaugh on 13 March 1930.

STARS NEAREST TO THE EARTH*

	STAR	DISTANCE (LIGHT YEARS)	(KM [MILLIONS])	(MILES [MILLIONS])
1	Proxima Centauri	4.22	39,923,310	24,792,500
2	Alpha Centauri	4.35	41,153,175	25,556,250
3	Barnard's Star	5.98	56,573,790	35,132,500
4	Wolf 359	7.75	73,318,875	45,531,250
5	Lalande 21185	8.22	77,765,310	48,292,500
6	Luyten 726-8	8.43	79,752,015	49,526,250
7	Sirius	8.65	81,833,325	50,818,750
8	Ross 154	9.45	89,401,725	55,518,750
9	Ross 248	10.40	98,389,200	61,100,000
10	Epsilon Eridani	10.80	102,173,400	63,450,000

Excluding the Sun

A spaceship travelling at 40,237 km/h (25,000 mph) – which is faster than any human has yet travelled in space – would take more than 113,200 years to reach the Earth's closest star, Proxima Centauri.

Exploring the Universe

LONGEST SPACE MISSIONS*

	COSMONAUT#	MISSION DATES	DURATION DAYS:HRS:MINS
1	Valeri V. Polyakov	8 Jan 1994–22 Mar 1995	437:17:59
2	Sergei V. Avdeyev	13 Aug 1998–28 Aug 1999	379:14:52
3 =	Musa K. Manarov	21 Dec 1987–21 Dec 1988	365:22:39
=	Vladimir G. Titov	21 Dec 1987–21 Dec 1988	365:22:39
5	Yuri V. Romanenko	5 Feb–5 Dec 1987	326:11:38
6	Sergei K. Krikalyov	18 May 1991–25 Mar 1992	311:20:01
7	Valeri V. Polyakov	31 Aug 1988–27 Apr 1989	240:22:35
8 =	Oleg Y. Atkov	8 Feb–2 Oct 1984	236:22:50
=	Leonid D. Kizim	8 Feb–2 Oct 1984	236:22:50
=	Anatoli Y. Solovyov	8 Feb–2 Oct 1984	236:22:50

* To 1 January 2003

\# All Soviet/Russian

Space-medicine specialist Valeri Vladimirovich Polyakov (born 27 April 1942) spent his 52nd birthday in space during his record-breaking mission aboard the Mir space station. One of the purposes of his mission was to study the effects on the human body of long-duration spaceflight.

LARGEST REFLECTING TELESCOPES

	TELESCOPE	LOCATION	APERTURE (M)	APERTURE (FT)
1 =	Keck I Telescope*	Mauna Kea, Hawaii	10.0	32.8
=	Keck II Telescope*	Mauna Kea, Hawaii	10.0	32.8
3	Hobby-Eberly Telescope	Mount Fowlkes, Texas	9.2	30.9
4	Subaru Telescope	Mauna Kea, Hawaii	8.3	27.2
5 =	Antu Telescope	Cerro Paranal, Chile	8.2	26.9
=	Kueyen Telescope	Cerro Paranal, Chile	8.2	26.9
=	Melipal Telescope	Cerro Paranal, Chile	8.2	26.9
=	Yepun Telescope	Cerro Paranal, Chile	8.2	26.9
9 =	Gemini North Telescope*	Mauna Kea, Hawaii	8.1	26.5
=	Gemini South Telescope*	Cerro Pachon, Chile	8.1	26.5

* Twins

Antu, Kueyen, Melipal, and Yepun are soon to be combined to form the appropriately named Very Large Telescope, which will take first place in this list with an aperture of 16.4 m (53.8 ft). The Keck telescopes work in tandem to produce the largest reflecting surface. They are to be combined with several smaller scopes to form the 14.6 m (47.9 ft) Keck Interferometer.

◀ **Callisto's craters**
First observed by Galileo, Callisto, the second largest of Jupiter's satellites, has the most heavily cratered surface of any body in the Solar System: Valhalla, the crater seen here on the right-hand side of Callisto, is 600 km (373 miles) in diameter.

FIRST PLANETARY MOONS TO BE DISCOVERED

	MOON	PLANET	DISCOVERER	YEAR
1	Moon	Earth	—	Ancient
2	Io	Jupiter	Galileo Galilei (Italian)	1610
3	Europa	Jupiter	Galileo Galilei	1610
4	Ganymede	Jupiter	Galileo Galilei	1610
5	Callisto	Jupiter	Galileo Galilei	1610
6	Titan	Saturn	Christian Huygens (Dutch)	1655
7	Iapetus	Saturn	Giovanni Cassini (Italian/French)	1671
8	Rhea	Saturn	Giovanni Cassini	1672
9	Tethys	Saturn	Giovanni Cassini	1684
10	Dione	Saturn	Giovanni Cassini	1684

While Earth's Moon has been observed since ancient times, it was not until the development of the telescope that Galileo was able to discover (on 7 January 1610) the first moons of another planet.

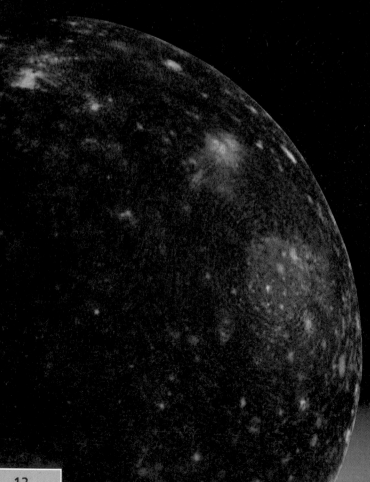

TOP 10 COUNTRIES WITH MOST SPACEFLIGHT EXPERIENCE*

	COUNTRY	ASTRONAUTS	(DAYS)	DURATION OF MISSION (HRS)	(MINS)	(SECS)
1	USSR/Russia#	96	15,806	13	16	36
2	USA	271	8,509	08	48	22
3	France	9	384	23	38	00
4	Kazakhstan	2	349	14	59	03
5	Germany	10	309	17	08	56
6	Canada	8	122	13	30	58
7	Japan	5	88	06	00	40
8	Italy	4	76	06	34	09
9	Switzerland	1	42	12	05	32
10	South Africa	1	24	22	28	22
	UK	1	7	21	13	45

* To 1 January 2003

 # Russia became a independent state on 25 December 1991

The USSR, and now Russia, has clocked up its considerable lead on the rest of the world (with 61 per cent of the total time spent by humans in space) largely through the long-duration stays of its cosmonauts on board the Mir space station. The USA has had almost three times as many astronauts in space – principally aboard the Space Shuttle – but its missions have been of shorter duration. Up to 1 January 2003, the USSR/Russia and the USA had hosted representatives of 28 further countries. Of these, Mexico's space experience is the shortest: a single six-day mission.

▲ **Space Shuttle**
The Space Shuttle's cargo bay is 18.3 m (60 ft) in length and 4.6 m (15 ft) in diameter. The bay has a Remote Manipulator System arm to manoeuvre and deploy the Shuttle's cargo, and also contains the docking systems that are used during missions to the Spacelab.

THE 10 FIRST UNMANNED MOON LANDINGS

	CRAFT	COUNTRY	DATE (LAUNCH/IMPACT)
1	Lunik 2	USSR	12/14 Sept 1959
2	Ranger 4*	USA	23/26 Apr 1962
3	Ranger 6	USA	30 Jan/2 Feb 1964
4	Ranger 7	USA	28/31 July 1964
5	Ranger 8	USA	17/20 Feb 1965
6	Ranger 9	USA	21/24 Mar 1965
7	Luna 5*	USSR	9/12 May 1965
8	Luna 7*	USSR	4/8 Oct 1965
9	Luna 8*	USSR	3/7 Dec 1965
10	Luna 9	USSR	31 Jan/3 Feb 1966

* Crash-landing

TOP 10 LONGEST SPACE SHUTTLE FLIGHTS*

	MISSION/SHUTTLE	FLIGHT DATES	(DAYS)	DURATION OF MISSION (HRS)	(MINS)	(SECS)
1	STS-80 Columbia	19 Nov–7 Dec 1996	17	08	53	18
2	STS-78 Columbia	20 June–7 July 1996	16	21	48	30
3	STS-67 Endeavour	2–18 Mar 1995	16	15	09	46
4	STS-73 Columbia	20 Oct–5 Nov 1995	15	21	53	16
5	STS-90 Columbia	17 Apr–3 May 1998	15	21	15	58
6	STS-75 Columbia	22 Feb–9 Mar 1996	15	17	41	25
7	STS-94 Columbia	1–17 July 1997	15	16	46	01
8	STS-87 Atlantis	25 Sept–6 Oct 1997	15	16	35	01
9	STS-65 Columbia	8–23 July 1994	14	17	55	00
10	STS-58 Columbia	18 Oct–1 Nov 1993	14	00	12	32

* To 1 January 2003

Water World

LARGEST OCEANS AND SEAS

OCEAN/SEA	APPROXIMATE AREA* (SQ KM)	(SQ MILES)
1 Pacific Ocean	166,242,500	64,186,600
2 Atlantic Ocean	86,557,800	33,420,160
3 Indian Ocean	73,427,800	28,350,640
4 Arctic Ocean	13,223,800	5,105,740
5 South China Sea	2,974,600	1,148,499
6 Caribbean Sea	2,515,900	971,400
7 Mediterranean Sea	2,510,000	969,120
8 Bering Sea	2,261,100	873,020
9 Sea of Okhotsk	1,527,570	589,800
10 Gulf of Mexico	1,507,600	582,100

Excluding tributary seas

The Coral, Weddell, and Tasman Seas would be eligible for this list, but most authorities consider them part of the Pacific Ocean. The Bering Sea is more commonly identified as an independent sea rather than part of the Pacific.

LONGEST RIVERS

RIVER	LOCATION	LENGTH (KM)	(MILES)
1 Nile	Burundi/Dem. Rep. of Congo/Egypt/Eritrea/ Ethiopia/Kenya/Rwanda/Sudan/Tanzania/Uganda	6,695	4,158
2 Amazon	Peru/Brazil	6,448	4,007
3 Chang Jiang (Yangtze)	China	6,378	3,964
4 Huang He (Yellow)	China	5,464	3,395
5 Amur	China/Russia	4,415	2,744
6 Lena	Russia	4,400	2,734
7 Congo	Angola/Dem. Rep. of Congo	4,373	2,718
8 Irtysh	China/Kazakhstan/Mongolia/Russia	4,248	2,640
9 Mackenzie	Canada	4,241	2,635
10 Mekong	Tibet/China/Myanmar/Laos/ Cambodia/Vietnam	4,183	2,600

TOP 10 DEEPEST DEEP-SEA TRENCHES

TRENCH*	DEEPEST POINT (M)	(FT)
1 Marianas	10,924	35,837
2 Tonga#	10,800	35,430
3 Philippine	10,497	34,436
4 Kermadec#	10,047	32,960
5 Bonin	9,994	32,786
6 New Britain	9,940	32,609
7 Kuril	9,750	31,985
8 Izu	9,695	31,805
9 Puerto Rico	8,605	28,229
10 Yap	8,527	27,973

* With the exception of the Puerto Rico (Atlantic), all the trenches are in the Pacific

\# Some authorities consider these parts of the same feature

TOP 10 HIGHEST WATERFALLS

WATERFALL	RIVER	LOCATION	TOTAL DROP (M)	(FT)
1 Angel	Carrao	Venezuela	979	3,212*
2 Tugela	Tugela	South Africa	947	3,107
3 Utigård	Jostedal Glacier	Nesdale, Norway	800	2,625
4 Mongefossen	Monge	Mongebekk, Norway	774	2,540
5 Yosemite	Yosemite Creek	California, USA	739	2,425
6 Østre Mardøla Foss	Mardals	Eikisdal, Norway	656	2,152
7 Tyssestrengane	Tysso	Hardanger, Norway	646	2,120
8 Cuquenán	Arabopo	Venezuela	610	2,000
9 Sutherland	Arthur	South Island, New Zealand	580	1,904
10 Kjellfossen	Naero	Gudvangen, Norway	561	1,841

* Longest single drop 807 m (2,648 ft)

TOP 10 COUNTRIES WITH THE LARGEST AREAS OF CORAL REEF

COUNTRY	REEF AREA (SQ KM)	PERCENTAGE OF WORLD TOTAL
1 Indonesia	51,020	17.95
2 Australia	48,960	17.22
3 The Philippines	25,060	8.81
4 France (overseas territories)	14,280	5.02
5 Papua New Guinea	13,840	4.87
6 Fiji	10,020	3.52
7 Maldives	8,920	3.14
8 Saudi Arabia	6,660	2.34
9 Marshall Islands	6,110	2.15
10 India	5,790	2.04
World total (including those not in Top 10)	284,300	100.00

Source: World Atlas of Coral Reefs

◄ **Beneath the waves**
Coral reefs have taken millions of years to form and, as habitats for a huge variety of sea life, are subject to stringent controls.

TOP 10 DEEPEST LAKES

LAKE	LOCATION	GREATEST DEPTH (M)	(FT)
1 Baikal	Russia	1,637	5,371
2 Tanganyika	Burundi/ Tanzania/ Dem. Rep. of Congo/ Zambia	1,471	4,825
3 Caspian Sea	Azerbaijan/ Iran/Kazakhstan/ Russia/Turkmenistan	1,025	3,363
4 Malawi	Malawi/ Mozambique/ Tanzania	706	2,316
5 Issyk-kul	Kyrgyzstan	688	2,257
6 Great Slave	Canada	614	2,015
7 Crater	Oregon, USA	589	1,932
8 Toba	Sumatra, Indonesia	529	1,736
9 Hornindals	Norway	514	1,686
10 = Sarez	Tajikistan	505	1,657
= Tahoe	California/ Nevada, USA	505	1,657

Lake Baikal contains some 20 per cent of the world's unfrozen fresh water, a volume of 23,000 km³ (5,518 miles³).

Island Treasure

LARGEST ISLANDS

	ISLAND	AREA* (SQ KM)	(SQ MILES)
1	Greenland (Kalaatdlit Nunaat)	2,175,600.0	840,003.9
2	New Guinea	785,753.0	303,381.0
3	Borneo (Indonesia/Malaysia/Brunei)	748,168.1	288,869.3
4	Madagascar (Malagasy Republic)	587,713.1	226,917.3
5	Baffin Island, Canada	503,944.0	194,573.9
6	Sumatra, Indonesia	443,065.8	171,068.7
7	Great Britain	229,957.0	88,786.9
8	Honshu, Japan	225,800.3	87,182.0
9	Victoria Island, Canada	220,548.2	85,154.2
10	Ellesmere Island, Canada	183,964.6	71,029.1

* Mainlands, including areas of inland water, but excluding offshore islands

Australia is regarded as a continental land mass rather than an island; otherwise it would rank first, at 7,618,493 sq km (2,941,517 sq miles), or 35 times the size of Great Britain. The largest US island is Hawaii, which measures 10,456 sq km (4,037 sq miles), and the largest off mainland USA is Kodiak, Alaska, at 9,510 sq km (3,672 sq miles).

LARGEST ISLAND COUNTRIES

	COUNTRY	AREA (SQ KM)	(SQ MILES)
1	Indonesia	1,826,440	705,192
2	Madagascar	581,540	224,534
3	Papua New Guinea	451,709	174,406
4	Japan	394,744	152,411
5	Malaysia	328,549	126,853
6	Philippines	298,171	115,124
7	New Zealand	268,671	103,734
8	Cuba	110,860	42,803
9	Iceland	100,251	38,707
10	Sri Lanka	64,740	24,996

Source: *US Census Bureau, International Data Base*

All of the countries on this list are completely self-contained island countries. Because Ireland and Northern Ireland share an island, the UK and Ireland are both excluded from this list. Had it been included, the UK would take 8th place with an area of 241,590 sq km (93,278 sq miles).

MOST IMPORTANT ISLANDS FOR CONSERVATION

	ISLAND/LOCATION	ENDEMIC SPECIES	THREATENED SPECIES	CONSERVATION IMPORTANCE INDEX
1	New Caledonia, South West Pacific	2,688	172	115
2	Mauritius, Indian Ocean	316	223	85
3	Malta, Mediterranean Sea	32	230	63
4	Lord Howe Island, Australia	130	79	58
5	St. Helena, South Atlantic	62	54	50
6	Rapa Iti, South West Pacific	225	51	49
7	Madeira, Atlantic Ocean	230	136	48
8	Henderson, Pitcairn, South Pacific	21	2	47
9	Viti Levu, Fiji, South West Pacific	9	4	44
10 =	Jamaica, Caribbean Sea	1,020	13	42
=	Vanua Levu, Fiji South West Pacific	2	3	42

Source: *United Nations System-wide Earthwatch*

The United Nations' Conservation Importance Index ranks islands according to terrestrial and marine conservation importance, endemic and threatened species, vulnerability, and features such as seabird rookeries and sea turtle nesting areas.

SMALLEST ISLAND COUNTRIES

	COUNTRY/LOCATION	AREA (SQ KM)	(SQ MILES)
1	Nauru, Pacific Ocean	21	8
2	Tuvalu, Pacific Ocean	26	10
3	Marshall Islands, Pacific Ocean	181	70
4	Maldives, Indian Ocean	300	116
5	Malta, Mediterranean Sea	321	124
6 =	Grenada, Caribbean Sea	339	131
=	St. Vincent and the Grenadines, Caribbean Sea	339	131
8	St. Kitts and Nevis, Caribbean Sea	360	139
9	Barbados, Caribbean Sea	430	166
10	Antigua and Barbuda, Caribbean Sea	440	170

Source: *US Census Bureau, International Data Base*

▶ **Easter Island**
Guarded by over 600 giant statues, or "moais", of mysterious origin, Easter Island was discovered by Jacob Roggeveen on Easter Day, 1722. It lies more than 3,200 km (2,000 miles) from the nearest population centres in Tahiti and Chile, making it the world's most isolated inhabited island.

TOP 10 MOST ISOLATED INHABITED ISLANDS

	ISLAND/LOCATION	ISOLATION INDEX
1	**Easter Island,** South Pacific	149
2	**Rapa Iti,** South West Pacific	130
3	**Kiritimati,** Line Islands, Central Pacific	129
4	**Jarvis Island,** Central Pacific	128
5 =	**Kosrae,** Micronesia, Pacific	126
=	**Malden,** Line Islands, Central Pacific	126
=	**Starbuck,** Line Islands, Central Pacific	126
=	**Vostok,** Line Islands, Central Pacific	126
9 =	**Bouvet Island,** South Atlantic	125
=	**Gough Island,** South Atlantic	125
=	**Palmyra Island,** Central Pacific	125

Source: *United Nations*

The United Nation's isolation index is calculated by adding together the square roots of the distances to the nearest island, group of islands, and continent.

TOP 10 LARGEST VOLCANIC ISLANDS

	ISLAND/LOCATION	TYPE	AREA (SQ KM)	AREA (SQ MILES)
1	**Sumatra,** Indonesia	Active volcanic	443,065.8	171,068.7
2	**Honshu,** Japan	Volcanic	225,800.3	87,182.0
3	**Java,** Indonesia	Volcanic	138,793.6	53,588.5
4	**North Island,** New Zealand	Volcanic	111,582.8	43,082.4
5	**Luzon,** Philippines	Active volcanic	109,964.9	42,457.7
6	**Iceland**	Active volcanic	101,826.0	39,315.2
7	**Mindanao,** Philippines	Active volcanic	97,530.0	37,656.5
8	**Hokkaido,** Japan	Active volcanic	78,719.4	30,394.7
9	**New Britain,** Papua New Guinea	Volcanic	35,144.6	13,569.4
10	**Halmahera,** Indonesia	Active volcanic	18,039.6	6,965.1

Source: *United Nations*

High & Mighty

TOP 10 HIGHEST MOUNTAINS

MOUNTAIN/LOCATION	FIRST ASCENT	TEAM LEADER(S)' NATIONALITY	HEIGHT* (M)	(FT)
1 Everest, Nepal/China	29 May 1953	British/ New Zealander	8,850	29,035
2 K2 (Chogori), Pakistan/China	31 July 1954	Italian	8,607	28,238
3 Kangchenjunga, Nepal/India	25 May 1955	British	8,598	28,208
4 Lhotse, Nepal/China	18 May 1956	Swiss	8,511	27,923
5 Makalu I, Nepal/China	15 May 1955	French	8,481	27,824
6 Lhotse Shar II, Nepal/China	12 May 1970	Austrian	8,383	27,504
7 Dhaulagiri I, Nepal	13 May 1960	Swiss/Austrian	8,172	26,810
8 Manaslu I (Kutang I), Nepal	9 May 1956	Japanese	8,156	26,760
9 Cho Oyu, Nepal	19 Oct 1954	Austrian	8,153	26,750
10 Nanga Parbat (Diamir), Kashmir	3 July 1953	German/ Austrian	8,126	26,660

* *Height of principal peak; lower peaks of the same mountain are excluded*

The current "official" height of Everest was announced in November 1999 following analysis of data beamed from sensors on Everest's summit to GPS (Global Positioning System) satellites. This superseded the previous "official" measurement of 8,848 m (29,028 ft), recorded on 20 April 1993.

TOP 10 HIGHEST ACTIVE VOLCANOES

VOLCANO/LOCATION	LATEST ACTIVITY	HEIGHT (M)	(FT)
1 Cerro Pular, Chile	1990	6,233	20,449
2 San Pedro, Chile	1960	6,145	20,161
3 Antofallar, Argentina	1911	6,100	20,013
4 Aracar, Argentina	1993	6,082	19,954
5 Guallatiri, Chile	1985	6,071	19,918
6 Tupungatito, Chile	1986	6,000	19,685
7 Tacora, Chile	1937	5,980	19,619
8 Sabancaya, Peru	2000	5,967	19,577
9 Cotopaxi, Ecuador	1942	5,911	19,393
10 Putana, Chile	1972	5,890	19,324

This list includes only volcanoes that were active at some time during the 20th century. Activity cannot always be confirmed beyond doubt, due to the remoteness of the volcanoes, which can often make it difficult to ascertain precisely which volcano has erupted. The tallest currently active volcano in Europe is Mt. Etna, Sicily, at 3,311 m (10,855 ft), which was responsible for numerous deaths in earlier times.

TOP 10 HIGHEST MOUNTAINS IN NORTH AMERICA

MOUNTAIN	COUNTRY	HEIGHT* (M)	(FT)
1 McKinley	Alaska, USA	6,194	20,320
2 Logan	Canada	5,959	19,545
3 Citlaltépetl (Orizaba)	Mexico	5,611	18,409
4 St. Elias	Alaska, USA/Canada	5,489	18,008
5 Popocatépetl	Mexico	5,452	17,887
6 Foraker	Alaska, USA	5,304	17,400
7 Ixtaccihuatl	Mexico	5,286	17,343
8 Lucania	Canada	5,226	17,147
9 King	Canada	5,173	16,971
10 Steele	Canada	5,073	16,644

* *Height of principal peak; lower peaks of the same mountain are excluded*

▶ **Peak performance**
The Andes, the world's longest mountain range, stretches the length of South America, from Lago de Maracaibo in the north to Tierra del Fuego in the south.

TOP 10 HIGHEST MOUNTAINS IN EUROPE

	MOUNTAIN/COUNTRY	HEIGHT* (M)	(FT)
1	**Mont Blanc**, France/Italy	4,807	15,771
2	**Monte Rosa**, Switzerland	4,634	15,203
3	**Zumsteinspitze**, Italy/Switzerland	4,564	14,970
4	**Signalkuppe**, Italy/Switzerland	4,555	14,941
5	**Dom**, Switzerland	4,545	14,911
6	**Liskamm**, Italy/Switzerland	4,527	14,853
7	**Weisshorn**, Switzerland	4,505	14,780
8	**Täschorn**, Switzerland	4,491	14,733
9	**Matterhorn**, Italy/Switzerland	4,477	14,688
10	**Mont Maudit**, France/Italy	4,466	14,649

* Height of principal peak; lower peaks of the same mountain are excluded

THE 10 FIRST MOUNTAINEERS TO CLIMB EVEREST

	MOUNTAINEER/NATIONALITY	DATE
1	**Edmund Hillary**, New Zealander	29 May 1953
2	**Tenzing Norgay**, Nepalese	29 May 1953
3	**Jürg Marmet**, Swiss	23 May 1956
4	**Ernst Schmied**, Swiss	23 May 1956
5	**Hans-Rudolf von Gunten**, Swiss	24 May 1956
6	**Adolf Reist**, Swiss	24 May 1956
7	**Wang Fu-chou**, Chinese	25 May 1960
8	**Chu Ying-hua**, Chinese	25 May 1960
9	**Konbu**, Tibetan	25 May 1960
10 =	**Nawang Gombu**, Indian	1 May 1963
=	**James Whittaker**, American	1 May 1963

Hillary and Tenzing's conquest of Everest followed at least 16 unsuccessful expeditions from 1921 to 1952. Whether George Leigh Mallory and Andrew Irvine, the British climbers who died on the 1924 expedition, reached the summit is still controversial. Mallory's body was discovered in 1999 at a height of 8,230 m (27,000 ft). Nawang Gombu and James Whittaker are 10th equal as neither wished to deny the other the privilege of being first, so they ascended the last steps to the summit side-by-side.

TOP 10 LONGEST MOUNTAIN RANGES

	RANGE/LOCATION	LENGTH (KM)	(MILES)
1	**Andes,** South America	7,242	4,500
2	**Rocky Mountains,** North America	6,035	3,750
3	**Himalayas/Karakoram/Hindu Kush,** Asia	3,862	2,400
4	**Great Dividing Range,** Australia	3,621	2,250
5	**Trans-Antarctic Mountains,** Antarctica	3,541	2,200
6	**Brazilian East Coast Range,** Brazil	3,058	1,900
7	**Sumatran/Javan Range,** Sumatra, Java	2,897	1,800
8	**Tien Shan,** China	2,253	1,400
9	**Eastern Ghats,** India	2,092	1,300
10 =	**Altai,** Asia	2,012	1,250
=	**Central New Guinean Range,** Papua New Guinea	2,012	1,250
=	**Urals,** Russia	2,012	1,250

Face of the Earth

LONGEST CAVES

CAVE/LOCATION	TOTAL KNOWN LENGTH (KM)	(MILES)
1 **Mammoth Cave System,** Kentucky, USA	557	346
2 **Optimisticheskaya,** Ukraine	212	131
3 **Jewel Cave,** South Dakota, USA	206	128
4 **Hölloch,** Switzerland	184	114
5 **Lechuguilla Cave,** New Mexico, USA	176	109
6 **Wind Cave,** South Dakota, USA	171	106
7 **Fisher Ridge System,** Kentucky, USA	169	105
8 **Siebenhengstehohle,** Switzerland	145	90
9 **Ozernaya,** Ukraine	117	73
10 **Gua Air Jernih,** Malaysia	109	68

Source: *Tony Waltham, BCRA*

The longest-known cave system in the UK is Ease Gill, West Yorkshire, at 70,500 m (231,300 ft).

▼ An immense and ancient land

The Sahara's boundaries are the Atlantic Ocean to the west, the Atlas Mountains and the Mediterranean Sea to the north, the Red Sea and Egypt to the east, and the Sudan and the Niger River to the south. Over 8,000 years ago the Sahara was a fertile area where millet and other crops were cultivated. As conditions gradually became drier, however, and the desert began to form, the farmers abandoned their land.

DEEPEST DEPRESSIONS

DEPRESSION/LOCATION	MAXIMUM DEPTH BELOW SEA LEVEL (M)	(FT)
1 **Dead Sea,** Israel/Jordan	400	1,312
2 **Lake Assal,** Djibouti	156	511
3 **Turfan Depression,** China	154	505
4 **Qattâra Depression,** Egypt	133	436
5 **Mangyshlak Peninsula,** Kazakhstan	132	433
6 **Danakil Depression,** Ethiopia	117	383
7 **Death Valley,** USA	86	282
8 **Salton Sink,** USA	72	235
9 **Zapadny Chink Ustyurta,** Kazakhstan	70	230
10 **Prikaspiyskaya Nizmennost',** Kazakhstan/Russia	67	220

The shore of the Dead Sea is the lowest exposed ground below sea level, but the bed of the Sea actually reaches 728 m (2,388 ft) below sea level, and that of Lake Baikal, Russia, attains 1,485 m (4,872 ft) below sea level. Much of Antarctica is below sea level – some as low as 2,538 m (8,326 ft) – but the land there is covered by an ice cap that averages 2,100 m (6,890 ft) in depth. Lake Assal is Africa's lowest point and reputedly the world's saltiest body of water, 10 times as salty as the average for seawater, and saltier even than the notorious Dead Sea, which causes intense irritation to the eyes of swimmers, who are advised instead to take advantage of their unusual buoyancy and simply float. The Top 10 includes the lowest elevations in the continents of Asia, Africa, Europe, and North America; the lowest point in South America is the Valdes Peninsula, Argentina, at 40 m (131 ft) below sea level, and in Australia, Lake Eyre, 16 m (52 ft) below sea level.

TOP 10 | LAND MASSES WITH THE LOWEST ELEVATIONS

	LAND MASS/LOCATION/COUNTRY	HIGHEST POINT (M)	(FT)
1	**Kingman Reef,** North Pacific (USA)	1	3.2
2	**Palmyra Atoll,** North Pacific (USA)	2	6.5
3 =	**Bassas da India,** Mozambique Channel, Southern Africa (French)	2.4	7.8
=	**Wingili Island in the Addu Atoll,** Maldives	2.4	7.8
5 =	**Ashmore and Cartier Islands,** Indian Ocean (Australian)	3	9.8
=	**Howland Island,** North Pacific (USA)	3	9.8
7	**Spratly Islands,** South China Sea (claimed by China, Taiwan, Vietnam, Malaysia, and the Philippines)	4	13.1
8 =	**Cocos (Keeling) Islands,** Indian Ocean (Australian)	5	16.4
=	**Johnston Atoll,** North Pacific (USA)	5	16.4
=	**Tokelau,** South Pacific (New Zealand)	5	16.4
=	**Tuvalu,** South Pacific	5	16.4

Source: *CIA, The World Factbook 2001*

These 10 locations are definitely off the agenda if you are planning a climbing vacation, none of them possessing a single elevation taller than a small house. Beyond these exceptionally low-lying places, several countries, including Gambia and the Marshall Islands, lack a rise greater than 10 m (33 ft). Compared with these, even the Netherlands' 321-m (1,050-ft) Vaalserberg hill makes the country's appellation as one of the "Low Countries" seem almost unfair.

TOP 10 | LARGEST DESERTS

	DESERT/LOCATION	APPROX. AREA (SQ KM)	(SQ MILES)
1	**Sahara,** Northern Africa	9,100,000	3,500,000
2	**Australian,** Australia*	3,400,000	1,300,000
3	**Arabian Peninsula,** Southwest Asia[#]	2,600,000	1,000,000
4	**Turkestan,** Central Asia[†]	1,900,000	750,000
5 =	**Gobi,** Central Asia	1,300,000	500,000
=	**North American Desert,** USA/Mexico[§]	1,300,000	500,000
7	**Patagonia,** Southern Argentina	670,000	260,000
8	**Thar,** Northwest India/Pakistan	600,000	230,000
9	**Kalahari,** Southwestern Africa	570,000	220,000
10	**Takla Makan,** Northwestern China	480,000	185,000

* *Includes Gibson, Great Sandy, Great Victoria, and Simpson*

[#] *Includes an-Nafud and Rub al-Khali*

[†] *Includes Kara-Kum and Kyzylkum*

[§] *Includes Great Basin, Mojave, Sonorah, and Chihuahuan*

This Top 10 presents the approximate areas and ranking of the world's great deserts, which are often broken down into smaller desert regions – the Australian Desert into the Gibson, Great Sandy, Great Victoria, and Simpson, for example. The world total is more than double that of the Top 10 at some 35,264,000 sq km (13,616,000 sq miles), or about one-quarter of the world's land area. However, deserts may range from the extremely arid and typical barren sandy desert (about 4 per cent of the total land surface of the globe), through arid (15 per cent) to semi-arid (almost 15 per cent), and most exhibit features that encompass all these degrees of aridity, with one zone merging almost imperceptibly into the next.

Elementary Matters

TOP 10 MOST COMMON ELEMENTS IN THE EARTH'S CRUST

ELEMENT	PARTS PER MILLION*
1 Oxygen	460,000
2 Silicon	270,000
3 Aluminium	82,000
4 Iron	63,000
5 Calcium	50,000
6 Magnesium	29,000
7 Sodium	23,000
8 Potassium	15,000
9 Titanium	6,600
10 Hydrogen	1,500

* mg per kg

This is based on the average percentages of the elements in igneous rock. Of every million atoms, some 200,000 are silicon, 63,000 aluminium, and 31,000 hydrogen – although in the Universe as a whole, hydrogen is by far the commonest element, comprising some 930,000 out of every million atoms.

TOP 10 HEAVIEST ELEMENTS

ELEMENT	DISCOVERER/ COUNTRY	YEAR DISCOVERED	DENSITY*
1 Osmium	Smithson Tennant, UK	1804	22.59
2 Iridium	Smithson Tennant, UK	1804	22.56
3 Platinum	Julius Caesar Scaliger[#], Italy/France; Charles Wood, UK[†]	1557 1741	21.45
4 Rhenium	Walter K. Noddack et al., Germany	1925	21.01
5 Neptunium	Edwin Mattison McMillan/Philip H. Abelson, USA	1940	20.47
6 Plutonium	Glenn Theodore Seaborg et al., USA	1940	20.26
7 Gold		Prehistoric	19.29
8 Tungsten	Juan José and Fausto de Elhuijar, Spain	1783	19.26
9 Uranium	Martin Heinrich Klaproth, Germany	1789	19.05
10 Tantalum	Anders Gustav Ekeberg, Sweden	1802	16.67

* Grams per cubic centimetre at 20° C

[#] Earliest reference to

[†] Discovered

The two heaviest elements, the metals osmium and iridium, were discovered at the same time by the British chemist Smithson Tennant (1761–1815), who was also the first to prove that diamonds are made of carbon. 0.028317 m³ (1 cubic foot) of osmium weighs 640 kg (1,410 lb).

TOP 10 MOST COMMON ELEMENTS ON THE MOON

ELEMENT	PERCENTAGE
1 Oxygen	40.0
2 Silicon	19.2
3 Iron	14.3
4 Calcium	8.0
5 Titanium	5.9
6 Aluminium	5.6
7 Magnesium	4.5
8 Sodium	0.33
9 Potassium	0.14
10 Chromium	0.002

This Top 10 is based on the analysis of the 20.77 kg (45.8 lb) of rock samples brought back to Earth by the crew of the 1969 Apollo 11 lunar mission. One of the minerals they discovered was named Armalcolite in honour of the three astronauts – Armstrong, Aldrin, and Collins.

ELEMENTARY FIRSTS

FIRST FACT

THE EXISTENCE OF HYDROGEN, the lightest and most abundant element in the Universe, was first demonstrated in 1766 by British scientist Henry Cavendish (1731–1810). He called it "inflammable air", but because it produces water when it burns in oxygen, it was given a name that means "water-forming". Soon after Cavendish's discovery, techniques for extracting hydrogen were developed, which led to one of its earliest practical uses by enabling the first hydrogen balloon flight, by Jacques Charles and Nicholas-Louis Robert, to take place in France on 1 December 1783. Following their debut two-hour flight from Paris to Nesle, Charles took off alone, thus becoming the world's first solo flier.

TOP 10 MOST COMMON ELEMENTS IN THE SUN

ELEMENT	PARTS PER MILLION*
1 Hydrogen	750,000
2 Helium	230,000
3 Oxygen	9,000
4 Carbon	3,000
5 = Iron	1,000
= Neon	1,000
= Nitrogen	1,000
8 Silicon	900
9 Magnesium	700
10 Sulphur	400

* mg per kg

More than 70 elements have been detected in the Sun, the most common of which correspond closely to those found in the Universe as a whole, but with some variations in their ratios, including a greater proportion of the principal element, hydrogen.

MOST COMMON ELEMENTS IN THE UNIVERSE

	ELEMENT	PARTS PER MILLION*
1	Hydrogen	750,000
2	Helium	230,000
3	Oxygen	10,000
4	Carbon	5,000
5	Neon	1,300
6	Iron	1,100
7	Nitrogen	1,000
8	Silicon	700
9	Magnesium	600
10	Sulphur	500

mg per kg

Hydrogen is the simplest atom – a single proton circled by a single electron. The atoms of hydrogen in the Universe outnumber those of all the other elements combined.

PRINCIPAL COMPONENTS OF AIR

	COMPONENT	VOLUME PER CENT
1	Nitrogen	78.110
2	Oxygen	20.953
3	Argon	0.934
4	Carbon dioxide	0.01–0.10
5	Neon	0.001818
6	Helium	0.000524
7	Methane	0.0002
8	Krypton	0.000114
9	= Hydrogen	0.00005
	= Nitrous oxide	0.00005

▶ **Gas light**
A cloud of electrons whirl round an atom of helium, the lightest and most abundant element after hydrogen. Helium was discovered in the Sun's spectrum during an eclipse in 1868, and isolated on Earth in 1895.

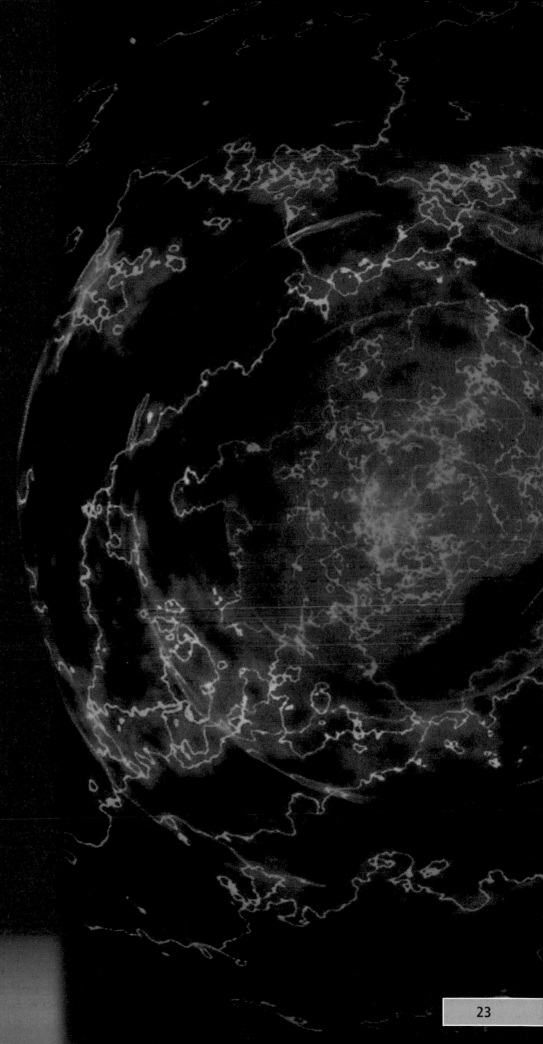

Weather Extremes

**HOTTEST PLACES –
EXTREMES**

	LOCATION	HIGHEST TEMPERATURE (°C)	(°F)
1	**Al'Azīzīyah,** Libya	58.0	136.4
2	**Greenland Ranch,** Death Valley, USA	56.7	134.0
3 =	**Ghudamis,** Libya	55.0	131.0
=	**Kebili,** Tunisia	55.0	131.0
5	**Tombouctou,** Mali	54.5	130.1
6	**Araouane,** Mali	54.4	130.0
7	**Tirat Tavi,** Israel	53.9	129.0
8	**Ahwāz,** Iran	53.5	128.3
9	**Agha Jārī,** Iran	53.3	128.0
10	**Wadi Halfa,** Sudan	52.8	127.0

Maximum of two places per country listed

Source: *Philip Eden*

The hottest temperature on Earth was that recorded by meteorologists from the National Geographic Society at Al'Azīzīyah, 40 km (25 miles) south of Tripoli, Libya, on 13 September 1922.

**COLDEST PLACES –
EXTREMES**

	LOCATION	LOWEST TEMPERATURE (°C)	(°F)
1	**Vostok*,** Antarctica	-89.2	-138.6
2	**Plateau Station*,** Antarctica	-84.0	-129.2
3	**Oymyakon,** Russia	-71.1	-96.0
4	**Verkhoyansk,** Russia	-67.7	-90.0
5	**Northice*,** Greenland	-66.0	-87.0
6	**Eismitte*,** Greenland	-64.9	-85.0
7	**Snag,** Yukon, Canada	-63.0	-81.4
8	**Prospect Creek,** Alaska, USA	-62.1	-79.8
9	**Fort Selkirk,** Yukon, Canada	-58.9	-74.0
10	**Rogers Pass,** Montana, USA	-56.5	-69.7

Maximum of two places per country listed

* *Present or former scientific research base*

Source: *Philip Eden*

▼ **Freezing point**
The Martin A. Pomerantz observatory at the Amundsen-Scott base at the South Pole. The American scientific research facility is located in almost the coldest place on Earth.

**PLACES WITH THE MOST
CONTRASTING SEASONS***

	LOCATION	WINTER (°C)	(°F)	SUMMER (°C)	(°F)	DIFFERENCE (°C)	(°F)
1	**Verkhoyansk,** Russia	-50.3	-58.5	13.6	56.5	63.9	115.0
2	**Yakutsk,** Russia	-45.0	-49.0	17.5	63.5	62.5	112.5
3	**Manzhouli,** China	-26.1	-15.0	20.6	69.0	46.7	84.0
4	**Fort Yukon,** Alaska, USA	-29.0	-20.2	16.3	61.4	45.3	81.6
5	**Fort Good Hope,** Northwestern Territory, Canada	-29.9	-21.8	15.3	59.5	45.2	81.3
6	**Brochet,** Manitoba, Canada	-29.2	-20.5	15.4	59.7	44.6	80.2
7	**Tunka,** Mongolia	-26.7	-16.0	16.1	61.0	42.8	77.0
8	**Fairbanks,** Alaska, USA	-24.0	-11.2	15.6	60.1	39.6	71.3
9	**Semipalatinsk,** Kazakhstan	-17.7	0.5	20.6	69.0	38.3	68.5
10	**Jorgen Bronlund Fjørd,** Greenland	-30.9	-23.6	6.4	43.5	37.3	67.1

Maximum of two places per country listed

* *Biggest differences between mean monthly temperatures in summer and winter*

Source: *Philip Eden*

Whether based on the differences in its mean winter and summer temperatures, or on its extremes, having recorded a winter temperature as low as -68° C (-90° F) and summer temperatures as high as 37° C (98° F), Verkhoyansk, a river port in northeast Siberia, has the most extreme climate on the planet.

TOP 10 PLACES WITH THE LEAST CONTRASTING SEASONS*

LOCATION	COOLEST (°C)	(°F)	WARMEST (°C)	(°F)	DIFFERENCE (°C)	(°F)
1 = Lorengau, New Guinea	26.7	80.0	27.2	81.0	0.5	1.0
= Malacca, Malaysia	26.7	80.0	27.2	81.0	0.5	1.0
= Malden Island, Kiribati	27.8	82.0	28.3	83.0	0.5	1.0
= Ocean Island, Kiribati	27.8	82.0	28.3	83.0	0.5	1.0
5 = Kavieng, New Guinea	27.2	81.0	27.8	82.0	0.6	1.0
= Quito, Ecuador	14.4	58.0	15.0	59.0	0.6	1.0
7 = Andagoya, Colombia	27.2	81.0	28.0	82.4	0.8	1.4
= Labuhan, Indonesia	27.2	81.0	28.0	82.4	0.8	1.4
= Mwanza, Tanzania	22.6	72.7	23.4	74.1	0.8	1.4
10 Belém, Brazil	26.1	79.0	26.9	80.5	0.8	1.5

Maximum of two places per country listed

* Smallest differences between mean monthly temperature of warmest and coolest months

Source: Philip Eden

TOP 10 WETTEST PLACES – AVERAGE

LOCATION	AVERAGE ANNUAL RAINFALL* (MM)	(IN)
1 Cherrapunji, India	12,649	498.0
2 Mawsynram, India	11,872	467.4
3 Waialeale, Hawaii, USA	11,455	451.0
4 Debundscha, Cameroon	10,277	404.6
5 Quibdó, Colombia	8,989	353.9
6 Bellenden Ker Range, Australia	8,636	340.0
7 Andagoya, Colombia	7,137	281.0
8 Henderson Lake, British Columbia, Canada	6,502	256.0
9 Kikori, Papua New Guinea	5,916	232.9
10 Tavoy, Myanmar	5,451	214.6

Maximum of two places per country listed

* Annual rainfall total, averaged over a long period of years

Source: Philip Eden

TOP 10 COLDEST PLACES – AVERAGE

LOCATION	AVERAGE TEMPERATURE* (°C)	(°F)
1 Plateau#, Antarctica	-56.7	-70.0
2 Amundsen-Scott#, Antarctica	-49.0	-56.2
3 Northice#, Greenland	-30.0	-22.0
4 Eismitte#, Greenland	-29.2	-20.5
5 Resolute, NWT, Canada	-24.2	-11.6
6 Eureka, NWT, Canada	-19.7	-3.5
7 Ostrov Bol'shoy, Lyakhovskiy, Russia	-14.7	5.5
8 Barrow Point, Alaska, USA	-12.3	9.8
9 Barter Island, Alaska, USA	-12.1	10.2
10 Ostrov Vrangela, Russia	-11.7	11.0

Maximum of two places per country listed

* Lowest long-term temperature averaged throughout the year

Present or former scientific research base

Source: Philip Eden

TOP 10 HOTTEST PLACES – AVERAGE

LOCATION*	AVERAGE TEMPERATURE* (°C)	(°F)
1 Dallol, Ethiopia	34.6	94.3
2 Assab, Eritrea	30.4	86.8
3 Néma, Mauritania	30.3	86.5
4 Berbera, Somalia	30.1	86.2
5 Hombori, Mali	30.1	86.1
6 Perm Island, South Yemen	30.0	86.0
7 Djibouti, Djibouti	29.9	85.8
8 Atbara, Sudan	29.8	85.7
9 = Bender Qaasim, Somalia	29.7	85.5
= Kamaran Island, North Yemen	29.7	85.5

Maximum of two places per country listed

* Highest long-term temperature averaged throughout the year

Source: Philip Eden

Natural Disasters

WORST EARTHQUAKES

	LOCATION	DATE	ESTIMATED NO. KILLED
1	**Near East/Mediterranean**	20 May 1202	1,100,000
2	**Shenshi,** China	2 Feb 1556	820,000
3	**Calcutta,** India	11 Oct 1737	300,000
4	**Antioch,** Syria	20 May 526	250,000
5	**Tang-shan,** China	28 July 1976	242,419
6	**Nan-Shan,** China	22 May 1927	200,000
7	**Yeddo,** Japan	30 Dec 1703	190,000
8	**Kansu,** China	16 Dec 1920	180,000
9	**Messina,** Italy	28 Dec 1908	160,000
10	**Tokyo/Yokohama,** Japan	1 Sept 1923	142,807

There are discrepancies between the "official" death tolls in many earthquakes and the estimates of other authorities: a figure of 750,000 is sometimes quoted for the 1976 Tang-shan earthquake, for example, and totals ranging from 58,000 to 250,000 for the quake that devastated Messina in 1908. In more recent times, the Armenian earthquake of 7 December 1988 killed more than 55,000 (28,854 officially), and that in Iran on 21 June 1990 killed over 55,000 (50,000 officially).

WORST TSUNAMIS

	LOCATIONS AFFECTED	DATE	ESTIMATED NO. KILLED
1	**Krakatoa,** Sumatra, Java*	27 Aug 1883	36,380
2	**Sanriku,** Japan	15 June 1896	28,000
3	**Agadir,** Morocco#	29 Feb 1960	12,000
4	**Lisbon,** Portugal	1 Nov 1755	10,000
5	**Papua New Guinea**	18 July 1998	8,000
6	**Chile/Pacific islands/Japan**	22 May 1960	5,700
7	**Philippines**	17 Aug 1976	5,000
8	**Hyuga to Izu,** Japan	28 Oct 1707	4,900
9	**Sanriku,** Japan	3 Mar 1933	3,000
10	**Japan#**	9 July 1854	2,400

* *Combined effect of volcanic eruption and tsunamis*

\# *Combined effect of earthquake and tsunamis*

Tsunamis (from the Japanese *tsu*, port and *nami*, wave) are waves caused by undersea disturbances such as earthquakes or volcanic eruptions. They are often mistakenly called tidal waves, which are another phenomenon. Tsunamis can cross entire oceans, devastating islands and coastal regions in their paths.

WORST VOLCANIC ERUPTIONS

	LOCATION	DATE	ESTIMATED NO. KILLED
1	**Tambora,** Indonesia	5–12 Apr 1815	92,000

The eruption of Tambora on the island of Sumbawa killed about 10,000 islanders immediately, with a further 82,000 dying subsequently from disease and famine resulting from crops being destroyed. An estimated 1,700,000 tonnes of ash were hurled into the atmosphere. This blocked out the sunlight and affected the weather over the globe during the following year. An effect of this was to produce brilliantly coloured sunsets, depicted strikingly in paintings from the period, especially in the works of J.M.W. Turner.

	LOCATION	DATE	ESTIMATED NO. KILLED
2	**Unsen,** Japan	1 Apr 1793	53,000

During a period of intense volcanic activity in the area, the island of Unsen, or Unzen, completely disappeared, killing all its inhabitants.

	LOCATION	DATE	ESTIMATED NO. KILLED
3	**Mont Pelée,** Martinique	8 May 1902	40,000

After lying dormant for centuries, Mont Pelée began to erupt in April 1902. Assured that there was no danger, the 30,000 residents of the main city, St. Pierre, stayed in their homes and were there when, at 7.30 a.m. on 8 May, the volcano burst apart and showered the port with molten lava, ash, and gas, destroying virtually all life and property.

	LOCATION	DATE	ESTIMATED NO. KILLED
4	**Krakatoa,** Sumatra/Java	26–27 Aug 1883	36,380

The uninhabited island of Krakatoa exploded after a series of eruptions over the course of several days, and was audible up to 4,800 km (3,000 miles) away. Some sources put the fatalities as high as 200,000, most of them killed by subsequent tsunamis that reached 30 m (100 ft) high. The events were portrayed in the 1969 film *Krakatoa, East of Java*, but purists should note that Krakatoa is actually *west* of Java.

	LOCATION	DATE	ESTIMATED NO. KILLED
5	**Nevado del Ruiz,** Colombia	13 Nov 1985	22,940

The Andean volcano gave signs of erupting, but the decision to evacuate came too late. The steam, rocks, and ash ejected from Nevado del Ruiz melted its ice cap, resulting in a mudslide that completely engulfed the town of Armero.

	LOCATION	DATE	ESTIMATED NO. KILLED
6	**Mt. Etna,** Sicily	11 Mar 1669	over 20,000

Europe's largest volcano at 3,280 m (10,760 ft) has erupted frequently, but killed most people in 1669 when lava engulfed Catania, killing at least 20,000.

	LOCATION	DATE	ESTIMATED NO. KILLED
7	**Laki,** Iceland	Jan–June 1783	20,000

Events on the Laki volcanic ridge in 1783 culminated on 11 June with the largest ever recorded lava flow, up to 80 km (50 miles) long and 30 m (100 ft) deep. Many villages were engulfed and those who managed to escape were killed by poisonous gases released from the lava.

	LOCATION	DATE	ESTIMATED NO. KILLED
8	**Vesuvius,** Italy	24 Aug AD 79	16–20,000

When the previously dormant Vesuvius erupted, Herculaneum was engulfed by a mud flow while Pompeii was buried under a vast layer of pumice and volcanic ash – which preserved it in a near-perfect state that was revealed by archaeological excavations that began in 1738 and continue to this day.

	LOCATION	DATE	ESTIMATED NO. KILLED
9	**Vesuvius,** Italy	16–17 Dec 1631	up to 18,000

The next major cataclysm after that of AD 79 was almost as disastrous when lava and mud flows poured into surrounding towns including Naples.

	LOCATION	DATE	ESTIMATED NO. KILLED
10	**Mt. Etna,** Sicily	1169	over 15,000

Large numbers died sheltering in Catania cathedral, and more were killed when a tsunami caused by the eruption hit the port of Messina.

THE 10 WORST AVALANCHES AND LANDSLIDES*

	LOCATION	INCIDENT	DATE	ESTIMATED NO. KILLED
1	**Alps,** Italy	Avalanche	Oct 218 BC	18,000
2	**Yungay,** Peru	Landslide	31 May 1970	17,500
3	**Italian Alps**	Avalanche	13 Dec 1916	10,000
4	**Huarás,** Peru	Avalanche	13 Dec 1941	5,000
5	**Nevada Huascaran,** Peru	Avalanche	10 Jan 1962	3,500
6	**Chiavenna,** Italy	Landslide	4 Sept 1618	2,427
7	**Plurs,** Switzerland	Avalanche	4 Sept 1618	1,496
8	**Goldau Valley,** Switzerland	Landslide	2 Sept 1806	800
9	**Medellin,** Colombia	Landslide	27 Sept 1987	683
10	**Chungar,** Peru	Avalanche	19 Mar 1971	600

* Excluding those where most deaths resulted from flooding, earthquakes, volcanoes etc., associated with landslides

▼ Landslide tragedy
The Villa Tina area of Medellin, Colombia, was engulfed in a mudslide in 1987. Although 183 bodies were recovered, a further 500 inhabitants disappeared completely and 200 were injured, leaving just 117 survivors.

THE 10 WORST FLOODS

	LOCATION	DATE	ESTIMATED NO. KILLED
1	**Huang He River,** China	Aug 1931	3,700,000
2	**Huang He River,** China	Spring 1887	1,500,000
3	**Holland**	1 Nov 1530	400,000
4	**Kaifong,** China	1642	300,000
5	**Henan,** China	Sept–Nov 1939	over 200,000
6	**Bengal,** India	1876	200,000
7	**Yangtze River,** China	Aug–Sept 1931	140,000
8	**Holland**	1646	110,000
9	**North Vietnam**	30 Aug 1971	over 100,000
10 =	**Friesland,** Holland	1228	100,000
=	**Dort,** Holland	16 Apr 1421	100,000
=	**Canton,** China	12 June 1915	100,000
=	**Yangtze River,** China	Sept 1911	100,000

Records of floods caused by China's Huang He, or Yellow River, date back to 2297 BC. Since then, it has flooded at least 1,500 times, resulting in millions of deaths and giving it the nickname "China's Sorrow". According to some accounts, the flood of 1887 may have resulted in as many as 6 million deaths.

LIFE ON EARTH

Land Animals

TOP 10 HEAVIEST PRIMATES

PRIMATE	LENGTH* (CM)	(IN)	WEIGHT (KG)	(LB)
1 Gorilla	200	79	220	485
2 Man	177	70	77	170
3 Orangutan	137	54	75	165
4 Chimpanzee	92	36	50	110
5 = Baboon	100	39	45	99
= Mandrill	95	37	45	99
7 Gelada baboon	75	30	25	55
8 Proboscis monkey	76	30	24	53
9 Hanuman langur	107	42	20	44
10 Siamung gibbon	90	35	13	29

* Excluding tail

The largest primates (including man) and all the apes derive from the Old World (Africa, Asia and Europe). Only one member of a New World species of monkey (the Guatemalan howler at 91 cm/36 in; 9 kg/20 lb) is a close contender for the Top 10. The difference between the prosimians (primitive primates), great apes, lesser apes, and monkeys is more to do with shape than size, though the great apes mostly top the table.

TEST-TUBE GORILLA!

FIRST FACT

ROSIE, A LOWLAND GORILLA at Cincinnati Zoo, Ohio, USA, produced her seventh baby, a female named Timu ("team" in Swahili), on 9 October 1995. Timu was the first gorilla ever born by *in vitro* fertilization, using the same technique that produced the first human test-tube baby, Louise Brown, in 1978. An egg from Rosie had been fertilized by sperm from Mosuba, a male gorilla at Henry Doorly Zoo, Omaha, Nebraska, as part of a programme to ensure the survival of this threatened species.

◀ **Great ape**
Gorillas are the heaviest primates. The largest on record was N'gagi, a male living at San Diego Zoo, California, USA, from 1931 to 1944, whose peak weight was 310 kg (683 lb).

SNAKES WITH THE DEADLIEST BITES

	SNAKE	EST. LETHAL DOSE FOR HUMANS (MG)	AVE. VENOM PER BITE (MG)	POTENTIAL HUMANS KILLED PER BITE
1	Coastal taipan (*Oxyuranus scutellatus*)	1	120	120
2	Common krait (*Bungarus caeruleus*)	0.5	42	84
3	Philippine cobra (*Naja naja philippinensis*)	2	120	60
4 =	King cobra (*Ophiophagus hannah*)	20	1,000	50
=	Russell's viper (*Daboia russelli*)	3	150	50
6	Black mamba (*Dendroaspis polyepis*)	3	135	45
7	Yellow-jawed tommygoff (*Bothrops asper*)	25	1,000	40
8 =	Multibanded krait (*Bungarus multicinctus*)	0.8	28	35
=	Tiger snake (*Notechis scutatus*)	1	35	35
10	Jararacussu (*Bothrops jarararcussu*)	25	800	32

This list represents the results of a comprehensive survey of the various factors that determine the relative danger posed by poisonous snakes. These include the strength of the venom (and hence the estimated lethal dose for an adult), and the amount injected per bite; most snakes inject about 15 per cent of their venom per bite. Some snakes are rare and seldom come into contact with humans, while the likelihood of death as a result of snake bite varies according to the availability of antivenom and medical treatment. The common krait has the highest fatality rate of any snake on record: in one study, of 32 victims admitted to hospital in India after bites, only two survived. Bites by Russell's vipers have been known to cause death within 15 minutes.

FASTEST MAMMALS

	MAMMAL	MAXIMUM RECORDED SPEED (KM/H)	(MPH)
1	Cheetah	105	65
2	Pronghorn antelope	89	55
3 =	Mongolian gazelle	80	50
=	Springbok	80	50
5 =	Grant's gazelle	76	47
=	Thomson's gazelle	76	47
7	Brown hare	72	45
8	Horse	69	43
9 =	Greyhound	68	42
=	Red deer	68	42

Although several animals on the list are capable of higher speeds, these figures are based on controlled measurements of average speeds over 0.4 km (0.25 miles). Charging lions can achieve 80 km/h (50 mph) over very short distances, while various members of the antelope family, wildebeests, elks, dogs, coyotes, foxes, hyenas, zebras, and Mongolian wild asses have all been credited with unsustained spurts of 64 km/h (40 mph) or more. Compare these figures with the top speed of the three-toed sloth, which is 0.2 km/h (0.12 mph).

HEAVIEST CARNIVORES

	CARNIVORE	LENGTH (M)	(FT)	(IN)	WEIGHT (KG)	(LB)
1	Southern elephant seal	6.5	21	4	3,500	7,716
2	Walrus	3.8	12	6	1,200	2,646
3	Steller sea lion	3.0	9	8	1,100	2,425
4	Grizzly bear	3.0	9	8	780	1,720
5	Polar bear	2.6	8	6	600	1,323
6	Tiger	2.8	9	2	300	661
7	Lion	1.9	6	3	250	551
8	American black bear	1.8	6	0	227	500
9	Giant panda	1.5	5	0	160	353
10	Spectacled bear	1.8	6	0	140	309

Only three marine carnivores have been included to make room for the terrestrial heavyweights. The polar bear is probably the largest land carnivore if shoulder height (when the animal is on all fours) is taken into account; it tops an awesome 1.6 m (5.3 ft) compared with the 1.2 m (4 ft) of its nearest rival, the grizzly.

HEAVIEST TERRESTRIAL MAMMALS

	MAMMAL	LENGTH (M)	(FT)	WEIGHT (KG)	(LB)
1	African elephant	7.3	24	7,000	14,432
2	White rhinoceros	4.2	14	3,600	7,937
3	Hippopotamus	4.0	13	2,500	5,512
4	Giraffe	5.8	19	1,600	3,527
5	American bison	3.9	13	1,000	2,205
6	Arabian camel (dromedary)	3.5	12	690	1,521
7	Polar bear	2.6	8	600	1,323
8	Moose	3.0	10	550	1,213
9	Siberian tiger	3.3	11	300	661
10	Gorilla	2.0	7	220	485

The list excludes domesticated cattle and horses. It also avoids comparing close kin such as the African and Indian elephants, highlighting instead the sumo stars within distinctive large mammal groups such as the bears, deer, big cats, primates, and bovines (ox-like mammals).

Flying Animals

HEAVIEST FLIGHTED BIRDS

BIRD*	WINGSPAN (CM)	(IN)	WEIGHT (KG)	(LB)	(OZ)
1 Mute swan	238	94	22.50	49	6
2 Kori bustard	270	106	19.00	41	8
3 = Andean condor	320	126	15.00	33	1
= Great white pelican	360	142	15.00	33	1
5 Black vulture (Old World)	295	116	12.50	27	5
6 Sarus crane	280	110	12.24	26	9
7 Himalayan griffon (vulture)	310	122	12.00	26	5
8 Wandering albatross	350	138	11.30	24	9
9 Steller's sea eagle	265	104	9.00	19	8
10 Marabou stork	287	113	8.90	19	6

* By species

Source: *Chris Mead*

Wing size does not necessarily correspond to weight in flighted birds: the huge wingspan of the marabou stork, for example, is greater than that of species twice its weight. When laden with a meal of carrion, however, the voracious marabou can double its weight and needs all the lift it can get to take off. It often fails altogether and has to put up with flightlessness until digestion takes its course.

FASTEST BIRDS

BIRD	SPEED (KM/H)	(MPH)
1 Common eider	76	47
2 Bewick's swan	72	44
3 = Barnacle goose	68	42
= Common crane	68	42
5 Mallard	65	40
6 = Red-throated diver	61	38
= Wood pigeon	61	38
8 Oyster catcher	58	36
9 = Pheasant	54	33
= White-fronted goose	54	33

Source: *Chris Mead*

Recent research reveals that, contrary to popular belief, swifts are not fast fliers, but very efficient with long thin wings like gliders and low wing-loading. Fast fliers generally have high wing-loading and fast wing beats. The fastest swimming birds are penguins that can achieve speeds of 35 km/h (21 mph). The fastest running bird is the ostrich which can reach a speed of 72 km/h (44 mph), and maintain it for 20 minutes – ostrich racing with human jockeys or drawing chariots is pursued in South Africa and other countries.

SMALLEST BATS

	BAT/HABITAT	LENGTH (CM)	(IN)	WEIGHT (GM)	(OZ)
1	**Kitti's hognosed bat** (*Craseonycteris thonglongyai*), Thailand	2.9	1.10	2.0	0.07
2	**Proboscis bat** (*Rhynchonycteris naso*), Central and South America	3.8	1.50	2.5	0.09
3 =	**Banana bat** (*Pipistrellus nanus*), Africa	3.8	1.50	3.0	0.11
=	**Smoky bat** (*Furipterus horrens*), Central and South America	3.8	1.50	3.0	0.11
5 =	**Little yellow bat** (*Rhogeessa mira*), Central America	4.0	1.57	3.5	0.12
=	**Lesser bamboo bat** (*Tylonycteris pachypus*), Southeast Asia	4.0	1.57	3.5	0.12
7	**Disc-winged bat** (*Thyroptera tricolor*), Central and South America	3.6	1.42	4.0	0.14
8 =	**Lesser horseshoe bat** (*Rhinolophus hipposideros*), Europe and Western Asia	3.7	1.46	5.0	0.18
=	**California myotis** (*Myotis californienses*), North America	4.3	1.69	5.0	0.18
10	**Northern blossom bat** (*Macroglossus minimus*), Southeast Asia to Australia	6.4	2.52	15.0	0.53

The minute Kitti's hognosed bat, the world's smallest mammal, is found only in a group of caves in Thailand. It is named after its 1973 discoverer, Dr. Kitti Thonglongya.

LONGEST BIRD MIGRATIONS

	BIRD	APPROXIMATE DISTANCE (KM)	(MILES)
1	Pectoral sandpiper	19,000*	11,806
2	Wheatear	18,000	11,184
3	Slender-billed shearwater	17,500*	10,874
4	Ruff	16,600	10,314
5	Willow warbler	16,300	10,128
6	Arctic tern	16,200	10,066
7	Arctic skua	15,600	9,693
8	Swainson's hawk	15,200	9,445
9	Knot	15,000	9,320
10	Swallow	14,900	9,258

* Thought to be only half of the path taken during a whole year

Source: *Chris Mead*

This list is of the likely extremes for a normal migrant, not one that has got lost and wandered into new territory. All migrant birds fly far longer than is indicated by the direct route. Many species fly all year, except when they come to land to breed or, in the case of seabirds, to rest on the sea. Such species include the albatross, petrel, tern, and some types of swift and house martin. The annual distance covered by these birds may range from 150,000 km (93,206 miles) to almost 300,000 km (186,413 miles).

HEAVIEST OWLS

	OWL*	WINGSPAN (CM)	(IN)	WEIGHT (KG)	(LB)	(OZ)
1	Eurasian eagle-owl	75	29	4.20	9	4
2	Verraux's eagle-owl	65	26	3.11	6	14
3	Snowy owl	70	28	2.95	6	8
4	Great horned owl	60	24	2.50	5	8
5	Pel's fishing-owl	63	25	2.32	5	2
6	Pharaoh eagle-owl	50	20	2.30	5	1
7	Cape eagle-owl	58	23	1.80	3	15
8	Great grey owl	69	27	1.70	3	12
9	Powerful owl	60	24	1.50	3	5
10	Ural owl	62	24	1.30	2	14

* Some owls closely related to these species may be of similar size; most measurements are from female owls as they are usually larger

Source: *Chris Mead*

◄ **Big wings**
The Andean condor has one of the greatest total wing areas of any bird. The celebrated British mountaineer Edward Whymper encountered one in Ecuador in 1892 with wings that measured 3.2 m (10 ft 6 in) from tip to tip.

Marine Animals

THE 10 COUNTRIES WITH THE MOST THREATENED FISH SPECIES

COUNTRY/MOST THREATENED SPECIES*	TOTAL NO. OF THREATENED FISH

1 USA — 131
Alabama sturgeon#, cu-cui#, Charalito chihuahua, White River spinedace#, Moapa dace#, Cahaba shiner#, Cape Fear shiner#, Leon Spring pupfish#, Pecos pupfish#, California black sea bass, Alabama cavefish#, shortnose cisco, Apache trout

2 Mexico — 88
Perrito de potosi# (extinct in the wild), Cachorrito de charco palmal# (extinct in the wild), black-blotch pupfish# (extinct in the wild), butterfly splitfin# (extinct in the wild), golden skiffia# (extinct in the wild), charal de Alchichica#, *Cyprinella alvarezdelvillari*# (no common name), sardinita bocagrande#, sardinita quijarrona#, charalito saltillo#, charalito chihuahua, sardinita de tepelmene#, cachorrito de Mezquital#, cachorrito cabezon#, cachorrito de dorsal larga#, cachorrito de charco azul#, Cuatrocienegas killifish#, blackspot allotoca#, Mexclapique#, Turners hocklandkärpfling#, balsas hocklandkärpfling#, guayacon bocon#, broad-spotted molly#, molly del Teapa#, Monterrey platyfish#, black sea bass, totoaba#, Boccacio rockfish

3 Indonesia — 67
Sentani rainbowfish#, duck-bill poso minnow#, elongate poso minnow#, *Betta miniopinna*# (no common name), *Betta spilotogena*# (no common name), poso bungu#, *Encheloclarias kelioides*# (no common name)

4 Australia — 44
Red-finned blue-eye#, spotted handfish#, swan galaxias#, barred galaxias#, Clarence galaxias#, pedder galaxias#, Elizabeth Springs goby#, Edgbaston goby#, Mary River cod#

5 China — 33
Dabry's sturgeon#, Chinese paddlefish#

6 South Africa — 30
Twee River redfin#, border barb#, Clanwilliam sandfish#, Berg redfin#, Barnard's rock-catfish#, Incomati suckermouth#, river pipefish#

7 Philippines — 28
Cephalakoompsus pachycheilus# (no common name), manumbok#, bagangan#, bitungu#, pait#, baolan#, disa#, katapa-tapa#, *Puntius herrei*# (no common name), katolo#, kandar#, manalak#, tras#, palata#, dwarf pygmy goby#

8 = Cameroon — 27
Dikume#, konye#, myaka#, pungu#, fissi#, blackbelly tilapia#, keppi#, kululu#, nsess#, mongo#, pindu#, *Clarias maclareni*# (no common name)

= Uganda — 27
Allochromis welcommei# (no common name), *Astatotilapia latifasciata*# (no common name), *Haplochromis annectidens*# (no common name), *Harpagochromis worthingtoni*# (no common name), *Lipochromis "backflash cryptodon"*# (no common name), *Paralabidochromis beadlei*# (no common name), *Xystichromis "Kyoga flameback"*# (no common name)

10 Turkey — 22
Baltic/European sturgeon, *Aphanius splendens*# (no common name), *Aphanius sureyanus*# (no common name), *Aphanius transgrediens*# (no common name), flathead trout#

* Listed as Critically Endangered on the IUCN Red List 2000, except where otherwise indicated

 # Found in no other countries

Source: 2000 IUCN Red List of Threatened Species/UNEP-WCMC Animals of the World Database

HEAVIEST MARINE MAMMALS

MAMMAL	LENGTH (M)	(FT)	WEIGHT (TONNES)
1 Blue whale	33.5	110.0	137.0
2 Bowhead whale (Greenland right)	20.0	65.0	86.0
3 Northern right whale (black right)	18.6	60.0	77.7
4 Fin whale (common rorqual)	25.0	82.0	63.4
5 Sperm whale	18.0	59.0	43.7
6 Grey whale	14.0	46.0	34.9
7 Humpback whale	15.0	49.2	34.6
8 Sei whale	18.5	60.0	29.4
9 Bryde's whale	14.6	47.9	20.0
10 Baird's whale	5.5	18.0	12.1

Source: *Lucy T. Verma*

Probably the largest animal that ever lived, the blue whale dwarfs even the other whales listed here, all but one of which far outweigh the biggest land animal, the elephant. The elephant seal, with a weight of 3.5 tonnes, is the largest marine mammal that is not a whale.

HEAVIEST SHARKS

SHARK	MAXIMUM WEIGHT (KG)	(LB)
1 Whale shark	30,500	67,240
2 Basking shark	9,258	20,410
3 Great white shark	3,507	7,731
4 Greenland shark	1,009	2,224
5 Tiger shark	927	2,043
6 Great hammerhead shark	857	1,889
7 Six-gill shark	602	1,327
8 Grey nurse shark	564	1,243
9 Mako shark	554	1,221
10 Thresher shark	498	1,097

Source: *Lucy T. Verma*

Such is the notoriety of sharks that many accounts of their size are exaggerated, and this list should be taken as an approximate ranking based on best available evidence. The rare whale shark is also the largest fish, measuring up to 12.65 m (41 ft 6 in). First discovered in 1828, it is a plankton-eater and consequently not a threat to swimmers.

HEAVIEST TURTLES

TURTLE	MAXIMUM WEIGHT (KG)	(LB)
1 Pacific leatherback turtle*	704.4	1,552
2 Atlantic leatherback turtle*	463.0	1,018
3 Green sea turtle	355.3	783
4 Loggerhead turtle	257.8	568
5 Alligator snapping turtle#	100.0	220
6 Flatback (sea) turtle	78.2	171
7 Hawksbill (sea) turtle	62.7	138
8 Kemps Ridley turtle	60.5	133
9 Olive Ridley turtle	49.9	110
10 Common snapping turtle#	38.5	85

* *One species, differing in size according to where they live*

\# *Freshwater species*

Source: *Lucy T. Verma*

The largest leatherback turtle ever recorded is a male found beached at Harlech, Wales, in 1988, measuring 2.9 m (9 ft 5½ in) and weighing 961 kg (2,120 lb). It is now displayed in the National Museum of Wales, Cardiff.

◄ Threatened turtle
Having been hunted as food and for their shells, many of the world's largest turtles are endangered and under threat of extinction.

A Bug's Life

 MOST COMMON INSECTS*

	SPECIES (SCIENTIFIC NAME)	APPROXIMATE NO. OF KNOWN SPECIES
1	Beetles (Coleoptera)	400,000
2	Butterflies and moths (Lepidoptera)	165,000
3	Ants, bees, and wasps (Hymenoptera)	140,000
4	True flies (Diptera)	120,000
5	Bugs (Hemiptera)	90,000
6	Crickets, grasshoppers, and locusts (Orthoptera)	20,000
7	Caddisflies (Trichoptera)	10,000
8	Lice (Phthiraptera/Psocoptera)	7,000
9	Dragonflies and damselflies (Odonata)	5,500
10	Lacewings (Neuroptera)	4,700

* By number of known species

This list includes only species that have been discovered and named; it is surmised that many thousands of species still await discovery. It takes no account of the absolute numbers of each species, which are truly colossal. There are at least one million insects for each of the Earth's 6.3 billion humans, which together would weigh at least 12 times as much as the human race and at least three times more than the combined weight of all other living animals. There are at least five quadrillion individuals, among the commonest of which are ants, flies, beetles, and the little-known springtails, which inhabit moist topsoil the world over. The latter alone probably outweigh the entire human race.

LARGEST MOLLUSCS*

	SPECIES (SCIENTIFIC NAME)	CLASS	LENGTH (MM)	LENGTH (IN)
1	Giant squid (Architeuthis species)	Cephalopod	16,764	660[#]
2	Giant clam (Tridacna gigas)	Marine bivalve	1,300	51
3	Australian trumpet (Syrus aruanus)	Marine snail	770	30
4	Hexabranchus sanguineus	Sea slug	520	20
5	Carinaria cristata	Heteropod	500	19
6	Steller's Coat of Mail shell (Cryptochiton stelleri)	Chiton	470	18
7	Freshwater mussel (Cristaria plicata)	Freshwater bivalve	300	11
8	Giant African snail (Achatina achatina)	Land snail	200	7
9	Tusk shell (Dentalium vernedi)	Scaphopod	138	5
10	Apple snail (Pila werneri)	Freshwater snail	125	4

* Largest species within each class

[#] Estimated; actual length unknown

There are over 60,000 species of molluscs, including octopuses, snails, slugs, and shellfish, of which these are the largest – although tales of the largest, the giant squid, attacking and sinking ships, are in the realm of sailors' tall stories. The giant clam is noted for its longevity, with lifespans of up to 150 years being claimed by some experts.

 LARGEST BUTTERFLIES

	BUTTERFLY (SCIENTIFIC NAME)	WINGSPAN (MM)	WINGSPAN (IN)
1	Queen Alexandra's birdwing (Ornithoptera alexandrae)	280	11.0
2	African giant swallowtail (Papilio antimachus)	230	9.1
3	Goliath birdwing (Ornithoptera goliath)	210	8.3
4 =	Buru opalescent birdwing (Troides prattorum)	200	7.9
=	Trogonoptera trojana	200	7.9
=	Troides hypolitus	200	7.9
7 =	Chimaera birdwing (Ornithoptera chimaera)	190	7.5
=	Ornithoptera lydius	190	7.5
=	Troides magellanus	190	7.5
=	Troides miranda	190	7.5

The rare Queen Alexandra's birdwing is found only in Papua New Guinea. Females, which are usually larger than males, weigh up to 25 gm (‰ oz).

▶ **Leaf beetle**
Almost one-third of all known animal species are beetles, with more than 25,000 species of leaf beetles among the 400,000 recorded.

TOP10 FASTEST INSECT FLIERS

SPECIES (SCIENTIFIC NAME)	SPEED (KM/H)	(MPH)
1 Hawkmoth (*Sphingidaei*)	53.6	33.3
2 = West Indian butterfly (*Nymphalidae prepona*)	48.0	30.0
= Deer bot fly (*Cephenemyia pratti*)	48.0	30.0
4 Deer bot fly (*Chrysops*)	40.0	25.0
5 West Indian butterfly (*Hesperiidae* species)	30.0	18.6
6 Dragonfly (*Anax parthenope*)	28.6	17.8
7 Hornet (*Vespa crabro*)	21.4	13.3
8 Bumble bee (*Bombus lapidarius*)	17.9	11.1
9 Horsefly (*Tabanus bovinus*)	14.3	8.9
10 Honey bee (*Apis mellifera*)	11.6	7.2

▶ **Hive of activity**
With its wings beating at an amazing rate of 11,000 times a minute, the honey bee can fly extremely fast.

TOP10 DEADLIEST SPIDERS

SPIDER (SCIENTIFIC NAME)	LOCATION
1 Banana spider (*Phonenutria nigriventer*)	Central and South America
2 Sydney funnel web (*Atrax robustus*)	Australia
3 Wolf spider (*Lycosa raptoria/erythrognatha*)	Central and South America
4 Black widow (*Latrodectus* species)	Widespread
5 Violin spider/Recluse spider	Widespread
6 Sac spider	Southern Europe
7 Tarantula (*Eurypelma rubropilosum*)	Neotropics
8 Tarantula (*Acanthoscurria atrox*)	Neotropics
9 Tarantula (*Lasiodora klugi*)	Neotropics
10 Tarantula (*Pamphobeteus* species)	Neotropics

This list ranks spiders according to their "lethal potential" – their venom yield divided by their venom potency. The banana spider, for example, yields 6 mg of venom, with 1 mg the estimated lethal dose in man. However, few spiders are capable of killing humans – there were just 14 recorded deaths caused by black widows in the USA in the whole of the 19th century – since their venom yield is relatively low compared with that of the most dangerous snakes; the tarantula, for example, produces 1.5 mg of venom, but its lethal dose for an adult human is 12 mg. Anecdotal evidence suggests that the Thailand and Sumatran black birdeaters may be equally dangerous, but insufficient data are available.

Man & Beast

TOP 10 MOST COMMON ANIMAL PHOBIAS

	ANIMAL	MEDICAL TERM
1	Spiders	Arachnephobia or arachnophobia
2	Bees and wasps	Bees: Apiphobia, apiophobia or melissophobia; wasps: spheksophobia
3	Reptiles	Batrachophobia
4	Snakes	Ophidiophobia, ophiophobia, ophiciophobia, herpetophobia or snakephobia
5	Mice	Musophobia or muriphobia
6	Dogs	Cynophobia or kynophobia
7	Birds	Ornithophobia
8	Frogs	Batrachophobia
9 =	Ants	Myrmecophobia
=	Horses	Hippophobia or equinophobia
=	Rats	No medical term

Not all phobias are completely irrational. Creatures that may bite or sting, or carry disease, such as rabid dogs or cats, are very wisely avoided.

▼ **Death rattle**
The fear of snakes is among the most common of all phobias – although with species such as this rattlesnake there are good reasons.

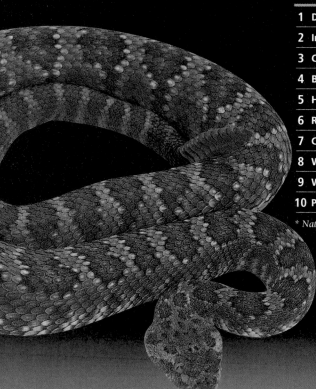

THE 10 COUNTRIES THAT CATCH THE MOST WHALES

		CATCH (2000)		
	COUNTRY	SPERM AND PILOT WHALES	BLUE AND FIN WHALES	TOTAL
1	Japan	16,937	552	17,489
2	Brazil	861	–	861
3	Norway	–	487	487
4	Argentina	445	–	445
5	France	213	–	213
6	USA	172	35	207
7	Russia	22	180	202
8	South Korea	95	79	174
9	Greenland	–	162	162
10	UK	46	3	49

Source: *Food and Agriculture Organization of the United Nations*

Whaling has been banned in the majority of these countries; most of the whales listed in this Top 10 have been caught accidentally in fishing nets.

THE 10 ANIMALS INVOLVED IN THE MOST ACCIDENTS IN THE UK

	ANIMAL	NO. OF INJURIES CAUSED PER ANNUM*
1	Dog	69,222
2	Insect (excluding bees and wasps)	17,009
3	Cat	15,118
4	Bee and wasp	10,565
5	Horse, pony, donkey	3,607
6	Rabbit, hamster, etc.	3,528
7	Chicken, swan, duck, etc.	986
8	Wild bird	907
9	Wild animal	631
10	Pet bird	453

* *National estimates*

Extrapolated from a survey of case histories from Accident and Emergency units of hospitals in the UK, a picture emerges of the creatures that cause injuries requiring medical treatment – many of them by the victims' own pets.

THE 10 COUNTRIES WITH THE MOST IVORY SEIZURES

	COUNTRY	SEIZURES (1989–99)
1	USA	1,435
2	Namibia	409
3	France	375
4	UK	367
5	Germany	261
6	Belgium	237
7	Tanzania	210
8	South Africa	155
9	Malawi	132
10	Zambia	104
	World	4,361

Source: *The Elephant Trade Information System (ETIS)*

The records indicate that nearly 120 tonnes of ivory have been seized across the world in the period 1989–99, representing some 28,319 tusks and pieces of raw ivory, 204,215 semi-worked ivory blocks, and 187,950 ivory products.

TOP 10 FILMS STARRING ANIMALS

	FILM	YEAR	ANIMAL
1	Jaws	1975	Shark
2	101 Dalmatians	1996	Dogs
3	Doctor Dolittle	1998	Various
4	Babe	1995	Pig
5	Jaws 2	1978	Shark
6	Cats & Dogs	2001	Cats/dogs
7	The Horse Whisperer	1998	Horses
8	102 Dalmatians	2000	Dogs
9	Doctor Dolittle 2	2001	Various
10	Deep Blue Sea	1999	Sharks

This list is of films where real animals are central, rather than secondary, characters. It excludes dinosaurs, fantasy creatures such as dragons, and humans disguised as animals (hence eliminating *Planet of the Apes*) as well as animated films and the eponymous stars of animated/live-action combinations such as *Who Framed Roger Rabbit*, *Stuart Little*, and *Scooby-Doo*. With new technology, the line between real, animatronic, and computer-generated animals is becoming increasingly blurred.

Jaws of death
Star of *Jaws*, the great white shark is responsible for more human attacks (254) and fatalities (67) than any other species in attacks recorded between 1580 and 2001.

PLACES WHERE MOST PEOPLE ARE ATTACKED BY SHARKS

COUNTRY/STATE	FATAL ATTACKS	LAST FATAL ATTACK	TOTAL ATTACKS*
1 USA (continental)	69	2001	855
2 Australia	152	2000	323
3 South Africa	43	1999	225
4 Hawaii	19	1992	99
5 Brazil	20	1998	78
6 Papua New Guinea	31	2000	65
7 New Zealand	9	1968	53
8 The Bahamas	1	1968	42
9 Mexico	21	1997	39
10 Fiji Islands	10	2000	25

* Including non-fatal

Source: *International Shark Attack File/American Elasmobranch Society/Florida Museum of Natural History*

The International Shark Attack File monitors worldwide incidents, a total of more than 2,000 of which have been recorded since the 16th century. The 1990s had the highest attack total (536) of any decade, while 76 unprovoked attacks were recorded in 2001 alone. This upward trend is believed to reflect the increase in the numbers of people engaging in scuba diving and other aquatic activities.

ANIMALS USED IN THE MOST EXPERIMENTS IN THE UK

ANIMAL	EXPERIMENTAL PROCEDURES (2000)
1 Rodents	2,213,436
2 Fish	243,019
3 Birds	124,209
4 Rabbits	39,683
5 Sheep	36,544
6 Reptiles/amphibians	15,637
7 Pigs	8,553
8 Dogs	7,632
9 Monkeys	3,690
10 Cats	1,813
Total including others not in Top 10	2,714,726

Source: *Fund for the Replacement of Animals in Medical Experiments (FRAME)/Home Office*

Rodents include 1,606,962 mice and 534,973 rats, while among dogs beagles, with 6,872, are the most used breed. Of the total, 446,694 animals were employed in pharmaceutical research and 258,354 in cancer research. Many tests – which do not necessarily result in the death of the animals involved – are carried out to test the safety of products ranging from medicines and vaccines to food additives.

Pet Power

PETS IN THE UK

PET	NO. OWNED (2001)
1 Goldfish	14,700,000
2 Tropical fish	9,300,000
3 Cat	7,500,000
4 Dog	6,100,000
5 Rabbit	1,100,000
6 Birds (excluding budgerigars and canaries)	1,060,000
7 Hamster	860,000
8 Budgerigar	750,000
9 Guinea pig	730,000
10 Canary	260,000

Source: *Pet Food Manufacturers' Association*

Just under half of households in the UK own a pet, but changes in lifestyle have affected the relative populations of cats and dogs. More people go out to work, which makes dog ownership more difficult, so many people have opted for the more independent cat.

PET DOG POPULATIONS

COUNTRY	EST. PET DOG POPULATION (2002)
1 USA	61,080,000
2 Brazil	30,051,000
3 China	22,908,000
4 Japan	9,650,000
5 Russia	9,600,000
6 South Africa	9,100,000
7 France	8,150,000
8 Italy	7,600,000
9 Poland	7,520,000
10 Thailand	6,900,000
UK	5,800,000

Source: *Euromonitor*

The estimate for the US dog population represents a ratio of more than one dog for every two of the 104,705,000 households in the country, but since multiple ownership is common, there are more dog-free homes than those with a canine inhabitant.

PET BIRD POPULATIONS

COUNTRY	EST. PET BIRD POPULATION (2002)
1 China	71,474,000
2 Japan	21,300,000
3 USA	18,740,000
4 Brazil	17,254,000
5 Indonesia	14,842,000
6 Italy	13,000,000
7 Turkey	9,200,000
8 Spain	7,734,000
9 Australia	7,100,000
10 France	6,500,000
UK	3,100,00

Source: *Euromonitor*

PET FISH POPULATIONS

COUNTRY	EST. PET FISH POPULATION (2002)
1 USA	168,990,000
2 China	121,852,000
3 Germany	50,000,000
4 Japan	34,100,000
5 Italy	30,000,000
6 France	28,000,000
7 UK	23,900,000
8 Russia	20,600,000
9 Australia	12,900,000
10 Sweden	9,480,000

Source: *Euromonitor*

◀ **Tanks a lot**
Fish are kept as domestic pets, rather than for food, the world over. China's particular fondness for them has a long-standing tradition.

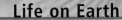

▲ Cool for cats
Ownership of pedigree cats, such as this Siamese, contributes to the substantial feline population of many Western countries. In developing parts of the world, cats continue their traditional role as domestic mouse-catchers.

THE 10 LATEST WINNERS OF "BEST IN SHOW" AT CRUFTS

YEAR	BREED	NAME
2003	Pekingnese	Danny
2002	Standard poodle	Nordic Champion Topscore Contradiction
2001	Basenji hound	Jethard Cidevant
2000	Kerry blue terrier	Torums Scarf Michael
1999	Irish setter	Caspians Intrepid
1998	Welsh terrier	Saredon Forever Young
1997	Yorkshire terrier	Ozmilion Mystification
1996	Cocker spaniel	Canigou Cambrai
1995	Irish setter	Starchelle Chicago Bear
1994	Welsh terrier	Purston Hit

Crufts Dog Show was the brainchild of Charles Cruft (1852–1939), an employee of pioneer dog biscuit manufacturer James Spratt. After managing the Allied Terrier Club Show at the Royal Aquarium, Westminster, London, in 1886, he started the first show to bear his name at the Royal Agricultural Hall, Islington, London, in 1891. After his death, his widow passed responsibility to the Kennel Club, which continues to stage it under its founder's name.

TOP 10 PET CAT POPULATIONS

	COUNTRY	EST. PET CAT POPULATION (2002)
1	USA	76,430,000
2	China	53,100,000
3	Russia	12,700,000
4	Brazil	12,466,000
5	France	9,600,000
6	Italy	9,400,000
7	UK	7,700,000
8	Ukraine	7,350,000
9	Japan	7,300,000
10	Germany	7,000,000

Source: *Euromonitor*

TOP 10 PET SMALL MAMMAL POPULATIONS

	COUNTRY	EST. PET SMALL MAMMAL POPULATION (2002)
1	USA	20,930,000
2	Germany	6,400,000
3	Russia	4,700,000
4	UK	4,200,000
5	Japan	3,000,000
6	France	2,400,000
7	Italy	2,100,000
8	China	1,748,000
9	Canada	1,153,000
10	Spain	1,112,000

Source: *Euromonitor*

TOP 10 PET INSURANCE CLAIMS IN THE UK

1 **Arthritis**

2 **Lameness**

3 **Dermatitis** (inflammation of the skin)

4 **Otitis** (inflammation of the ear)

5 **Heart disorders**

6 **Tumours**

7 **Growths**

8 **Pyoderma** (skin infection)

9 **Teeth and gum disorders**

10 **Skin disorders**

Source: *Petplan*

Trees & Forests

COUNTRY	AREA (2000) (SQ KM)	(SQ MILES)
1 Russia	8,513,920	3,287,243
2 Brazil	5,439,905	2,100,359
3 Canada	2,445,710	944,294
4 USA	2,259,930	872,564
5 China	1,634,800	631,200
6 Australia	1,545,390	596,678
7 Dem. Rep. of Congo	1,352,070	522,037
8 Indonesia	1,049,860	405,353
9 Angola	697,560	269,329
10 Peru	652,150	251,796
World	*38,561,590*	*14,888,715*
UK	*27,940*	*10,788*

Source: *Food and Agriculture Organization of the United Nations*, State of the World's Forests, 2001

The world's forests occupy some 29 per cent of the total land area of the planet. Just under half of Russia is forested – a total area that is almost the size of the whole of Brazil.

COUNTRY	AREA (SQ KM)	(SQ MILES)
1 Brazil	3,012,730	1,163,222
2 Dem. Rep. of Congo	1,350,710	521,512
3 Indonesia	887,440	343,029
4 Peru	756,360	292,032
5 Bolivia	686,380	265,012
6 Venezuela	556,150	214,730
7 Colombia	531,860	205,352
8 Mexico	457,650	176,700
9 India	444,500	171,622
10 Angola	375,640	145,035
World	*14,076,490*	*5,434,964*

▼ Tropical forest

The world's tropical forests are among Earth's most important resources, and are home to more than half the planet's plant and animal species. The vast forests of Brazil occupy an area greater than the whole of India.

TOP 10 LARGEST FORESTS IN THE UK*

	FOREST	AREA (SQ KM)	(SQ MILES)
1	**Galloway Forest Park,** Dumfries and Galloway	760	293
2	**Kielder Forest Park,** Northumberland	720	278
3	**New Forest,** Hampshire	270	104
4	**Dornoch Forest,** Highland	260	100
5	**Argyll Forest Park,** Argyll and Bute	220	85
6	**Queen Elizabeth Forest Park,** Stirling	210	81
7	**Thetford Forest Park,** Norfolk/Suffolk	190	73
8	= **Affric Forest** (Fort Augustus), Highland	180	69
	= **Tay Forest Park,** Perthshire	180	69
10	**Glengarry Forest** (Lochaber Forest District), Highland	165	64

* Forestry Commission forests, including areas designated as Forest Parks, which can include areas not covered by woodland

Source: *Forestry Commission*

Seized by William the Conqueror in 1079, the New Forest is the largest surviving royal forest in Britain. It was transferred from the Crown to the Forestry Commission in 1923.

▲ Deforesting countries

In the 1990s the net loss of the world's forest (the difference between deforestation and increase by new planting) declined from 39,634,290 sq km (15,302,887 sq miles) to 38,694,550 sq km (14,940,051 sq miles), an average of 939,740 sq km (362,836 sq miles) a year.

TOP 10 COUNTRIES WITH THE HIGHEST DEFORESTATION RATE

	COUNTRY	ANNUAL FOREST COVER LOSS (1990–2000) (SQ KM)	(SQ MILES)
1	**Brazil**	23,090	8,915
2	**Indonesia**	13,120	5,065
3	**Sudan**	9,590	3,702
4	**Zambia**	8,510	3,286
5	**Mexico**	6,310	2,436
6	**Dem. Rep. of Congo**	5,320	2,054
7	**Myanmar**	5,170	1,996
8	**Nigeria**	3,980	1,537
9	**Zimbabwe**	3,200	1,235
10	**Argentina**	2,850	1,100

Source: *Food and Agriculture Organization of the United Nations, State of the World's Forests, 2001*

During the 1990s, deforestation – the permanent loss of forest when trees are felled to enable the land to be used for other purposes – resulted in the decline of Brazil's rainforests from 5,669,980 sq km (2,189,192 sq miles) to 5,439,050 sq km (2,100,029 sq miles).

TOP 10 MOST FORESTED COUNTRIES

	COUNTRY	PERCENTAGE FOREST COVER (2000)
1	**French Guiana**	90.0
2	**Solomon Islands**	87.8
3	**Suriname**	86.4
4	**Gabon**	81.5
5	**Guyana**	78.5
6	**Brunei**	76.6
7	**Palau**	76.1
8	**Finland**	72.0
9	**North Korea**	68.1
10	**Sweden**	66.8
	UK	*11.6*

Source: *Food and Agriculture Organization of the United Nations*

These countries have the greatest area of forest as a percentage of their total land area. Deforestation has caused the world average to fall from about 32 per cent in 1972 to its present 29 per cent.

TOP 10 TIMBER-PRODUCING COUNTRIES

	COUNTRY	ROUNDWOOD PRODUCTION (2001) (CU M)	(CU FT)
1	**USA**	481,092,992	16,989,640,251
2	**India**	296,234,016	10,461,406,317
3	**China**	284,910,024	10,061,503,477
4	**Brazil**	236,422,218	8,349,172,609
5	**Canada**	176,692,000	6,239,819,672
6	**Russia**	162,300,000	5,731,570,941
7	**Indonesia**	119,208,572	4,210,053,374
8	**Ethiopia**	91,283,543	3,223,648,197
9	**Dem. Rep. of Congo**	69,733,688	2,462,622,179
10	**Nigeria**	69,115,552	2,440,792,910
	World	*3,327,616,024*	*117,513,661,774*
	UK	*7,609,000*	*268,709,324*

Source: *Food and Agriculture Organization of the United Nations*

Enough roundwood is produced annually to build more than 3,000 buildings with the volume of the Empire State Building, all constructed in solid wood!

Crops & Livestock

TOP 10 CEREAL CROPS

	CROP	PRODUCTION (2001) (TONNES)
1	Maize	614,219,025
2	Rice (paddy)	595,267,724
3	Wheat	589,871,831
4	Barley	143,067,330
5	Sorghum	58,732,210
6	Millet	28,900,100
7	Oats	26,950,177
8	Rye	23,283,404
9	Triticale (wheat/rye hybrid)	10,414,390
10	Buckwheat	2,577,044

Source: *Food and Agriculture Organization of the United Nations*

◄ Top of the crops

Terraced rice cultivation in Indonesia, a leading producer of one of the world's most important crops. Worldwide, more than 1.5 million sq km (579,000 sq miles) are devoted to rice growing.

TOP 10 RICE-PRODUCING COUNTRIES

	COUNTRY	PRODUCTION* (2001) (TONNES)
1	China	179,303,895
2	India	136,580,992
3	Indonesia	50,096,000
4	Bangladesh	38,500,000
5	Vietnam	31,970,100
6	Thailand	26,954,068
7	Myanmar	20,600,000
8	Philippines	12,954,900
9	Japan	11,320,000
10	Brazil	10,195,400
	World	595,267,724

* Paddy

Source: *Food and Agriculture Organization of the United Nations*

Rice has been cultivated in Southeast Asia since at least 4000 BC, from where it spread to India and the Mediterranean region and on to Brazil.

TOP 10 VEGETABLE CROPS

	CROP*	PRODUCTION (2001) (TONNES)
1	Sugar cane	1,273,370,750
2	Potatoes	309,306,566
3	Sugar beets	229,417,606
4	Soya beans	176,506,154
5	Sweet potatoes	135,447,539
6	Tomatoes	105,069,537
7	Cabbages	59,267,364
8	Onions (dry)	49,415,090
9	Yams	38,569,348
10	Cucumbers and gherkins	35,017,554

* Excluding cereals

Source: *Food and Agriculture Organization of the United Nations*

The two leading crops exemplify the two-way traffic history of vegetable cultivation: sugar cane originated in India but was taken to the Carribean, while the potato, indigenous to the Americas, was transported to Europe, where it became a staple crop.

TOP 10 TRACTOR COUNTRIES

	COUNTRY	AGRICULTURAL TRACTORS IN USE (2000) TOTAL	PER 1,000 INHABITANTS
1	Slovenia	114,188	57.44
2	Ireland	167,000	43.91
3	Austria	330,000	40.84
4	Yugoslavia	397,391	37.66
5	Finland	194,000	37.51
6	Estonia	50,624	36.34
7	Poland	1,306,700	33.85
8	Iceland	9,019	32.33
9	Italy	1,750,000	30.42
10	Norway	133,000	29.76
	World	26,409,666	4.36
	UK	500,000	8.38

Source: *Food and Agriculture Organization of the United Nations*

TOP 10 CATTLE COUNTRIES

	COUNTRY	CATTLE (2001)
1	India	219,642,000
2	Brazil	176,000,000
3	China	106,175,000
4	USA	96,700,000
5	Argentina	50,369,000
6	Sudan	38,325,000
7	Ethiopia	34,500,000
8	Mexico	30,600,000
9	Australia	28,768,000
10	Colombia	27,000,000
	World	*1,360,475,620*
	UK	*10,430,000*

Source: *Food and Agriculture Organization of the United Nations*

In addition to its symbolic and religious significance, the dairy cow has long been a crucial component of India's economy. The country's cattle population has more than quadrupled in the past century.

TOP 10 TYPES OF LIVESTOCK

	ANIMAL	WORLD STOCKS (2001)
1	Chickens	15,420,137,000
2	Cattle	1,360,475,620
3	Sheep	1,044,045,120
4	Ducks	947,525,000
5	Pigs	939,318,631
6	Rabbits	497,082,000
7	Geese	245,731,000
8	Turkeys	242,802,000
9	Buffaloes	166,418,998
10	Goats	146,514,641

Source: *Food and Agriculture Organization of the United Nations*

In sheer numbers, chickens clearly rule the roost, with more than two chickens for every human on the planet. As well as providing meat, they produce some 880 billion eggs per annum, 337 billion of them in China alone – enough to make an omelette larger than Denmark!

▶ **Getting the goat**
There are more than 60 countries in the world with one million or more goats. Worldwide, goats produce over 12 million tonnes of milk a year, while more than 300 million are slaughtered annually to provide meat and goatskin.

Fruit & Nuts

TOP 10 | FRUIT-PRODUCING COUNTRIES

	COUNTRY	PRODUCTION* (2001) (TONNES)
1	China	68,738,224
2	India	48,570,920
3	Brazil	31,795,266
4	USA	30,100,045
5	Italy	18,274,570
6	Spain	14,920,852
7	Mexico	14,217,004
8	Iran	11,768,628
9	Philippines	11,122,028
10	France	11,037,748
	World	468,261,602
	UK	318,100

* Excluding melons

Source: *Food and Agriculture Organization of the United Nations*

TOP 10 | ALMOND-PRODUCING COUNTRIES

	COUNTRY	PRODUCTION (2001) (TONNES)
1	USA	376,480
2	Spain	257,000
3	Italy	112,812
4	Iran	97,144
5	Morocco	81,820
6	Greece	55,267
7	Syria	49,487
8	Turkey	42,000
9	Pakistan	33,236
10	Lebanon	33,000
	World	1,330,321

Source: *Food and Agriculture Organization of the United Nations*

TOP 10 | FRUIT CROPS

	CROP	PRODUCTION (2001) (TONNES)
1	Watermelons	78,341,249
2	Bananas	68,487,734
3	Oranges	62,566,069
4	Grapes	61,247,694
5	Apples	58,673,116
6	Coconuts	50,556,959
7	Plantains	28,829,889
8	Mangoes	25,646,285
9	Cantaloupes and other melons	21,136,774
10	Tangerines, etc.	18,172,950

Source: *Food and Agriculture Organization of the United Nations*

About 70 per cent of watermelons, the world's top fruit crop, are grown in China, where they have been cultivated since the 10th century.

TOP 10 | WALNUT-PRODUCING COUNTRIES

	COUNTRY	PRODUCTION (2001) (TONNES)
1	USA	276,690
2	China	252,347
3	Iran	168,031
4	Turkey	116,000
5	Ukraine	55,130
6	Romania	33,942
7	India	31,000
8	France	29,176
9	Yugoslavia	23,600
10	Greece	21,927
	World	1,246,259

Source: *Food and Agriculture Organization of the United Nations*

◄ In a nutshell

Walnuts were exported to the USA from England and introduced in California in 1867, starting a state industry that today produces 99 per cent of the US total and a major proportion of the world's supply.

TOP 10 | NUT CROPS

	CROP	PRODUCTION (2001) (TONNES)
1	Groundnuts (in shell)	36,123,906
2	Cashew nuts	1,604,569
3	Almonds	1,330,321
4	Walnuts	1,246,259
5	Chestnuts	959,954
6	Hazelnuts	870,475
7	Karite nuts (sheanuts)	647,500
8	Areca nuts (betel)	645,166
9	Tung nuts	558,390
10	Pistachios	294,439

Source: *Food and Agriculture Organization of the United Nations*

Groundnuts, or peanuts, are natives of Peru and Brazil, from where they spread to Asia and Africa. The modern peanut industry owes its origins to African-American agriculturalist George Washington Carver (1864–1943), who pioneered improved methods of cultivation, devising no fewer than 325 products based on peanuts, ranging from shampoo to shoe polish.

TOP 10 GRAPE-PRODUCING COUNTRIES

	COUNTRY	PRODUCTION (2001) (TONNES)
1	Italy	8,988,388
2	France	7,281,550
3	USA	5,944,350
4	Spain	5,111,300
5	China	3,765,017
6	Turkey	3,250,000
7	Iran	2,516,695
8	Argentina	2,457,599
9	Chile	1,570,000
10	Australia	1,551,000
	World	*61,247,694*
	UK	*1,500*

Source: *Food and Agriculture Organization of the United Nations*

TOP 10 DATE-PRODUCING COUNTRIES

	COUNTRY	PRODUCTION (2001) (TONNES)
1	Egypt	1,113,270
2	Iran	874,985
3	United Arab Emirates	757,600
4	Saudi Arabia	735,000
5	Iraq	650,000
6	Pakistan	631,695
7	Algeria	370,000
8	Oman	248,458
9	Sudan	177,000
10	Libya	132,500
	World	*6,132,921*

Source: *Food and Agriculture Organization of the United Nations*

▶ It's a date

There are some 90 million date palms in the world, 64 million of them in Arab countries, for which dates are an important export crop. Only female trees produce fruit – as much as 68 kg (150 lb) a year each.

THE HUMAN
WORLD

Human Body & Health

TOP 10 HEALTHIEST COUNTRIES

	COUNTRY	HEALTHY LIFE EXPECTANCY AT BIRTH*
1	Japan	73.6
2	Switzerland	72.8
3	San Marino	72.2
4	Sweden	71.8
5	Australia	71.6
6 =	France	71.3
=	Monaco	71.3
8	Iceland	71.2
9 =	Austria	71.0
=	Italy	71.0
	UK	69.6

* Average number of years expected to be spent in good health

Source: *World Health Organization,* World Health Report 2002

▶ Long life
Diet and other factors have enabled Japanese healthy life expectancy to top the world league table.

THE 10 LEAST HEALTHY COUNTRIES

	COUNTRY	HEALTHY LIFE EXPECTANCY AT BIRTH*
1	Sierra Leone	26.5
2	Malawi	29.8
3	Zambia	30.9
4	Botswana	32.9
5	Niger	33.2
6 =	Afghanistan	33.4
=	Lesotho	33.4
8	Burundi	33.7
9	Rwanda	33.8
10	Swaziland	33.9

* Average number of years expected to be spent in good health

Source: *World Health Organization,* World Health Report 2002

THE 10 MOST COMMON HEALTH DISORDERS

DISORDERS AFFECTING MALES	% TOTAL*		DISORDERS AFFECTING FEMALES	% TOTAL*
Depression	9.7	1	Depression	14.0
Alcohol-use disorders	5.5	2	Iron-deficiency disorders	4.9
Hearing loss, adult onset	5.1	3	Hearing loss, adult onset	4.2
Iron-deficiency anaemia	4.1	4	Osteoarthritis	3.5
Chronic obstructive pulmonary disease	3.8	5	Chronic obstructive pulmonary disease	2.9
Injuries resulting from falls	3.3	6	Schizophrenia	2.7
Schizophrenia	3.0	7	Manic depression	2.4
Injuries resulting from road traffic accidents	2.7	8	Injuries resulting from falls	2.3
Manic depression	2.6	9	Alzheimer's/other dementias	2.2
Osteoarthritis	2.5	10	Obstructed labour	2.1

* Total includes other disorders not listed above

Source: *World Health Organization,* World Health Report 2001

TOP 10 LONGEST BONES IN THE HUMAN BODY

	BONE	AVERAGE LENGTH (CM)	(IN)
1	**Femur** (thighbone – upper leg)	50.50	19.88
2	**Tibia** (shinbone – inner lower leg)	43.03	16.94
3	**Fibula** (outer lower leg)	40.50	15.94
4	**Humerus** (upper arm)	36.46	14.35
5	**Ulna** (inner lower arm)	28.20	11.10
6	**Radius** (outer lower arm)	26.42	10.40
7	**7th rib**	24.00	9.45
8	**8th rib**	23.00	9.06
9	**Innominate bone** (hipbone – half pelvis)	18.50	7.28
10	**Sternum** (breastbone)	17.00	6.69

These are average dimensions of the bones of an adult male measured from their extremities (ribs are curved, and the pelvis measurement is taken diagonally). The same bones in the female skeleton are usually 6 to 13 per cent smaller, with the exception of the sternum, which is virtually identical.

THE 10 MOST COMMON ALLERGENS

FOOD		ENVIRONMENTAL
Nuts	1	House dust mite (*Dermatophagoldes pteronyssinus*)
Shellfish/seafood	2	Grass pollens
Milk	3	Tree pollens
Wheat	4	Cats
Eggs	5	Dogs
Fresh fruit (apples, oranges, strawberries, etc)	6	Horses
Fresh vegetables (potatoes, cucumber, etc)	7	Moulds (*Aspergillus fumigatus, Alternaria cladosporium,* etc.)
Cheese	8	Birch pollen
Yeast	9	Weed pollen
Soya protein	10	Wasp/bee venom

An allergy has been defined as "an unpleasant reaction to foreign matter, specific to that substance, which is altered from the normal response and peculiar to the individual concerned".

TOP 10 LARGEST HUMAN ORGANS

	ORGAN	AVERAGE WEIGHT (G)	(OZ)
1	**Skin**	10,886	384.0
2	**Liver**	1,560	55.0
3	**Brain**		
	male	1,408	49.7
	female	1,263	44.6
4	**Lungs**		
	right	580	20.5
	left	510	18.0
	total	1,090	38.5
5	**Heart**		
	male	315	11.1
	female	265	9.3
6	**Kidneys**		
	right	140	4.9
	left	150	5.3
	total	290	10.2
7	**Spleen**	170	6.0
8	**Pancreas**	98	3.5
9	**Thyroid**	35	1.2
10	**Prostate** (male only)	20	0.7

THE 10 MOST COMMON PHOBIAS

	OBJECT OF PHOBIA	MEDICAL TERM
1	**Spiders**	Arachnephobia or arachnophobia
2	**People and social situations**	Anthropophobia or sociophobia
3	**Flying**	Aerophobia or aviatophobia
4	**Open spaces**	Agoraphobia, cenophobia, or kenophobia
5	**Confined spaces**	Claustrophobia, cleisiophobia, cleithrophobia, or clithrophobia
6 =	**Heights**	Acrophobia, altophobia, hypsophobia, or hypsiphobia
=	**Vomiting**	Emetophobia or emitophobia
8	**Cancer**	Carcinomaphobia, carcinophobia, carcinomatophobia, cancerphobia, or cancerophobia
9	**Thunderstorms**	Brontophobia or keraunophobia; related phobias are those associated with lightning (astraphobia), cyclones (anemophobia), and hurricanes and tornadoes (lilapsophobia)
10 =	**Death**	Necrophobia or thanatophobia
=	**Heart disease**	Cardiophobia

A phobia is a morbid fear out of all proportion to the object of the fear. Many people would admit to being uncomfortable about these principal phobias, as well as others, but most do not become obsessive or allow such fears to rule their lives. True phobias often arise from an incident in childhood when a person has been afraid of some object and develops an irrational fear that persists into adulthood. Perhaps surprisingly, the Top 10 does not remain static, as "new" phobias become more common; although outside the Top 10, "technophobia", fear of modern technology such as computers, is increasingly reported. Nowadays, phobias can be cured by taking special desensitization courses, for example to conquer one's fear of flying.

Medicine & Healthcare

TOP 10 COUNTRIES WITH THE MOST HOSPITALS

	COUNTRY	BEDS PER 10,000 (1990–99)	HOSPITALS (1998)
1	China	17	69,105
2	India	8	15,067
3	Vietnam	17	12,500
4	Nigeria	2	11,588*
5	Russia	121	11,200
6	Japan	164	9,413#
7	Egypt	21	7,411
8	South Korea	55	6,446#
9	Brazil	31	6,410#
10	USA	36	6,097
	UK	41	no data

* 1993 data

 # 1997 data

▼ Babes in arms
Despite its single-child policy, China's hospitals still have to deal with a proportion of the country's 20 million births a year.

TOP 10 COUNTRIES THAT SPEND THE MOST ON HEALTHCARE

	COUNTRY	HEALTH SPENDING PER CAPITA (1995–99) ($)
1	USA	4,271
2	Switzerland	3,857
3	Norway	3,182
4	Denmark	2,785
5	Germany	2,697
6	France	2,288
7	Japan	2,243
8	Netherlands	2,173
9	Sweden	2,145
10	Belgium	2,137
	UK	1,675

Source: *World Bank*, World Development Indicators 2002

An annual average of $12 per capita is estimated to provide the minimum health services, but many poor countries fall short of this figure. Ethiopia, for example, spends only $4 per capita on healthcare.

TOP 10 PRESCRIPTION ITEMS IN ENGLAND

	PRODUCT	ITEMS PRESCRIBED (2001)
1	Analgesics	44,017,300
2	Antibacterial drugs	37,917,000
3	Diuretics	30,203,300
4	Nitrates, calcium blockers, and potassium activators	26,813,500
5	Antihypertensive therapy	25,046,900
6	Bronchodilators	24,919,500
7	Antidepressant drugs	24,342,700
8	Drugs used in rheumatic diseases and gout	22,451,900
9	Beta-adrenoceptor blocking drugs	20,438,800
10	Ulcer-healing drugs	18,951,300

Source: *Department of Health*

In 2001, a total of 587,049,000 prescriptions were dispensed in England – an average of almost 10 per head of the population – at a cost of £6,116,568,900.

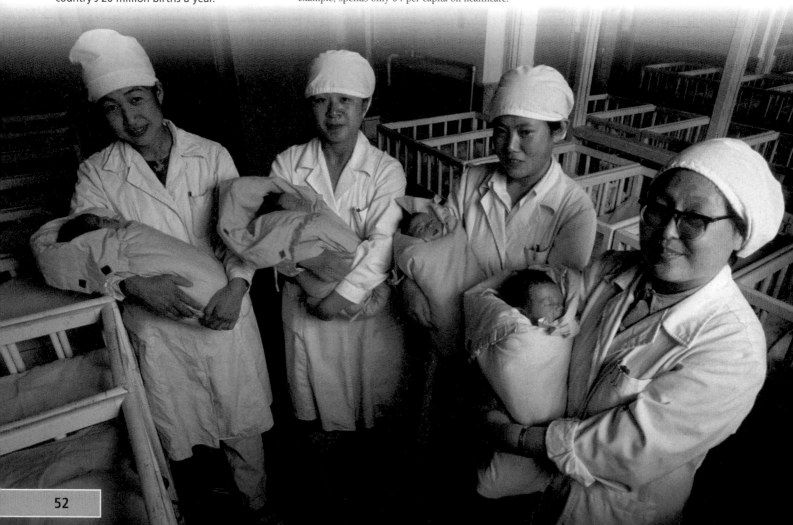

 COUNTRIES THAT SPEND THE MOST ON PRIVATE HEALTHCARE

	COUNTRY	PRIVATE HEALTH SPENDING AS PERCENTAGE OF GDP* (1995–99)
1	Lebanon	9.7
2	United Arab Emirates	7.6
3	Uruguay	7.3
4	USA	7.1
5	Cambodia	6.3
6	Argentina	6.1
7	Kenya	5.5
8	Honduras	4.7
9	El Salvador	4.6
10	Sierra Leone	4.4
	UK	*1.2*

* Gross domestic product

Source: *World Bank*, World Development Indicators 2002

Expenditure on private healthcare is high both in countries where inhabitants are sufficiently wealthy to choose this option and in some where the lack of state medicine makes it a necessity.

COUNTRIES THAT SPEND THE MOST ON PUBLIC HEALTHCARE

	COUNTRY	PUBLIC HEALTH SPENDING AS PERCENTAGE OF GDP* (1995–99)
1	Croatia	9.5
2	Nicaragua	8.5
3	Bosnia and Herzegovina	8.0
4	Germany	7.9
5	Switzerland	7.6
6	France	7.3
7	Norway	7.0
8	Denmark	6.9
9	Slovenia	6.7
10 =	Canada	6.6
=	Czech Republic	6.6
=	Sweden	6.6
	UK	*5.8*

* Gross domestic product

Source: *World Bank*, World Development Indicators 2002

BUSIEST AMBULANCE SERVICES IN ENGLAND

	AMBULANCE SERVICE*	PATIENT JOURNEYS (2000–01)
1	Lincolnshire	1,499,000
2	London	1,335,000
3	East Midlands	1,242,000
4	West Yorkshire Metropolitan	1,154,000
5	Greater Manchester	972,000
6	Essex	922,000
7	Tees, East and North Yorkshire	916,000
8	Mersey Regional	898,000
9	West Midlands Metropolitan	847,000
10	East Anglian	819,000

* All NHS Trust services

Source: *Department of Health*

Lincolnshire's Ambulance and Health Transport Service covers the mainly rural county of Lincolnshire, which extends from the Humber to the Wash – an area of approximately 8,800 sq km (3,400 sq miles). This is the largest cover provided by a single ambulance service in England.

COUNTRIES WITH THE MOST PATIENTS PER DOCTOR

	COUNTRY	PATIENTS PER DOCTOR*
1	Malawi	49,118
2	Liberia	43,434
3	Mozambique	36,320
4	Eritrea	33,240
5	Chad	30,260
6	Ethiopia	30,195
7	The Gambia	28,791
8	Central African Republic	28,600
9	Niger	28,560
10	Burkina Faso	27,158
	UK	*716*

* In those countries/latest year for which data available

COUNTRIES WITH THE FEWEST PATIENTS PER DOCTOR

	COUNTRY	PATIENTS PER DOCTOR*
1	Italy	169
2	Monaco	170
3	Cuba	188
4 =	Belarus	227
=	Georgia	227
6	Russia	238
7	Greece	243
8	Lithuania	250
9	Israel	256
10	Belgium	263
	UK	*716*

* In latest year for which data available

MOST COMMON HOSPITAL OPERATIONS IN ENGLAND

	OPERATION	NO. PERFORMED (2001–02)
1	Birth inducement and delivery	516,870
2	Upper gastrointestinal endoscopy	481,006
3	Normal birth delivery	331,342
4	Colon endoscopy	298,442
5	Bladder endoscopy	267,108
6	Eye lens replacement	241,354
7	Skin/tissue lesion removal	173,972
8	Evacuation of uterus contents	117,069
9	Caesarean delivery	116,883
10	Bone fracture reduction	133,252
	All operations	*6,443,782*

Source: *Department of Health*, Hospital Episode Statistics

Birth & Lifespan

TOP 10 COUNTRIES WITH THE HIGHEST BIRTH RATE

	COUNTRY	EST. BIRTH RATE (LIVE BIRTHS PER 1,000 POPULATION IN 2004)
1	Niger	48.8
2	Mali	47.5
3	Chad	46.7
4	Uganda	46.6
5	Somalia	46.0
6	Angola	45.4
7	Liberia	45.0
8 =	Dem. Rep. of Congo	44.7
=	Marshall Islands	44.7
10	Ethiopia	43.7

Source: *US Census Bureau, International Data Base*

The countries with the highest birth rates are often among the poorest in the world. In these places, people often have large families so that their children can contribute to the family income.

TOP 10 COUNTRIES WITH THE LOWEST BIRTH RATE

	COUNTRY	EST. BIRTH RATE (LIVE BIRTHS PER 1,000 POPULATION IN 2004)
1	Bulgaria	8.0
2	Italy	8.6
3	Germany	8.7
4 =	Czech Republic	8.9
=	Latvia	8.9
6 =	Hungary	9.2
=	Slovenia	9.2
8 =	Andorra	9.3
=	Austria	9.3
=	Spain	9.3
	UK	11.0

Source: *US Census Bureau, International Data Base*

◄ **Baby boom**
Mali and most of the other countries with high birth rates have rural economies that depend on large families to provide the required labour force.

TOP 10 COUNTRIES WITH THE HIGHEST LIFE EXPECTANCY

	COUNTRY	LIFE EXPECTANCY AT BIRTH (2004)
1	Andorra	83.5
2	San Marino	81.5
3	Japan	81.1
4	Singapore	80.5
5	Australia	80.2
6 =	Sweden	80.1
=	Switzerland	80.1
8 =	Canada	79.9
=	Iceland	79.9
10 =	Italy	79.4
=	Liechtenstein	79.4
=	Monaco	79.4
	UK	*78.3*

Source: *US Census Bureau, International Data Base*

Life expectancy represents the average life span of a newborn child. A century ago the world average life expectancy was about 30 years; today it is more than double that, but to achieve this average there are countries with a much higher expectancy, as well as those that fall below it.

THE 10 COUNTRIES WITH THE HIGHEST INFANT MORTALITY

	COUNTRY	EST. DEATH RATE PER 1,000 LIVE BIRTHS (2004)
1	Angola	187.5
2	Afghanistan	140.2
3	Sierra Leone	140.0
4	Mozambique	137.2
5	Liberia	125.7
6	Guinea	123.1
7	Niger	119.5
8	Somalia	118.5
9	Malawi	117.6
10	Mali	115.9
	UK	*5.2*

Source: *US Census Bureau, International Data Base*

With the exception of Afghanistan, which has experienced its own unique range of social and medical problems, all the countries in the Top 10 are in sub-Saharan Africa.

◄ **Lease of life**
Japan was the first country to attain an average lifespan of over 80 years – more than double that of many less-developed countries.

THE 10 COUNTRIES WITH THE LOWEST LIFE EXPECTANCY

	COUNTRY	LIFE EXPECTANCY AT BIRTH (2004)
1	Botswana	32.3
2	Mozambique	33.7
3	Swaziland	34.2
4	Zimbabwe	35.3
5	Malawi	35.6
6	Namibia	36.1
7	Zambia	37.4
8	Rwanda	38.0
9	Central African Republic	43.1
10	Ethiopia	43.3

Source: *US Census Bureau, International Data Base*

TOP 10 COUNTRIES WITH THE MOST BIRTHS

	COUNTRY	EST. BIRTHS (2004)
1	India	24,579,788
2	China	19,506,042
3	Nigeria	5,220,326
4	Indonesia	5,057,950
5	Pakistan	4,423,638
6	USA	4,025,868
7	Bangladesh	3,379,322
8	Ethiopia	3,111,374
9	Brazil	3,094,876
10	Dem. Rep. of Congo	2,614,438
	World	*131,471,559*
	UK	*660,805*

Source: *US Census Bureau, International Data Base*

TOP 10 COUNTRIES WITH THE LOWEST INFANT MORTALITY

	COUNTRY	EST. DEATH RATE PER 1,000 LIVE BIRTHS (2004)
1	Sweden	3.40
2	Iceland	3.48
3	Singapore	3.55
4	Finland	3.70
5	Japan	3.77
6	Norway	3.83
7	Andorra	4.05
8	Netherlands	4.21
9	Austria	4.28
10	Switzerland	4.30

Source: *US Census Bureau, International Data Base*

Marriage & Divorce

TOP 10 COUNTRIES WITH THE HIGHEST DIVORCE RATES

	COUNTRY	DIVORCE RATE PER 1,000*
1	Maldives	10.97
2	Belarus	4.65
3	USA	4.19
4	Panama	3.82
5	Russia	3.66
6	Estonia	3.65
7	Puerto Rico	3.61
8	Ukraine	3.59
9	Costa Rica	3.58
10	Cuba	3.54
	UK	2.91

* In those countries/latest year for which data available

Source: United Nations

TOP 10 COUNTRIES WITH THE LOWEST DIVORCE RATES

	COUNTRY	DIVORCE RATE PER 1,000*
1	Libya	0.24
2	Georgia	0.36
3	Mongolia	0.38
4 =	Armenia	0.42
=	Chile	0.42
6	Italy	0.47
7	Mexico	0.48
8	El Salvador	0.49
9 =	Macedonia	0.51
=	Turkey	0.51

* In those countries/latest year for which data available

Source: United Nations

THE 10 FIRST WEDDING ANNIVERSARY GIFTS

	GIFT
1	Cotton
2	Paper
3	Leather
4	Fruit and flowers (or silk)
5	Wood
6	Sugar (or iron)
7	Wool (or copper)
8	Bronze (or electrical appliances)
9	Pottery (or willow)
10	Tin (or aluminium)

The custom of celebrating different wedding anniversaries by presenting specific types of gift has a long tradition, but has been much modified over the years, the association of electrical appliances with the 8th anniversary testifying to the intrusion of modern commercialism into the practice.

TOP 10 COUNTRIES WITH THE HIGHEST PROPORTION OF TEENAGE BRIDES

	COUNTRY	PERCENTAGE OF 15–19-YEAR-OLD GIRLS WHO HAVE EVER BEEN MARRIED*
1	Dem. Rep. of Congo	74.2
2	Congo	55.0
3	Afghanistan	53.7
4	Bangladesh	51.3
5	Uganda	49.8
6	Mali	49.7
7	Guinea	49.0
8	Chad	48.6
9	Mozambique	47.1
10	Senegal	43.8
	UK	1.7

* In latest year for which data available

Source: United Nations

TOP 10 COUNTRIES WITH THE HIGHEST PROPORTION OF TEENAGE HUSBANDS

	COUNTRY	PERCENTAGE OF 15–19-YEAR-OLD BOYS WHO HAVE EVER BEEN MARRIED*
1	Iraq	14.9
2	Nepal	13.5
3	Congo	11.8
4	Uganda	11.4
5	India	9.5
6	Afghanistan	9.2
7	Guinea	8.2
8	Central African Republic	8.1
9	Guatemala	7.8
10	Colombia	7.7
	UK	0.5

* In latest year for which data available

Source: United Nations

IN-FLIGHT WEDDINGS!

HOLDING WEDDINGS IN UNUSUAL locations is not a strictly modern phenomenon: the first marriage to take place in the air was in a balloon a mile above Cincinnati, Ohio, on 19 October 1874. A publicity stunt for showman Phineas T. Barnum's Great Roman Hippodrome circus, the balloonist was daredevil Washington Harrison Donaldson, the first person to ride a bicycle on a tightrope. Before 50,000 spectators, Donaldson piloted a huge gas balloon named P. T. Barnum, which also carried the bride, Mary Elizabeth Walsh (a horseback rider in Barnum's circus), the groom, Charles M. Colton, and, to conduct the airborne ceremony, minister Rev. Howard B. Jeffries.

FIRST FACT

TOP 10 | COUNTRIES WITH THE HIGHEST MARRIAGE RATES

	COUNTRY	MARRIAGES PER 1,000 PER ANNUM*
1	Antigua and Barbuda	21.0
2	Maldives	20.1
3	Barbados	13.5
4	Liechtenstein	12.8
5	Cyprus	12.1
6 =	Seychelles	11.5
=	South Africa	11.5
8	Jamaica	10.3
9 =	Ethiopia	10.2
=	Iran	10.2
	UK	5.1

* In those countries/latest year for which data available

Source: United Nations

TOP 10 | COUNTRIES WITH THE MOST MARRIAGES

	COUNTRY	MARRIAGES PER ANNUM*
1	USA	2,244,000
2	Bangladesh	1,181,000
3	Russia	911,162
4	Japan	784,595
5	Brazil	734,045
6	Mexico	704,456
7	Ethiopia	630,290
8	Iran	511,277
9	Egypt	493,787
10	Turkey	485,112
	UK	304,800

* In those countries/latest year for which data available

Source: United Nations

This list, based on United Nations statistics, regrettably excludes certain large countries such as India, Indonesia, and Pakistan, which fail to provide accurate data.

▼ **Viva Las Vegas**
More than 110,000 people tie the knot in Las Vegas each year, including celebrities such as Frank Sinatra and Mia Farrow (1966), Elvis Presley and Priscilla Beaulieu (1967), and Bruce Willis and Demi Moore (1987).

Death & Disease

MOST COMMON CAUSES OF DEATH BY NON-COMMUNICABLE DISORDERS

	CAUSE	APPROXIMATE DEATHS (2001)
1	Ischaemic heart disease	7,181,000
2	Cancers	7,115,000
3	Cerebrovascular disease	5,454,000
4	Chronic obstructive pulmonary disease	2,672,000
5	Perinatal conditions	2,504,000
6	Road traffic accidents	1,194,000
7	Neuropsychiatric disorders	1,023,000
8	Diabetes mellitus	895,000
9	Hypertensive heart disease	874,000
10	Self-inflicted injury	849,000

Source: *World Health Organization*, World Health Report 2002

WHO estimates identify 33,077,000 deaths in 2001 resulting from non-communicable conditions. These exclude a further 5,103,000 caused by injuries such as road traffic accidents, fires, and drowning.

WORST GLOBAL DISEASES*

	DISEASE	PERCENTAGE OF TOTAL BURDEN OF DISEASE[#†]
1	Neuropsychiatric disorders	13.0
2	Cardiovascular diseases	9.8
3	Lower respiratory infections	6.2
4	HIV/AIDS	6.0
5	Cancers	5.2
6 =	Diarrhoeal diseases	4.3
=	Respiratory diseases (non-communicable)	4.3
8	Digestive diseases	3.4
9	Childhood diseases	3.3
10	Malaria	2.9

* *Those diseases that cause the highest total levels of disability worldwide*

[#] *Measured in Disability-Adjusted Life Years (DALYs): a measure of the difference between a population's health and a normative goal of living in full health*

[†] *Total percentage includes injuries at 12.2%, maternal conditions at 2.1%, nutritional deficiencies at 2.2%, perinatal conditions at 6.7%*

Source: *World Health Organization*, World Health Report 2002

MOST COMMON CAUSES OF DEATH BY INFECTIOUS AND PARASITIC DISEASES

	CAUSE	APPROXIMATE DEATHS (2001)
1	Lower respiratory infections	3,871,000
2	HIV/AIDS	2,866,000
3	Diarrhoea (including dysentery)	2,001,000
4	Tuberculosis	1,644,000
5	Malaria	1,124,000
6	Measles	745,000
7	Whooping cough (pertussis)	285,000
8	Neonatal tetanus	282,000
9	Meningitis	173,000
10	Syphilis	167,000

Source: *World Health Organization*, World Health Report 2002

Infectious and parasitic diseases – those listed here and many outside the 10 principal causes – were responsible for 10,937,000 deaths worldwide in 2001. Extending the parameters to encompass all communicable diseases, maternal and perinatal conditions, and nutritional deficiencies increases the total to 18,374,000.

COUNTRIES WITH THE HIGHEST DEATH RATE

	COUNTRY	EST. DEATH RATE PER 1,000 (2004)
1	Botswana	33.6
2	Mozambique	30.9
3	Angola	25.9
4	Lesotho	24.8
5	Zambia	24.4
6	Zimbabwe	23.3
7	Swaziland	23.1
8	Malawi	23.0
9	Rwanda	21.9
10	Niger	21.5

Source: *US Census Bureau, International Data Base*

All 10 of the countries with the highest death rates are in Africa, with all but Niger and Rwanda located between 10° and 30° south latitude.

WORST EPIDEMICS

	EPIDEMIC	LOCATION	DATES	EST. DEATHS
1	Black Death	Europe/Asia	1347–51	75,000,000
2	AIDS	Worldwide	1981–	21,800,000
3	Influenza	Worldwide	1918–20	21,640,000
4	Bubonic plague	India	1896–1948	12,000,000
5	Typhus	Eastern Europe	1914–15	3,000,000
6 =	"Plague of Justinian"	Europe/Asia	541–90	millions*
=	Cholera	Worldwide	1846–60	millions*
=	Cholera	Europe	1826–37	millions*
=	Cholera	Worldwide	1893–94	millions*
10	Smallpox	Mexico	1530–45	>1,000,000

* *No precise figures available*

Pandemics – epidemics spread over widespread geographical areas – have affected human populations since ancient times. The Black Death – bubonic plague – was the worst of all time, annihilating entire communities and decimating countries. After spreading throughout Asia, it reached Constantinople in 1347 and then spread to Europe, where it killed half the population of many cities, recurring at intervals in later centuries.

THE 10 MOST SUICIDAL COUNTRIES

	COUNTRY	SUICIDES PER 100,000 POPULATION*
1	Lithuania	42.0
2	Russia	35.3
3	Belarus	33.5
4	Estonia	33.2
5	Hungary	33.1
6	Latvia	31.4
7	Slovenia	29.7
8	Ukraine	28.8
9	Kazakhstan	26.8
10	Finland	23.8
	UK	7.4

* In those countries/latest year for which data available

Source: United Nations

It is perhaps surprising that the highest suicide rates are not generally recorded in the poorest countries in the world. Suicide rates in many African countries are very low, maybe because of the strong extended family networks, as well as the cultural and religious taboo attached to suicide. It is also difficult to obtain reliable figures for such countries.

THE 10 COUNTRIES WITH THE HIGHEST DEATH RATE FROM LUNG CANCER

	COUNTRY	DEATH RATE PER 100,000 FEMALE	MALE*
1	Hungary	36.02	123.92
2	Belgium	18.69	119.73
3	Croatia	18.61	105.65
4	Italy	18.60	98.08
5	Greece	15.42	92.69
6	Netherlands	24.70	90.72
7	Luxembourg	19.61	86.66
8	Poland	17.84	86.55
9	Estonia	17.09	85.17
10	UK	44.19	84.58
	World	9.74	26.58

* Ranked by incidence in male population

Source: International Agency for Research on Cancer, Globocan 2000

Denmark has the highest incidence of deaths from lung cancer among women, with an average of 50.4 women in every 100,000 dying from the disease.

THE 10 COUNTRIES WITH THE HIGHEST DEATH RATE FROM HEART DISEASE

	COUNTRY	DEATH RATE PER 100,000
1	Ukraine	896.0
2	Bulgaria	891.2
3	Russia	746.6
4	Latvia	745.7
5	Belarus	741.3
6	Romania	736.8
7	Hungary	728.4
8	Estonia	715.6
9	Georgia	603.7
10	Croatia	594.5
	UK	435.9

* In those countries/latest year for which data available

Source: United Nations

▼ Buried alive!

The spectre of premature burial heightened the terror as the Black Death swept across Europe and Asia.

What's in a Name?

TOP 10 FEMALE NAMES IN ENGLAND & WALES

	NAME	OCCURRENCES
1	Margaret Smith	7,640
2	Margaret Jones	7,068
3	Susan Smith	6,531
4	Susan Jones	5,108
5	Mary Smith	5,049
6	Patricia Smith	4,743
7	Margaret Williams	4,636
8	Elizabeth Jones	4,604
9	Mary Jones	4,522
10	Sarah Jones	4,359

Source: *Office for National Statistics*

The Office for National Statistics conducted a survey of the most common combinations of first names and surnames based on the National Health Service Register, which accounts for everyone currently registered with a GP, or who has been registered since 1991. The extended survey revealed that there are 2,409 Catherine (though not Zeta-) Joneses in 58th place, and in 95th position 2,018 people who share their name with another British-born actress, Elizabeth Taylor.

TOP 10 MALE NAMES IN ENGLAND & WALES

	NAME	OCCURRENCES
1	David Jones	15,763
2	David Smith	14,341
3	John Smith	12,793
4	David Williams	11,392
5	Michael Smith	10,516
6	John Jones	10,021
7	John Williams	8,738
8 =	Paul Smith	8,348
=	Peter Smith	8,348
10	David Evans	8,103

Source: *Office for National Statistics*

The full survey indicated a number of differences between the male and female lists: there are 24 different surnames in the male top 100, but only 11 different female surnames. Smith appears 44 times in the male list, but only 22 times in the female version. Although John is the most common first male name overall, its 18 occurrences in the top 100 is fewer than that of David (22), since it appears less frequently in combination with the most common surnames. There are 4,470 people (in 54th position) who share their name with Welsh singer Tom (Thomas) Jones.

TOP 10 FIRST NAMES IN ENGLAND & WALES, 2002

GIRLS				BOYS
Chloe		1		Jack
Emily		2	+1	Joshua
Jessica	+1	3	-1	Thomas
Ellie	+7	4		James
Sophie		5		Daniel
Megan	-3	6	+8	Benjamin
Charlotte		7	+6	William
Lucy	+2	8	-1	Samuel
Hannah	-1	9	-1	Joseph
Olivia	-1	10	+2	Oliver

+ Indicates rise in popularity since previous year

– Indicates decline in popularity since previous year

Jack has been the top boy's name for eight years, in 2002 increasing its popularity, while Chloe, at No. 1 for six consecutive years, has declined slightly.

TOP 10 | GIRLS' & BOYS' NAMES IN ENGLAND & WALES 50 YEARS AGO*

GIRLS		BOYS
Susan	1	David
Linda	2	John
Christine	3	Stephen
Margaret	4	Michael
Janet	5	Peter
Patricia	6	Robert
Carol	7	Paul
Elizabeth	8	Alan
Mary	9	Christopher
Anne	10	Richard

* Based on birth registrations in 1954

TOP 10 | SURNAMES IN SCOTLAND*

	NAME	FREQUENCY* (1999–2001)
1	Smith	4,291
2	Brown	3,030
3	Wilson	2,876
4	Campbell	2,657
5	Stewart	2,626
6	Thomson	2,616
7	Robertson	2,536
8	Anderson	2,297
9	Macdonald	1,844
10	Scott	1,839

* Based on a survey of names appearing on birth and death registers, and both names on marriage registers

The first two surnames on the list are borne, respectively, by Scottish economist Adam Smith (1723–90) and Labour Chancellor Gordon Brown.

▼ Jack and Chloe?
The fraught business of choosing names for their children results in many parents opting for those in the list of the most popular.

TOP 10 | SURNAMES IN THE UK

	SURNAME	OCCURRENCES
1	Smith	538,369
2	Jones	402,489
3	Williams	279,150
4	Brown	260,652
5	Taylor	251,058
6	Davies/Davis	209,584
7	Wilson	191,006
8	Evans	170,391
9	Thomas	152,945
10	Johnson	146,535

This survey of British surnames is based on an analysis of almost 50 million appearing in the British electoral rolls – hence enumerating only those aged over 18 and eligible to vote. Some 10.77 people out of every 1,000 in the UK are called Smith, compared with 14.55 per 1,000 of names appearing in a sample from the 1851 Census. This decline may be accounted for by considering the diluting effect of immigrant names, the same survey indicating, for example, that 66,663 people, or 1.33 per 1,000, now bear the name Patel, whereas none with that name was listed in 1851.

Pomp & Power

FIRST FEMALE PRIME MINISTERS AND PRESIDENTS

	PRIME MINISTER OR PRESIDENT	COUNTRY	FIRST PERIOD IN OFFICE
1	Sirimavo Bandaranaike (PM)	Sri Lanka	July 1960–Mar 1965
2	Indira Gandhi (PM)	India	Jan 1966–Mar 1977
3	Golda Meir (PM)	Israel	Mar 1969–June 1974
4	Maria Estela Perón (President)	Argentina	July 1974–Mar 1976
5	Elisabeth Domitien (PM)	Central African Republic	Jan 1975–Apr 1976
6	Margaret Thatcher (PM)	UK	May 1979–Nov 1990
7	Dr Maria Lurdes Pintasilgo (PM)	Portugal	Aug 1979–Jan 1980
8	Mary Eugenia Charles (PM)	Dominica	July 1980–June 1995
9	Vigdís Finnbogadóttir (President)	Iceland	Aug 1980–Aug 1996
10	Gro Harlem Brundtland (PM)	Norway	Feb–Oct 1981

Sirimavo Bandaranaike (1916–2000) became the world's first female prime minister on 21 July 1960 when the Sri Lanka Freedom Party, founded by her assassinated husband Solomon Bandaranaike, won the general election. She held the position on three occasions, and her daughter, Chandrika Kumaratunga, also became prime minister and later president.

PARLIAMENTS WITH THE HIGHEST PERCENTAGE OF WOMEN MEMBERS*

	PARLIAMENT/ELECTION	WOMEN MEMBERS	TOTAL MEMBERS	PERCENTAGE WOMEN
1	Sweden, 2002	158	349	45.3
2	Denmark, 2001	68	179	38.0
3	Netherlands, 2003	55	150	36.7
4	Finland, 1999	73	200	36.5
5	Norway, 2001	60	165	36.4
6	Costa Rica, 2002	20	57	35.1
7	Iceland, 1999	22	63	34.9
8	Austria, 2002	62	183	33.9
9	Germany, 2002	194	603	32.2
10	Argentina, 2001	79	257	30.7
	UK, 2001	118	659	17.9

As at 1 March 2003

Source: *Inter-Parliamentary Union*

This list is based on the most recent general election results for all democracies, and based on the lower chamber where the parliament comprises two chambers. Forty-one countries now have at least 20 per cent female members of parliament.

LONGEST-REIGNING MONARCHS

	MONARCH	COUNTRY	REIGN	AGE AT ACCESSION	REIGN YEARS
1	King Louis XIV	France	1643–1715	5	72
2	King John II	Liechtenstein	1858–1929	18	71
3	Emperor Franz-Josef	Austria-Hungary	1848–1916	18	67
4	Queen Victoria	Great Britain	1837–1901	18	63
5	Emperor Hirohito	Japan	1926–89	25	62
6	Emperor K'ang Hsi	China	1661–1722	8	61
7	King Sobhuza II*	Swaziland	22 Dec 1921– 21 Aug 1982	22	60
8	Emperor Ch'ien Lung	China	18 Oct 1735– 9 Feb 1796	25	60
9	King Christian IV	Denmark	4 Apr 1588– 21 Feb 1648	11	59
10	King George III	Great Britain	26 Oct 1760– 29 Jan 1820	22	59

Paramount chief until 1967, when Great Britain recognized him as king with the granting of internal self-government

LONGEST-REIGNING LIVING MONARCHS*

	MONARCH	COUNTRY	DATE OF BIRTH	ACCESSION
1	Bhumibol Adulyadej	Thailand	5 Dec 1927	9 June 1946
2	Prince Rainier III	Monaco	31 May 1923	9 May 1949
3	Elizabeth II	UK	21 Apr 1926	6 Feb 1952
4	Malietoa Tanumafili II	Samoa	4 Jan 1913	1 Jan 1962#
5	Taufa'ahau Tupou IV	Tonga	4 July 1918	16 Dec 1965†
6	Haji Hassanal Bolkiah	Brunei	15 July 1946	5 Oct 1967
7	Sayyid Qaboos ibn Saidal-Said	Oman	18 Nov 1942	23 July 1970
8	Margrethe II	Denmark	16 Apr 1940	14 Jan 1972
9	Jigme Singye Wangchuk	Bhutan	11 Nov 1955	24 July 1972
10	Carl XVI Gustaf	Sweden	30 Apr 1946	19 Sept 1973

Including hereditary rulers of principalities, dukedoms, etc.

Sole ruler since 15 April 1963

† *Full sovereignty from 5 June 1970, when British protectorate ended*

There are 28 countries that have emperors, kings, queens, princes, dukes, sultans, or other hereditary rulers as their heads of state. This list formerly included Birendra Bir Bikram Shah Dev, King of Nepal since 31 January 1972. On 1 June 2001, he was shot dead by his own son, Crown Prince Dipendra, who then committed suicide.

TOP 10 LONGEST-SERVING PRESIDENTS TODAY

	PRESIDENT	COUNTRY	TOOK OFFICE
1	General Gnassingbé Eyadéma	Togo	14 Apr 1967
2	El Hadj Omar Bongo	Gabon	2 Dec 1967
3	Colonel Mu`ammar Gadhafi	Libya	1 Sept 1969*
4	Zayid ibn Sultan al-Nuhayyan	United Arab Emirates	2 Dec 1971
5	Fidel Castro	Cuba	2 Nov 1976
6	France-Albert René	Seychelles	5 June 1977
7	Ali Abdullah Saleh	Yemen	17 July 1978
8	Maumoon Abdul Gayoom	Maldives	11 Nov 1978
9	Teodoro Obiang Nguema Mbasogo	Equatorial Guinea	3 Aug 1979
10	José Eduardo Dos Santos	Angola	21 Sept 1979

Since a reorganization in 1979, Colonel Gadhafi has held no formal position, but continues to rule under the ceremonial title of "Leader of the Revolution"

All the presidents in this list have been in power for more than 20 years, some for over 30 years. Fidel Castro was Prime Minister of Cuba from February 1959. As he was also chief of the army, and there was no opposition party, he effectively ruled as dictator from then, but he was not technically president until the Cuban constitution was revised in 1976. Among those no longer in office, Abu Sulayman Hafiz al-Assad, President of Syria, died on 10 June 2000 after serving as leader of his country since 22 Feb 1971.

THE 10 FIRST COUNTRIES TO GIVE WOMEN THE VOTE

	COUNTRY	YEAR
1	New Zealand	1893
2	Australia (South Australia 1894; Western Australia 1898; Australia united in 1901)	1902
3	Finland (then a Grand Duchy under the Russian Crown)	1906
4	Norway (restricted franchise; all women over 25 in 1913)	1907
5	Denmark and Iceland (a Danish dependency until 1918)	1915
6 =	Netherlands	1917
=	USSR	1917
8 =	Austria	1918
=	Canada	1918
=	Germany	1918
=	Great Britain and Ireland (Ireland part of the United Kingdom until 1921; women over 30 only – lowered to 21 in 1928)	1918
=	Poland	1918

Although not a country, the Isle of Man was the first place to give women the vote, in 1880. Until 1920 the only other European countries to enfranchise women were Sweden in 1919 and Czechoslovakia in 1920. Certain states of the USA gave women the vote at earlier dates (Wyoming in 1869, Colorado in 1894, Utah in 1895, and Idaho in 1896), but it was not granted nationally until 1920. A number of countries, such as France and Italy, did not give women the vote until 1945. In certain countries, such as Saudi Arabia, women are not allowed to vote at all – but neither can men.

◀ **Head of state**
Leader of the Revolution and Supreme Commander of the Armed Forces, Colonel Mu`ammar Gadhafi has been the controversial leader of Libya since the overthrow of the monarchy in 1969.

Crime & Punishment

COUNTRIES WITH THE MOST EXECUTIONS

	COUNTRY	EXECUTIONS (1998)
1	China	1,067
2	Dem. Rep. of Congo	100
3	USA	68
4	Iran	66
5	Egypt	48
6	Belarus	33
7	Taiwan	32
8	Saudi Arabia	29
9	Singapore	28
10 =	Rwanda	24
=	Sierra Leone	24

Source: *Amnesty International*

At least 80 countries in the world retain the death penalty, with China consistently the leading practitioner of this ultimate sanction.

► **Hot seat**

The electric chair has been introduced in few countries outside the USA, where it has been used since 1890. It remains the official execution method in 10 of the 38 states that retain the death penalty.

THE 10 COUNTRIES WITH THE HIGHEST REPORTED BURGLARY RATES

	COUNTRY	RATE*
1	Netherlands	3,100.40
2	Australia	2,280.82
3	New Zealand	2,153.66
4	Scotland	2,118.73
5	Antigua and Barbuda	2,071.99
6	Denmark	1,868.06
7	England and Wales	1,832.69
8	St. Kitts and Nevis	1,790.00
9	Estonia	1,699.95
10	Finland	1,690.52

* Reported crime per 100,000 population, in latest year for which data available

Source: *Interpol*

TOP 10 COUNTRIES WITH THE LOWEST REPORTED CRIME RATES

	COUNTRY	RATE*
1	Burkina Faso	9.30
2	Mali	10.03
3	Syria	42.26
4	Cambodia	47.97
5	Yemen	63.22
6	Myanmar	64.54
7	Angola	71.52
8	Cameroon	78.17
9	Vietnam	83.56
10	Bangladesh	89.66

* Reported crime per 100,000 population, in latest year for which data available

Source: *Interpol*

There are just 12 countries in the world with reported crime rates of fewer than 100 per 100,000 inhabitants; the other two are Mauritania (95.40) and Niger (99.09). It should be noted that these figures are based on reported crimes. For propaganda purposes, many countries do not publish accurate figures, while in certain countries crime is so common and law enforcement so inefficient or corrupt that countless incidents are unreported.

THE 10 COUNTRIES WITH THE HIGHEST PRISON POPULATION RATES

	COUNTRY	TOTAL PRISON POPULATION*	PRISONERS PER 100,000
1	USA	1,962,220	686
2	Russia	919,330	638
3	Belarus	56,000	554
4	Kazakhstan	84,000	522
5	Turkmenistan	22,000	489
6	Belize	1,097	459
7	Suriname	1,933	437
8	Dominica	298	420
9	Bahamas	1,280	416
10	Maldives	1,098	414
	England and Wales	*72,669*	*139*

* Includes pre-trial detainees; most figures relate to dates between 1999–2002

Source: *UK Home Office,* World Prison Population List (4th ed.)

The US incarceration rate has increased dramatically in recent years. The total first exceeded 100,000 in 1927 and 200,000 in 1958, since when it has escalated rapidly, far outstripping the rate of population increase.

THE 10 MOST COMMON OFFENCES IN ENGLAND AND WALES

	OFFENCE	NUMBER RECORDED*
1	Theft and handling stolen goods (excluding car theft)	1,363,500
2	Criminal damage	1,089,500
3	Car theft (including theft from vehicles)	998,400
4	Violence against the person	742,900
5	Burglary (excluding domestic)	463,300
6	Domestic burglary	447,100
7	Fraud and forgery	326,300
8	Drug offences	130,200
9	Robbery	120,700
10	Sexual offences	45,700
	Total (including those not in Top 10)	*5,797,100*

* In 12 months to Sept 2002

Source: *UK Home Office*

Changes in recording methods make it unreliable to compare figures from year to year, but all categories show increases, with that of robbery escalating by 24 per cent – linked in part with the burgeoning street crime of stealing mobile phones.

THE 10 COUNTRIES WITH THE HIGHEST REPORTED CRIME RATES

	COUNTRY	RATE*
1	Iceland	14,726.95
2	Sweden	13,455.08
3	New Zealand	12,586.64
4	Grenada	10,177.89
5	Norway	10,086.72
6	England and Wales	9,823.28
7	Denmark	9,460.38
8	Finland	8,697.37
9	Scotland	8,428.73
10	Canada	4,123.97

* Reported crime per 100,000 population, in latest year for which data available

Source: *Interpol*

THE 10 COUNTRIES WITH THE HIGHEST REPORTED CAR THEFT RATES

	COUNTRY	RATE*
1	Switzerland	962.80
2	New Zealand	818.01
3	England and Wales	752.95
4	Sweden	738.47
5	Australia	726.19
6	Denmark	604.18
7	Scotland	555.33
8	Italy	537.00
9	Canada	521.20
10	Norway	518.25

* Reported crime per 100,000 population, in latest year for which data available

Source: *Interpol*

FIRST SPEEDING TICKET!

FIRST FACT

THE WORLD'S FIRST TRAFFFIC speeding ticket was issued in the UK on 28 January 1896 to Walter Arnold. He was charged with driving at 8 mph in an area of Paddock Wood, Kent, that had a limit of 2 mph, hurtling past the house of a policeman, who gave chase on his bicycle. Arnold was fined one shilling. In the USA on 20 May 1899, Jacob German became the first driver arrested for speeding when he was caught driving an electric taxicab at a "breakneck speed" of 12 mph on New York's Lexington Avenue – for which he was jailed.

Murder by Numbers

 ## COUNTRIES WITH THE LOWEST MURDER RATES

	COUNTRY	REPORTED MURDERS PER 100,000 POPULATION (2000*)
1	Iceland	0.00
2	Senegal	0.33
3 =	Burkina Faso	0.38
=	Cameroon	0.38
5 =	Finland	0.71
=	Gambia	0.71
=	Mali	0.71
=	Saudi Arabia	0.71
9	Mauritania	0.76
10	Oman	0.91

* Or latest year for which data are available

Source: *Interpol*

The murder rate in Iceland has been so exceptionally low for many years that it is often excluded altogether from comparative international statistics.

COUNTRIES WITH THE HIGHEST MURDER RATES

	COUNTRY	REPORTED MURDERS PER 100,000 POPULATION (2000*)
1	Honduras	154.02
2	South Africa	121.91
3	Swaziland	93.32
4	Colombia	69.98
5	Lesotho	50.41
6	Rwanda	45.08
7	Jamaica	37.21
8	El Salvador	36.88
9	Venezuela	33.20
10	Bolivia	31.98
	England and Wales	2.75

* Or latest year for which data are available

Source: *Interpol*

These figures should be viewed with caution: not all countries record or define crimes identically or use the same statistical methods in reporting rates.

MOST COMMON MURDER WEAPONS AND METHODS IN ENGLAND AND WALES

	WEAPON OR METHOD	VICTIMS (2001–02)
1	Sharp instrument	198
2	Hitting and kicking	124
3	Shooting	90
4	Other/unknown	55
5	Blunt instrument	35
6	Poison or drugs	23
7	Strangulation	20
8	Motor vehicle	16
9	Burning	14
10	Drowning	7

Source: *Home Office,* Criminal Statistics England and Wales 2001/2002: Supplementary Volume

The comparative figure for shootings in 1980 was 19, confirming the popular perception that guns have increasingly become the murder weapon of choice.

 ## WORST GUN MASSACRES*

	PERPETRATOR/LOCATION/DATE/CIRCUMSTANCES	KILLED
1	**Woo Bum Kong** Sang-Namdo, South Korea, 28 Apr 1982. Off-duty policeman Woo Bum Kong, 27, killed 57 and injured 38 during a drunken rampage with rifles and hand grenades before blowing himself up with a grenade.	57
2	**Martin Bryant** Port Arthur, Tasmania, Australia, 28 Apr 1996. Bryant, a 28-year-old Hobart resident, began killing with a high-powered rifle and was eventually captured when he fled in flames from a guesthouse in which he had held three hostages.	35
3	**Baruch Goldstein** Hebron, occupied West Bank, Israel, 25 Feb 1994. Goldstein, a 42-year-old US immigrant doctor, massacred Palestinians at prayer at the Tomb of the Patriarchs before being beaten to death by the crowd.	29
4	**Campo Elias Delgado** Bogota, Colombia, 4 Dec 1986. Delgado, a Vietnamese war veteran, stabbed two and shot a further 26 people before being killed by police.	28
5 =	**George Jo Hennard** Killeen, Texas, USA, 16 Oct 1991. Hennard drove his truck through a café window and killed 22 with semi-automatic guns before shooting himself.	22
=	**James Oliver Huberty** San Ysidro, California, USA, 18 July 1984. Huberty, aged 41, opened fire in a McDonald's restaurant before being shot dead by a SWAT marksman.	22

	PERPETRATOR/LOCATION/DATE/CIRCUMSTANCES	KILLED
7 =	**Thomas Hamilton** Dunblane, Stirling, UK, 13 Mar 1996. Hamilton, 43, shot 16 children and a teacher in Dunblane Primary School before killing himself in the UK's worst shooting incident ever.	17
=	**Robert Steinhäuser** Erfurt, Germany, 26 Apr 2002. Former student Steinhäuser returned to Johann Gutenberg secondary school and killed 14 teachers, two students, and a police officer with a handgun before shooting himself.	17
9 =	**Michael Ryan** Hungerford, Berkshire, UK, 19 Aug 1987. Ryan, 26, shot 14 dead and wounded 16 others (two of whom died later) before shooting himself.	16
=	**Ronald Gene Simmons** Russellville, Arkansas, USA, 28 Dec 1987. Simmons killed 16, including 14 members of his own family, by shooting or strangling. After being caught, he was sentenced to death on 10 Feb 1989.	16
=	**Charles Joseph Whitman** Austin, Texas, USA, 31 July–1 Aug 1966. Twenty-five-year-old ex-Marine marksman Whitman killed his mother and wife and the following day went to the University of Texas at Austin, where he took the lift to the 27th floor of the campus tower and ascended to the observation deck. From here he shot 14 and wounded 34 before being shot dead by police officers Romero Martinez and Houston McCoy.	16

* By individuals, excluding terrorist and military actions; totals exclude perpetrator

MOST PROLIFIC SERIAL KILLERS*

MURDERER/COUNTRY/CRIMES	VICTIMS
1 Behram (India)	931

Behram (or Buhram) was the leader of the Thugee cult in India, which it is thought was responsible for the deaths of up to two million people. At his trial Behram was found guilty of 931 murders between 1790 and 1830, mostly by ritual strangulation with the cult's traditional cloth, known as a "ruhmal".

2 Countess Erszébet Báthory (Hungary)	up to 650

In the period up to 1610 in Hungary, Báthory (1560–1614), known as "Countess Dracula", was alleged to have murdered between 300 and 650 girls (her personal list of 610 victims was described at her trial) in the belief that drinking their blood would prevent her from ageing. She was eventually arrested in 1611; tried and found guilty, she died on 21 August 1614 walled up in her own castle at Csejthe.

3 Pedro Alonso López (Colombia)	300

Captured in 1980, López, nicknamed the "Monster of the Andes", led police to 53 graves, but probably murdered at least 300 in Colombia, Ecuador, and Peru. He was sentenced to life imprisonment.

4 Dr Harold Shipman (UK)	215

In January 2000, Manchester doctor Shipman was found guilty of the murder of 15 women patients; the official enquiry into his crimes put the figure at 215, with 45 possible further cases, but some authorities believe that the total could be as high as 400.

5 Henry Lee Lucas (USA)	200

Lucas (1936–2001) admitted in 1983 to 360 murders, many with his partner-in-crime Ottis Toole. He died while on Death Row in Huntsville Prison, Texas.

MURDERER/COUNTRY/CRIMES	VICTIMS
6 Gilles de Rais (France)	up to 200

A wealthy aristocrat, Gilles de Laval, Baron de Rais (1404–40), was accused of having kidnapped between 60 and 200 children, and killed them as sacrifices during black magic rituals. After being tried, tortured, and found guilty, he was strangled and his body burnt at Nantes on 25 October 1440.

7 Hu Wanlin (China)	196

Posing as a doctor specializing in Chinese medicine, Hu Wanlin was given a 15-year sentence on 1 October 2000 for three deaths, but he is thought to have been responsible for 20 in Taiyuan, 146 in Shanxi, and 30 in Shangqui.

8 Luis Alfredo Garavito (Colombia)	189

Garavito confessed in 1999 to a spate of murders. On 28 May 2000 he was sentenced to a total of 835 years imprisonment.

9 Hermann Webster Mudgett (USA)	up to 150

Mudgett (1860–96) was believed to have lured over 150 women to his Chicago "castle" of soundproofed cells equipped for torture, murder, and the disposal of bodies. Arrested and found guilty of the murder of an ex-partner, he confessed to 27 killings, but 200 victims' remains were thought to have been found. Mudgett was hanged at Moyamensing Prison on 7 May 1896.

10 Dr. Jack Kevorkian (USA)	130

In 1999, Kevorkian, who admitted to assisting in 130 suicides since 1990, was convicted of second-degree murder. His appeal against his 10- to 25-year prison sentence was rejected on 21 November 2001.

* Includes only individual murderers; excludes murders by bandits, terrorist groups, political and military atrocities, and gangland slayings

▶ **Hand gun**
Despite being outlawed in many countries (hand guns were completely banned in the UK in 1997 in the wake of the Dunblane tragedy) guns continue to figure prominently in the world's murder statistics.

War & Peace

THE 10 BATTLES WITH THE MOST CASUALTIES

	BATTLE/WAR/DATES	CASUALTIES*
1	**Stalingrad,** World War II, 1942–43	2,000,000
2	**Somme River I,** World War I, 1916	1,073,900
3	**Po Valley,** World War II, 1945	740,000
4	**Moscow,** World War II, 1941–42	700,000
5	**Verdun,** World War I, 1916	595,000
6	**Gallipoli,** World War I, 1915	500,000
7	**Artois-Loos,** World War I, 1915	428,000
8	**Berezina,** War of 1812	400,000
9	**38th Parallel,** Korean War, 1951	320,000
10	**Somme River II,** World War I, 1918	300,000

* Estimated total of military and civilian dead, wounded, and missing

Source: *Alexis Tregenza*

Total numbers of casualties in the Battle of Stalingrad are at best estimates, but it was undoubtedly one of the longest and almost certainly the bloodiest battles of all time. Fought between German (with Hungarian, Romanian, and Italian troops also under German command) and Soviet forces, it continued from 19 August 1942 to 2 February 1943, with huge losses on both sides.

THE 10 20TH-CENTURY WARS WITH THE MOST MILITARY FATALITIES

	WAR	DATES	EST. MILITARY FATALITIES
1	**World War II**	1939–45	15,843,000
2	**World War I**	1914–18	8,545,800
3	**Korean War**	1950–53	1,893,100
4	**Sino-Japanese War**	1937–41	1,200,000
5	**Biafra–Nigeria Civil War**	1967–70	1,000,000
6	**Spanish Civil War**	1936–39	611,000
7	**Vietnam War**	1961–75	546,000
8	**French Vietnam War**	1945–54	300,000
9	**= India–Pakistan War**	1947	200,000
	= USSR invasion of Afghanistan	1979–89	200,000
	= Iran–Iraq War	1980–88	200,000

The statistics of warfare have always been an imperfect science. Not only are battle deaths seldom recorded accurately, but figures are often deliberately inflated by both sides in a conflict. These figures thus represent military historians' "best guesses" – and fail to take into account the enormous toll of deaths among civilian populations during the many wars that beset the 20th century.

THE 10 COUNTRIES SUFFERING THE GREATEST CIVILIAN LOSSES IN WORLD WAR II

	COUNTRY	EST. CIVILIAN FATALITIES
1	**China**	8,000,000
2	**USSR**	6,500,000
3	**Poland**	5,300,000
4	**Germany**	2,350,000
5	**Yugoslavia**	1,500,000
6	**France**	470,000
7	**Greece**	415,000
8	**Japan**	393,400
9	**Romania**	340,000
10	**Hungary**	300,000

Civilian deaths in World War II – many resulting from famine and internal purges, such as those in China and the USSR – were colossal, but they were less well documented than those among fighting forces. An estimate of 60,600 civilian deaths resulting from bomb and rocket attacks on the UK represent less than one-quarter of the total military deaths. Although the figures are the best available from authoritative sources, and present a broad picture of the scale of civilian losses, the precise numbers will never be known.

SHORTEST WAR EVER!

THE SHORTEST WAR ON RECORD was that between Britain and Zanzibar. On Thursday, 27 August 1896, the British fleet under Admiral Sir Henry Rawson arrived in Zanzibar harbour. Sultan Said Khaled, who had seized power two days earlier, regarded this as a provocative act and declared war, firing on the British from his sole warship, the *Glasgow*. The British fleet retaliated, sinking the ship, destroying the sultan's palace, and killing some 500 of his men. The sultan escaped to exile in Mombasa. The entire action had lasted 38 minutes, from 9.02 to 9.40 a.m.

THE 10 LATEST YEARS OF THE NOBEL PEACE PRIZE

PRIZE YEAR	WINNER(S)	COUNTRY
2002	Jimmy Carter Jr.	USA
2001	Kofi Annan/United Nations	Ghana/International body
2000	Kim Dae Jung	South Korea
1999	Médecins Sans Frontières	Belgium
1998	John Hume/David Trimble	UK
1997	International Campaign to Ban Landmines/Jody Williams	International body/USA
1996	Carlos Filipe Ximenes Belo/José Ramos-Horta	East Timor
1995	Joseph Rotblat	UK
1994	Yasir Arafat/Shimon Peres/Itzhak Rabin	Palestine/Israel
1993	Nelson Rolihlahla Mandela/Frederik Willem de Klerk	South Africa

Former US president, Jimmy Carter Jr., was awarded the Nobel Peace Prize in 2002 "for his decades of untiring effort to find peaceful solutions to international conflicts, to advance democracy and human rights, and to promote economic and social development".

THE 10 COUNTRIES SUFFERING THE GREATEST MILITARY LOSSES IN WORLD WAR II

	COUNTRY	EST. MILITARY FATALITIES
1	USSR	13,600,000*
2	Germany	3,300,000
3	China	1,324,516
4	Japan	1,140,429
5	British Empire#	357,116
6	Romania	350,000
7	Poland	320,000
8	Yugoslavia	305,000
9	USA	292,131
10	Italy	279,800
	Total	21,268,992

* Total, of which 7,800,000 are battlefield deaths

Including Australia, Canada, India, New Zealand, etc.; UK figure 264,000

The massive losses among the 30 million Soviet troops who bore arms include 7 million battlefield deaths, 2 million from wounds or disease received in battle, and 3 million prisoners who died in captivity.

THE 10 LONGEST WARS

	WAR	COMBATANTS	DATES	YEARS
1	Hundred Years War	France and England	1337–1453	116
2	Greco-Persian Wars	Greece and Persia	499–448 BC	51
3 =	Wars of the Roses	Lancaster and York	1455–85	30
=	Thirty Years War	Catholics and Protestants	1618–48	30
5	Second Peloponnesian War	Peloponnesian League (Sparta, Corinth, etc.) and Delian League (Athens, etc.)	432–404 BC	28
6 =	First Punic War	Rome and Carthage	264–241 BC	23
=	Napoleonic Wars	France and other European countries	1792–1815	23
8	Second Great Northern War	Russia and Sweden and Baltic states	1700–21	21
9	Vietnam War	South Vietnam (with US support) and North Vietnam	1957–75	18
10	Second Punic War	Rome and Carthage	219–202 BC	17

Source: Alexis Tregenza

It may be argued that the total period of the Crusades (fought by Christians and Muslims) constitutes one long single conflict spanning a total of 195 years from 1096 to 1291, rather than a series of nine short ones, in which case it ranks as the longest war ever. Similarly, if all the Punic Wars between 264 and 146 BC are taken as one, they would rank second at 118 years. The War of the Spanish Succession (1701–14) is the only other major conflict to have lasted more than 10 years, with the War of the Austrian Succession (1740–48), the American War of Independence (1775–83), and the Chinese–Japanese War (1937–45) each lasting eight years.

▼ Siege of Stalingrad
The German army besieged Stalingrad, USSR, in 1942. The ensuing battle lasted almost six months and was the bloodiest in history.

▲ Sub power

The US submarine fleet, the world's largest, is principally composed of Los Angeles Class nuclear-powered hunter-killers, named after the first, USS *Los Angeles*, which was commissioned in 1976.

TOP 10 COUNTRIES WITH THE MOST SUBMARINES

	COUNTRY	SUBMARINES
1	USA	73
2	China	69
3	Russia (and associated states)	56
4	North Korea	26
5	South Korea	19
6 =	India	16
=	Japan	16
=	UK	16
9	Germany	14
10	Turkey	13

TOP 10 COUNTRIES WITH THE MOST COMBAT AIRCRAFT*

	COUNTRY	COMBAT AIRCRAFT
1	USA	3,939
2	China	2,900
3	Russia	2,636
4	India	738
5	North Korea	621
6	Egypt	580
7	South Korea	555
8	Ukraine	543
9	Taiwan	482
10	France	473
	UK	427

* Air force only, excluding long-range strike/attack aircraft

Modern air forces rely more on technology than strength of numbers, in contrast to World War II, when the USAF deployed over 40,000 combat aircraft.

TOP 10 COUNTRIES WITH THE LARGEST ARMIES

	COUNTRY	ARMY PERSONNEL
1	China	1,600,000
2	India	1,100,000
3	North Korea	950,000
4	South Korea	560,000
5	Pakistan	550,000
6	USA	477,800
7	Vietnam	412,000
8	Turkey	402,000
9	Iraq	375,000
10	Russia	321,000
	UK	113,950

Slight reductions in numbers have been made over the past few years, but recent heightenings in international tension since the 11 September 2001 terrorist attacks and ongoing disputes have put further reductions "on hold".

TOP 10 COUNTRIES WITH THE LARGEST NAVIES

	COUNTRY	NAVY PERSONNEL*
1	USA	366,100
2	China	250,000
3	Russia	171,500
4	Taiwan	62,000
5	South Korea	60,000
6 =	India	53,000
=	Turkey	53,000
8	North Korea	46,000
9	France	45,600
10	UK	43,530

* Including naval air forces and marines

Along with other factors, the increasing reliance on technology rather than manpower in modern naval warfare led to reductions in numbers during the 1990s. Though modern navies are considerably smaller than those of the cold war era, when the US navy was almost twice as large, all the major powers remain capable of putting substantial forces to sea.

TOP 10 COUNTRIES WITH THE LARGEST DEFENCE BUDGETS

	COUNTRY	BUDGET ($)
1	USA	291,100,000,000
2	Russia	44,000,000,000
3	Japan	40,400,000,000
4	UK	34,000,000,000
5	Saudi Arabia	27,200,000,000
6	France	25,300,000,000
7	Germany	21,000,000,000
8	China	17,000,000,000
9	India	15,600,000,000
10	Italy	15,500,000,000

The so-called "peace dividend" – the savings made as a consequence of the end of the Cold War between the West and the former Soviet Union – means that both the numbers of personnel and the defence budgets of many countries have been cut. That of the USA has gone down from its 1989 peak of $303.6 billion.

TOP 10 COUNTRIES WITH THE HIGHEST MILITARY/ CIVILIAN RATIO

	COUNTRY	RATIO (2002)*
1	North Korea	441
2	Israel	258
3	United Arab Emirates	253
4	Qatar	202
5	Syria	195
6	Iraq	190
7	Bahrain	176
8	Taiwan	167
9	Oman	162
10	Jordan	146
	UK	36

* Military personnel per 10,000 population

▶ **People's army**
China's armed forces make up the world's largest military machine. At 18, male citizens are officially drafted into service for two years, but in practice conscription is selective.

World Religions

TOP 10 — RELIGIOUS BELIEFS

	RELIGION	FOLLOWERS (2002)
1	Christianity	2,050,616,000
2	Islam	1,239,029,000
3	Hinduism	836,543,000
4	Non-religion	780,557,000
5	Buddhism	367,538,000
6	Ethnic religion	234,341,000
7	Atheism	150,804,000
8	New religion	104,280,000
9	Sikhism	24,124,000
10	Judaism	14,670,000

Source: *David B. Barrett & Todd M. Johnson,*
International Bulletin of Missionary Research,
January 2002

TOP 10 — CHRISTIAN TRADITIONS IN THE MOST COUNTRIES

	CHRISTIAN TRADITION	COUNTRIES
1	Roman Catholic	235
2	Protestant	231
3	Independent	230
4	Jehovah's Witnesses	212
5	Adventist	199
6	Baptist	163
7	Anglican	162
8	New Apostolic	149
9	Reformed, Presbyterian	141
10	Orthodox	133

Source: *David B. Barrett & Todd M. Johnson,* World
Christian Trends, *William Carey Library, 2001*

◀ **Buddhist statue in China**
Despite its suppression during the
Cultural Revolution, Buddhism has
survived in China, where it now has
more than 100 million followers.

TOP 10 LARGEST BUDDHIST POPULATIONS

	COUNTRY	BUDDHIST POPULATION (2000)
1	China	105,829,000
2	Japan	69,931,000
3	Thailand	52,383,000
4	Vietnam	39,534,000
5	Myanmar	33,145,000
6	Sri Lanka	12,879,000
7	Cambodia	9,462,000
8	India	7,249,000
9	South Korea	7,174,000
10	Taiwan	4,686,000
	World	359,981,757

Source: *David B. Barrett & Todd M. Johnson,* World Christian Trends, *William Carey Library, 2001*

Buddhism originated in India in the 6th century BC. Its espousal of peace and tolerant coexistence ensured its appeal and encouraged its spread throughout Asia and beyond.

TOP 10 LARGEST HINDU POPULATIONS

	COUNTRY	HINDU POPULATION (2000)
1	India	755,135,000
2	Nepal	18,354,000
3	Bangladesh	15,995,000
4	Indonesia	7,259,000
5	Sri Lanka	2,124,000
6	Pakistan	1,868,000
7	Malaysia	1,630,000
8	USA	1,032,000
9	South Africa	959,000
10	Myanmar	893,000

Source: *David B. Barrett & Todd M. Johnson,* World Christian Trends, *William Carey Library, 2001*

Claimed as the world's oldest organized religion, Hinduism is also the third largest after Christianity and Islam, with an estimated total world population of at least 900 million.

TOP 10 RELIGIONS IN THE UK

	RELIGION	MEMBERS (2002)
1	Anglican	25,440,000
2	Roman Catholic	5,840,000
3	Presbyterian	2,560,000
4	Muslim	1,440,000
5	Methodist	1,160,000
6	Sikh	640,000
7	Baptist	600,000
8	Orthodox	540,000
9 =	Church of Scientology	500,000
=	Hindu	500,000

Source: *Christian Research*

Membership of Christian churches in the UK has fallen since the 1970s, while membership of other religions, particularly Sikh and Muslim has risen. This list represents the number of people belonging to a religion – not necessarily practicing members, but according to whether they stated that they belonged to a particular religion or denomination.

TOP 10 LARGEST MUSLIM POPULATIONS

	COUNTRY	MUSLIM POPULATION (2000)
1	Pakistan	150,365,000
2	India	122,570,000
3	Indonesia	116,105,000*
4	Bangladesh	110,849,000
5	Turkey	64,714,000
6	Iran	64,707,000
7	Egypt	57,780,000
8	Nigeria	49,000,000
9	Algeria	30,442,000
10	Morocco	27,736,000

* An additional 46 million people are considered Muslims by the Indonesian government but are more properly categorized as New Religionists (Islamisized syncretistic religions)

Source: *David B. Barrett & Todd M. Johnson,* World Christian Trends, *William Carey Library, 2001*

TOP 10 RELIGIOUS BRANCHES

	BRANCH/RELIGION	FOLLOWERS (2000)
1	Roman Catholic, Christianity	1,057,328,093
2	Sunni, Islam	1,002,542,801
3	Vaishnavite, Hinduism	549,583,323
4	Protestant, Christianity	342,001,605
5	Sufi, Islam	237,400,000
6	Shaivite, Hinduism	216,260,000
7	Animist, ethno-religion	216,160,890
8	Orthodox, Christianity	215,128,717
9	Mahayana, Buddhism	202,232,757
10	Shia, Islam	170,100,000

Source: *David B. Barrett & Todd M. Johnson,* World Christian Trends, *William Carey Library, 2001*

The world's religions are far from homogenous: within each major religion there are often numerous branches often conflicting – sometimes fiercely – with others. This list represents the 10 largest branches that share a common historical heritage and a proportion of doctrines or practices.

TOP 10 RELIGIOUS TRADITIONS WITH THE MOST MARTYRS

	RELIGIOUS TRADITION	MARTYRS
1	Russian Orthodox	21,626,000
2	Assyrian or Nestoran (East Syrian, Messihaye)	12,379,000
3	Latin-rite Catholic	11,024,000
4	Ukrainian Orthodox	3,500,000
5	Armenian Orthodox (Gregorian)	1,215,000
6	Coptic Orthodox	1,068,000
7	Pentecostal (Protestant, Classical Pentecostal)	1,021,000
8 =	Messianic Jewish	1,000,000
=	Quasi-Christians	1,000,000
10	Lutheran	987,000

Source: *David B. Barrett & Todd M. Johnson,* World Christian Trends, *William Carey Library, 2001*

According to some authorities, some 70 million Christians have been martyred for their faith during the past 2,000 years, while other major religions also claim figures running into the millions.

TOWN &
COUNTRY

World Cities

TOP 10 | MOST URBANIZED COUNTRIES

COUNTRY	POPULATION LIVING IN URBAN AREAS (2001) TOTAL	PERCENTAGE
1 = Hong Kong	6,961,000	100.0
= Monaco	34,000	100.0
= Nauru	13,000	100.0
= Singapore	4,108,000	100.0
= The Vatican	1,000	100.0
6 Belgium	5,444,000	97.4
7 Kuwait	1,894,000	96.1
8 Qatar	534,000	92.9
9 Iceland	261,000	92.7
10 Bahrain	603,000	92.5
World	2,923,182,000	47.7
UK	53,313,000	89.5

Source: *United Nations Population Division*, World Urbanization Prospects: The 2001 Revision

TOP 10 | FASTEST-GROWING CITIES*

	CITY/COUNTRY	AVERAGE ANNUAL POPULATION GROWTH RATE (PER CENT) (2000–05)
1	Ansan, South Korea	9.15
2	Toluca, Mexico	6.15
3	Sana`a, Yemen	5.83
4	Niamey, Niger	5.70
5	Songnam, South Korea	5.47
6	P'ohang, South Korea	5.43
7	Rajshahi, Bangladesh	5.29
8	Kabul, Afghanistan	5.10
9 =	Antananarivo, Madagascar	5.05
=	Campo Grande, Brazil	5.05

* Of urban agglomerations with 750,000 inhabitants or more

Source: *United Nations Population Division*, World Urbanization Report: The 2001 Revision

TOP 10 | COUNTRIES WITH THE MOST PEOPLE LIVING IN LARGE CITIES

	COUNTRY	% POPULATION IN CITIES OF OVER 1 MILLION* (2002)
1	Hong Kong	100
2	Singapore	89
3	Dominican Republic	61
4	Kuwait	60
5	Portugal	57
6	Australia	56
7 =	Lebanon	47
=	South Korea	47
9 =	Argentina	41
=	Congo	41
=	Germany	41
	UK	23

* In those countries for which data available

Source: *World Bank*, World Development Indicators, 2002

TOP 10 | COUNTRIES WITH THE LARGEST URBAN POPULATIONS

	COUNTRY	EST. TOTAL URBAN POPULATION (2005)
1	China	535,958,000
2	India	312,887,000
3	USA	232,080,000
4	Brazil	151,925,000
5	Indonesia	104,048,000
6	Russia	102,731,000
7	Japan	101,831,000
8	Mexico	80,073,000
9	Germany	72,405,000
10	Nigeria	62,623,000
	World	3,176,892,000
	UK	53,842,000

* In those countries for which data available

Source: *United Nations Population Division*, World Urbanization Prospects: The 2001 Revision

▶ **City and state**
Singapore City and the state are synonymous, as a result of which Singapore is considered a totally urbanized country.

TOP 10 LARGEST CITIES 100 YEARS AGO

	CITY/COUNTRY	POPULATION*
1	**London,** UK	6,581,000
2	**New York,** USA	3,437,000
3	**Paris,** France	2,714,000
4	**Berlin,** Germany	1,889,000
5	**Chicago,** USA	1,699,000
6	**Vienna,** Austria	1,675,000
7	**Wuhan,** China	1,500,000
8	**Tokyo,** Japan	1,440,000
9	**Philadelphia,** USA	1,294,000
10	**St. Petersburg,** Russia	1,265,000

* Including adjacent suburban areas

TOP 10 LARGEST CITIES

	CITY/COUNTRY	EST. POPULATION (2002)
1	**Tokyo,** Japan	35,100,000
2	**New York,** USA	21,650,000
3	**Seoul,** South Korea	21,350,000
4	**Mexico City,** Mexico	20,950,000
5	**São Paulo,** Brazil	19,900,000
6	**Mumbai** (Bombay), India	18,400,000
7	**Osaka,** Japan	18,050,000
8	**Delhi,** India	17,500,000
9	**Los Angeles,** USA	16,900,000
10	**Jakarta,** Indonesia	16,050,000

Source: *Th. Brinkhoff:* The Principal Agglomerations of the World, *http://www.citypopulation.de,* *12 November 2002*

TOP 10 LARGEST CITIES IN THE UK

	CITY	POPULATION (2001) PER SQ KM	TOTAL
1	**London**	4,572	7,188,000
2	**Birmingham**	3,647	976,000
3	**Leeds**	1,297	716,000
4	**Glasgow**	3,298	579,000
5	**Sheffield**	1,395	513,000
6	**Bradford**	1,277	468,000
7	**Edinburgh**	1,703	449,000
8	**Liverpool**	3,927	439,000
9	**Manchester**	3,398	393,000
10	**Kirklees**	952	389,000

CULTURE & LEARNING

MUSIC & MUSICIANS

Songs & Songwriters

TOP 10 | SONGWRITERS IN THE UK CHARTS

	SONGWRITER(S)	CHART HITS
1	John Lennon and Paul McCartney	131
2	Mike Stock, Matt Aitken, and Pete Waterman	90
3	Stevie Wonder	88
4	Mick Jagger and Keith Richard	82
5	Brian Holland, Lamont Dozier, and Eddie Holland	80
6	Sting	77
7	Bee Gees (Barry, Robin, and Maurice Gibb)	65
8	Nicky Chinn and Mike Chapman	64
9	Elton John and Bernie Taupin	63
10	Burt Bacharach and Hal David	57

Source: *Music Information Database*

▼ **Wonder land**
Prodigious singer-songwriter Stevie Wonder (Steveland Judkins) had his first UK chart success in 1966 with *Uptight (Everything's Alright)*, followed by an array of major hits.

THE 10 | LATEST GRAMMY SONGS OF THE YEAR

YEAR	SONG	SONGWRITER(S)
2002	Don't Know Why	Jesse Harris
2001	Fallin'	Alicia Keys
2000	Beautiful Day	U2
1999	Smooth	Itaal Shur and Rob Thomas
1998	My Heart Will Go On	James Horner and Will Jennings
1997	Sunny Came Home	Shawn Colvin
1996	Change the World	Gordon Kennedy, Wayne Kirkpatrick, and Tommy Sims
1995	Kiss From a Rose	Seal
1994	Streets of Philadelphia	Bruce Springsteen
1993	A Whole New World	Alan Menken and Tim Rice

The National Academy of Recording Arts & Sciences was founded in 1957. Awards have been presented annually since 1959, for recordings of the preceding year. In the category "Song of the Year", the award is made to the songwriter rather than performer. The first winner was *Nel Blu Dipinto di Blu*, written by Domenico Modugno. Subsequent winners represent many songs that are now regarded as classics, as well as some of the biggest-selling singles of all time, among them *Moon River* by Henry Mancini and Johnny Mercer, from the film *Breakfast at Tiffany's* (1961), and *We Are The World*, by Michael Jackson and Lionel Richie (1985).

THE 10 LATEST WINNERS OF THE Q MAGAZINE AWARD FOR CLASSIC SONGWRITER

YEAR	SONGWRITER(S)
2002	Jimmy Cliff
2001	Kate Bush
2000	Guy Chambers and Robbie Williams
1999	Ian Dury and Chas Jankel
1998	Paul Weller
1997	Paul McCartney
1996	Elvis Costello
1995	Van Morrison
1994	Morissey
1993	Neil Finn

The *Q Magazine* Songwriter (latterly Classic Songwriter) Award, based on a readers' poll, has been presented since the ceremony's first year, 1990, when it was won by Prince.

TOP 10 SONGS MOST PLAYED BY DJS IN THE UK, 2002

	SONG/SONGWRITER(S)	ORIGINAL/POPULAR PERFORMER
1	**Can't Get You Outa My Head,** Cathy Dennis and Robert Davis	Kylie Minogue
2	**Murder on the Dancefloor,** Gregg Alexander and Sophie Ellis Bextor	Sophie Ellis Bextor
3	**Just a Little,** Michael Escoffery, John Hammond, and George Hammond	Liberty X
4	**Like a Prayer,** Madonna Ciccone and Patrick Leonard	Madonna/Madhouse
5	**Whenever Wherever,** Shakira Mebarak, Timothy Mitchell, and Gloria Estefan	Shakira
6	**Get the Party Started,** Linda Perry	Pink
7	**Don't Stop Movin',** Sheppard Solomon, Simon Ellis, Rachel Stevens, Hannah Spearritt, Bradle Mcintosh, Jonathan Lee, Paul Cattermole, Joanne O'Meara, and Tina Barrett	S Club
8	**Hey Baby,** Bruce Channel and Margaret Cobb	DJ Otzi
9	**It's Raining Men,** Paul Shaffer and Paul Jabara	Weather Girls
10	**Billy Jean,** Michael Jackson	Michael Jackson

Source: *Performing Right Society*

These are the songs most played by DJs in live sets, as monitored by the MCPS (Mechanical-Copyright Protection Society) and PRS (Performing Right Society), which represent copyright owners (composers, songwriters, and music publishers), licensing their music and collecting and distributing royalties. In the present century, the DJ lists have been headed in 2000 by *Don't Call Me Baby* (written by Giuseppe Chierchia, April Coates, and Andy Van Dorsselae), and in 2001 by *Rock DJ* (Robbie Williams, Guy Chambers, Kelvin Andrews, Ekundayo Paris, and Nelson Pickford).

TOP 10 MOST-COVERED BEATLES SONGS

	SONG	WRITTEN
1	**Yesterday**	1965
2	**Eleanor Rigby**	1966
3	**Something**	1969
4	**Hey Jude**	1968
5	**Let It Be**	1969
6	**Michelle**	1965
7	**With a Little Help from My Friends**	1967
8	**Day Tripper**	1965
9	**Come Together**	1969
10	**The Long and Winding Road**	1969

Yesterday is one of the most-covered songs of all time, with the number of recorded versions now in four figures. Although most of these songs are Lennon and McCartney compositions, the No. 3 song, *Something*, was written by George Harrison, and released in 1969 as his first A-side single.

TOP 10 ROCK SONGS OF ALL TIME*

	SONG	ARTIST OR GROUP
1	**(I Can't Get No) Satisfaction**	The Rolling Stones
2	**Respect**	Aretha Franklin
3	**Stairway to Heaven**	Led Zeppelin
4	**Like a Rolling Stone**	Bob Dylan
5	**Born to Run**	Bruce Springsteen
6	**Hotel California**	The Eagles
7	**Light My Fire**	The Doors
8	**Good Vibrations**	The Beach Boys
9	**Hey Jude**	The Beatles
10	**Imagine**	John Lennon

* Determined by a panel of 700 voters assembled by the music network VH1

The Top 10 from an all-time top 100 list is dominated by songs dating from the 1960s. Within it are no fewer than nine Beatles songs (in addition to John Lennon's *Imagine*), as well as five by the Rolling Stones, four by Elvis Presley, and three each by the Beach Boys, Bob Dylan, Marvin Gaye, and Led Zeppelin. A number of notable artists are perhaps surprisingly represented by a single song, including Chuck Berry's *Johnny B Goode,* David Bowie's *Space Oddity,* the Doors' *Light My Fire,* the Eagles' *Hotel California,* Jimi Hendrix's *Purple Haze,* Little Richard's *Good Golly, Miss Molly,* Roy Orbison's *Oh, Pretty Woman,* and Stevie Wonder's *Superstition.*

Record Firsts

THE 10 | ALBUMS IN THE FIRST UK ALBUMS TOP 10*

	TITLE	ARTIST
1	South Pacific	Soundtrack
2	Come Fly With Me	Frank Sinatra
3	Elvis' Golden Records	Elvis Presley
4	King Creole	Elvis Presley
5	My Fair Lady	Broadway Cast
6	Warm	Johnny Mathis
7	The King and I	Soundtrack
8	Dear Perry	Perry Como
9	Oklahoma!	Soundtrack
10	Songs by Tom Lehrer	Tom Lehrer

Source: Melody Maker

* 8 November 1958

THE 10 | FIRST GRAMMY RECORDS OF THE YEAR

YEAR	TITLE	ARTIST
1958	Nel Blu Dipinto di Blu (Volare)	Domenico Modugno
1959	Mack the Knife	Bobby Darin
1960	Theme from A Summer Place	Percy Faith
1961	Moon River	Henry Mancini
1962	I Left My Heart in San Francisco	Tony Bennett
1963	The Days of Wine and Roses	Henry Mancini
1964	The Girl from Ipanema	Stan Getz & Astrud Gilberto
1965	A Taste of Honey	Herb Alpert & the Tijuana Brass
1966	Strangers in the Night	Frank Sinatra
1967	Up Up and Away	5th Dimension

◀ **The King rules**
Elvis Presley's *It's Now or Never*, an English version of the Italian song *O Sole Mio* (1901), was the fourth ever million-selling single in the UK, where it topped the chart for nine weeks.

THE 10 SINGLES IN THE FIRST UK TOP 10

	TITLE	ARTIST
1	Here in My Heart	Al Martino
2	You Belong to Me	Jo Stafford
3	Somewhere Along the Way	Nat "King" Cole
4	Isle of Innisfree	Bing Crosby
5	Feet Up	Guy Mitchell
6	Half as Much	Rosemary Clooney
7 =	Forget Me Not	Vera Lynn
=	High Noon	Frankie Lane
8 =	Blue Tango	Ray Martin
=	Sugarbush	Doris Day & Frankie Laine
9	Homing Waltz	Vera Lynn
10	Auf Wiedersehen (Sweetheart)	Vera Lynn

Source: New Musical Express

The first UK singles chart was published in the *New Musical Express* for the week ending 15 November 1952. Curiously, the Top 10 contained 12 entries because those of equal rank shared the same placing. Other singles in the list steadily fell out of the chart, but Jo Stafford's continued to sell strongly until the following year, thus becoming the first woman to top the UK chart.

THE 10 FIRST FEMALE SINGERS TO HAVE A NO. 1 HIT IN THE UK

	ARTIST	TITLE	DATE AT NO. 1
1	Jo Stafford	You Belong to Me	16 Jan 1953
2	Kay Starr	Comes A-Long A-Love	23 Jan 1953
3	Lita Roza	(How Much is That) Doggie in the Window?	17 Apr 1953
4	Doris Day	Secret Love	16 Apr 1954
5	Kitty Kallen	Little Things Mean a Lot	10 Sept 1954
6	Vera Lynn	My Son, My Son	5 Nov 1954
7	Rosemary Clooney	This Ole House	26 Nov 1954
8	Ruby Murray	Softly Softly	18 Feb 1955
9	Alma Cogan	Dreamboat	15 July 1955
10	Anne Shelton	Lay Down Your Arms	21 Sept 1956

Source: *Music Information Database*

The UK singles chart was launched in November 1952, and in replacing the inaugural chart-topper (Al Martino's *Here in My Heart*), Jo Stafford's *You Belong to Me* was only the second single to reach No. 1 on it. The girls were briefly ahead of their male counterparts in these early days, when Kay Starr's *Comes A-Long A-Love* became Britain's third chart-topper only a week after Ms Stafford's single. Lita Roza, covering a US No. 1 by Patti Page, was the first British female artist to reach the summit, six months into the life of the chart.

THE 10 SINGLES IN THE FIRST UK RAP TOP 10

	TITLE	ARTIST
1	The Boomin' System	L.L. Cool J featuring Uncle J
2	Gangsta Gangsta	N.W.A.
3	Simba Groove/Cult of Snap	Hi Power
4	Bonita Applebum	A Tribe Called Quest
5	Raise (63 Steps to Heaven)	Bocca Juniors
6	Superfly 1990	Curtis Mayfield & Ice T
7	Amerikkka's Most Wanted	Ice Cube
8	Steppin' to the A.M.	3rd Bass
9	100 Miles and Runnin'	N.W.A.
10	U Can't Touch This	MC Hammer

Source: *MRIB*

Regarded as a musical fad until the late 1980s, the advent of London's Kiss FM radio station in 1990 led to MRIB compiling, on 8 September 1990, the first UK rap singles survey for weekly broadcast on the ground-breaking dance-oriented station.

THE 10 FIRST MILLION-SELLING SINGLES IN THE UK

	TITLE/ARTIST	YEAR
1	Rock Around the Clock, Bill Haley & His Comets	1955
2	Mary's Boy Child, Harry Belafonte	1957
3	Diana, Paul Anka	1957
4	It's Now or Never, Elvis Presley	1960
5	Stranger on the Shore, Mr Acker Bilk	1961
6	The Young Ones, Cliff Richard	1962
7	I Remember You, Frank Ifield	1962
8	Telstar, Tornados	1962
9	The Next Time/Bachelor Boy, Cliff Richard & the Shadows	1962
10	She Loves You, The Beatles	1963

The Beatles are the all-time platinum singles sales kings: they amassed five million-selling UK singles in the 1960s, while John Lennon added one with *Imagine* and Paul McCartney another with Wings' *Mull of Kintyre/Girls School* in 1978.

FIRST MILLION-SELLER!

THE SOUNDTRACK ALBUM of *South Pacific* was released in 1958. It was the biggest-selling soundtrack album ever until it was overtaken by *The Sound of Music* (1965), by which time it had sold five million copies, going on to sell eight million worldwide by 1970. It broke all records on both sides of the Atlantic: in the USA the album stayed at No. 1 for 54 weeks, was in the Top 10 for two years, and remained in the charts for 259 weeks. In the UK it was the first LP ever to sell a million copies, while it spent a record 115 weeks at No. 1, 70 of them consecutive. The film from which it was derived was the highest-earning of the year, making some $36.8 million in the USA alone.

FIRST FACT

Stars of the Decades

TOP 10 | SOLO SINGERS OF THE 1970s IN THE UK

	SINGER	TOTAL HITS*
1	Elvis Presley	40
2 =	David Bowie	23
=	Elton John	23
4	Cliff Richard	21
5	Diana Ross	20
6	Rod Stewart	19
7 =	Donna Summer	16
=	Stevie Wonder	16
9 =	David Essex	15
=	Gary Glitter	15

* Includes only records that entered the charts in the 1970s

Source: *Music Information Database*

Elvis Presley's 1970s career represents a continuation of his triumphs of the 1960s, when he scored a record 44 UK chart hits. Although his career was cut short by his death in 1977, posthumous successes continued.

▲ **Material girl**
Since her first chart hit, *Holiday*, in 1984, Madonna has achieved more chart hits than any other female artist.

TOP 10 | SOLO SINGERS OF THE 1980s IN THE UK

	SINGER	TOTAL HITS*
1	Shakin' Stevens	29
2 =	Prince	25
=	Cliff Richard	25
4 =	Elton John	23
=	Diana Ross	23
6 =	Michael Jackson	22
=	Madonna	22
8 =	David Bowie	21
=	Gary Numan	21
10 =	Rod Stewart	18
=	Donna Summer	18
=	Kim Wilde	18
=	Stevie Wonder	18

* Includes only records that entered the charts in the 1980s

Source: *Music Information Database*

TOP 10 | SOLO SINGERS OF THE 1990s IN THE UK

	SINGER	TOTAL HITS*
1	Madonna	29
2	Gloria Estefan	23
3	Mariah Carey	21
4	Cher	19
5 =	Janet Jackson	18
=	Morrissey	18
=	Cliff Richard	18
=	Diana Ross	18
=	Sting	18
=	Paul Weller	18

* Includes only records that entered the charts in the 1990s

Source: *Music Information Database*

The careers of some of the most successful solo singers of the decade began in previous decades – the 1950s in the case of Cliff Richard, and 1960s for Cher and Diana Ross.

TOP 10 | GROUPS OF THE 1970s IN THE UK

	GROUP	TOTAL HITS*
1 =	T. Rex	21
=	Wings	21
3	Hot Chocolate	20
4 =	The Carpenters	19
=	Slade	19
6 =	Electric Light Orchestra	18
=	Showaddywaddy	18
8	Abba	17
9 =	Status Quo	16
=	The Stylistics	16
=	Sweet	16

* Includes only records that entered the charts in the 1970s

Source: *Music Information Database*

Sharing the honours as one of the leading groups of the 1970s, the initial line-up of T. Rex (originally Tyrannosaurus Rex) comprised Marc Bolan, killed in a car crash in 1977, and Steve Took (died 1980).

TOP 10 | GROUPS OF THE 1980s IN THE UK

	GROUP	TOTAL HITS*
1	UB40	24
2 =	Depeche Mode	23
=	Level 42	23
4	Madness	22
5 =	Eurythmics	21
=	Kool & the Gang	21
=	Queen	21
=	Status Quo	21
9 =	Bananarama	20
=	Bucks Fizz	20
=	Duran Duran	20
=	Iron Maiden	20
=	Orchestral Manoeuvres in the Dark	20
=	Siouxsie & the Banshees	20

* Includes only records that entered the charts in the 1980s

Source: *Music Information Database*

ROCK 'N' ROLL

THE ROCK 'N' ROLL ERA is generally dated from the release of Bill Haley and his Comets' single (*We're Gonna*) *Rock Around the Clock*. Recorded in New York's Pythian Temple Studios on 12 April 1954, it was first released later that year, but became a smash hit only after it appeared in the teen film *Blackboard Jungle*, which opened in the USA on 25 March 1955. On 9 July it became the first rock record to top the US chart, where it stayed for eight weeks, and on 14 October became the first rock record ever to top the UK chart.

▶ **All the right moves**
Led by Michael Stipe, American band R.E.M., named after the Rapid Eye Movement dream phase of the sleep cycle, was among the most successful of the 1990s.

TOP 10 GROUPS OF THE 1990s IN THE UK

	GROUP	TOTAL HITS*
1	The Manic Street Preachers	29
2 =	Blur	23
=	R.E.M.	23
4	Roxette	22
5 =	Beautiful South	20
=	James	20
=	Pet Shop Boys	20
=	Wedding Present	20
9 =	The Charlatans	19
=	M People	19
=	Wet Wet Wet	19

* Includes only records that entered the charts in the 1990s

Source: *Music Information Database*

Wet Wet Wet not only gain a place in this Top 10, but with one of their 1990s hits, *Love is All Around*, in the film *Four Weddings and a Funeral*, achieved the record for a UK group with 15 weeks at No.1.

All-Time Greats

SINGLES OF ALL TIME

	TITLE/ARTIST OR GROUP/YEAR OF ENTRY	SALES EXCEED
1	Candle in the Wind (1997)/Something About the Way You Look Tonight, Elton John, 1997	37,000,000
2	White Christmas, Bing Crosby, 1945	30,000,000
3	Rock Around the Clock, Bill Haley and His Comets, 1954	17,000,000
4	I Want to Hold Your Hand, The Beatles, 1963	12,000,000
5 =	Hey Jude, The Beatles, 1968	10,000,000
=	It's Now or Never, Elvis Presley, 1960	10,000,000
=	I Will Always Love You, Whitney Houston, 1992	10,000,000
8 =	Hound Dog/Don't Be Cruel, Elvis Presley, 1956	9,000,000
=	Diana, Paul Anka, 1957	9,000,000
10 =	I'm a Believer, The Monkees, 1966	8,000,000
=	(Everything I Do) I Do it for You, Bryan Adams, 1991	8,000,000

Global sales are notoriously difficult to calculate, since for many decades, little statistical research on record sales was done in a large part of the world. "Worldwide" is thus usually taken to mean the known minimum "western world" sales. It took 55 years for a record to overtake Bing Crosby's 1942 *White Christmas*, although the song, as also recorded by others and sold as sheet music, has achieved such enormous total sales that it would still appear in first position in any list of bestselling songs.

SINGLES OF ALL TIME IN THE UK

	TITLE/ARTIST OR GROUP/YEAR OF ENTRY	EST. UK SALES
1	Candle in The Wind (1997)/Something About the Way You Look Tonight, Elton John, 1997	4,864,611
2	Do They Know It's Christmas?, Band Aid, 1984	3,550,000
3	Bohemian Rhapsody, Queen, 1975/91	2,130,000
4	Mull of Kintyre, Wings, 1977	2,050,000
5	Rivers of Babylon/Brown Girl in the Ring, Boney M, 1978	1,985,000
6	You're the One that I Want, John Travolta and Olivia Newton-John, 1978	1,975,000
7	Relax, Frankie Goes to Hollywood, 1984	1,910,000
8	She Loves You, The Beatles, 1963	1,890,000
9	Unchained Melody, Robson Green and Jerome Flynn, 1995	1,843,701
10	Mary's Boy Child/Oh My Lord, Boney M, 1978	1,790,000

Source: *The Official UK Charts Company*

Seventy-six singles have sold over a million copies apiece in the UK in the last 50 years: these are the cream of that crop. The Band Aid single was surrounded by special circumstances, and it took the remarkable response to the death of Diana, Princess of Wales, to generate sales capable of overtaking it. Two years, 1978 and 1984, were the all-time strongest for million-selling singles. The only act to appear twice is Boney M, who had a string of UK chart singles, but none came close to the sales figures achieved by their two 1978 mega-hits.

"GREATEST HITS" ALBUMS IN THE UK

	TITLE/ARTIST OR GROUP	YEAR OF ENTRY
1	Abba Gold Greatest Hits, Abba	1992
2	Greatest Hits (Volume One), Queen	1981
3	The Immaculate Collection, Madonna	1990
4	The Very Best of Elton John, Elton John	1990
5	1, The Beatles	2000
6	Ladies and Gentleman – The Best of George Michael, George Michael	1998
7	Legend, Bob Marley and The Wailers	1984
8	Carry On Up the Charts – The Best of the Beautiful South, Beautiful South	1994
9	Texas – The Greatest Hits, Texas	2000
10	Greatest Hits II, Queen	1991

Source: *BPI*

Some of the biggest of these hits compilations have achieved truly immense sales in the UK – far more, in most cases, than the hit singles they anthologize. All the albums here have sold at least 1.5 million copies, while Abba's album has topped 3.5 million – more than doubling its sales in the past three years – no doubt helped by the long-running West End show *Mamma Mia*.

NORTH AMERICAN CONCERT TOURS

	ARTIST OR GROUP	TOUR/YEAR	GROSS ($)
1	The Rolling Stones	Voodoo Lounge, 1994	121,200,000
2	U2	Elevation, 2001	109,700,000
3	Pink Floyd	The Division Bell, 1994	103,500,000
4	Paul McCartney	Driving USA, 2002	103,300,000
5	The Rolling Stones	Steel Wheels, 1989	98,000,000
6	The Rolling Stones	Bridges to Babylon, 1997	89,300,000
7	The Rolling Stones	Licks, 2002	87,900,000
8	*NSYNC	Popodyssey, 2001	86,800,000
9	The Backstreet Boys	Black and Blue, 2001	82,100,000
10	Tina Turner	Twenty-Four Seven, 2000	80,200,000

Source: Fortune/*Pollstar*

The most recent member of this élite is Paul McCartney, who beat the Rolling Stones into second place during 2002 – the first time during the past 20 years that the Stones failed to top the list in a year when they have toured. While the Rolling Stones' 2002–03 *Licks* world tour was in progress, it was estimated that the group has earned more than $1 billion from ticket sales alone since its 1989 sell-out *Steel Wheels* tour.

 ARTISTS WITH THE MOST GRAMMY AWARDS

	ARTIST	YEARS	AWARDS*
1	Sir Georg Solti	1962–97	38
2	Pierre Boulez	1969–2001	29
3	= Vladimir Horowitz	1962–92	26
	= Quincy Jones	1963–93	26
5	Stevie Wonder	1973–2002	22
6	= Leonard Bernstein	1961–2001	20
	= Henry Mancini	1958–70	20
8	John T. Williams	1975–2000	18
9	= Eric Clapton	1972–2001	16
	= Itzhak Perlman	1977–95	16

Excludes Lifetime Achievements

The Grammy Awards are considered to be the most prestigious in the music industry. The proliferation of classical artists reflects the number of classical award categories at the Grammys, which have only latterly been overshadowed by pop and rock.

ALBUMS OF ALL TIME IN THE UK

	TITLE/ARTIST OR GROUP	YEAR OF ENTRY
1	Sgt. Pepper's Lonely Hearts Club Band, The Beatles	1967
2	(What's the Story) Morning Glory, Oasis	1995
3	Bad, Michael Jackson	1987
4	Brothers in Arms, Dire Straits	1985
5	Stars, Simply Red	1991
6	Abba Gold Greatest Hits, Abba	1992
7	The Immaculate Collection, Madonna	1990
8	Thriller, Michael Jackson	1982
9	Greatest Hits (Volume One), Queen	1981
10	Come On Over, Shania Twain	1998

Source: *BPI*

Even the lowest entry in this list of Top 10 bestsellers, Shania Twain's *Come On Over*, has been certified for nine platinum awards (for sales of 300,000 copies each) in the UK.

ARTISTS WITH THE MOST WEEKS ON THE UK SINGLES CHART

	ARTIST OR GROUP	TOTAL WEEKS*
1	Elvis Presley	1,172
2	Cliff Richard	1,146
3	Elton John	583
4	Madonna	534
5	Michael Jackson	485
6	Rod Stewart	466
7	The Beatles	456
8	David Bowie	449
9	Frank Sinatra	440
10	Diana Ross	434

To end of 2002

Source: *Music Information Database*

▼ Bell ringer

Along with the majority of the top-earning concert tours, the dramatic stage set for Pink Floyd's 1994 *The Division Bell* tour was designed by British architect Mark Fisher.

Today's Stars

TOP 10 · ALBUMS OF 2002 IN THE UK

	ALBUM	ARTIST OR GROUP
1	Escapology	Robbie Williams
2	M!ssundaztood	Pink
3	Escape	Enrique Iglesias
4	A Rush of Blood to the Head	Coldplay
5	One Love	Blue
6	By the Way	Red Hot Chili Peppers
7	The Eminem Show	Eminem
8	Unbreakable – The Greatest Hits – Vol. 1	Westlife
9	Elv1s – 30 #1 Hits	Elvis Presley
10	Heathen Chemistry	Oasis

Source: *The Official Charts Company*

TOP 10 · SINGLES OF 2002 IN THE UK

	SINGLE	ARTIST OR GROUP
1	Anything is Possible/Evergreen	Will Young
2	Unchained Melody	Gareth Gates
3	Hero	Enrique Iglesias
4	Dilemma	Nelly featuring Kelly Rowland
5	A Little Less Conversation	Elvis vs. JXL
6	Anyone of Us (Stupid Mistake)	Gareth Gates
7	Whenever Wherever	Shakira
8	The Ketchup Song (Aserejé)	Las Ketchup
9	Just a Little	Liberty X
10	Without Me	Eminem

Source: *The Official Charts Company*

Will Young and Gareth Gates shot to stardom by respectively winning and becoming runner-up in the year's TV *Pop Idol* contest.

THE 10 · LATEST GRAMMY RECORDS OF THE YEAR

YEAR	RECORD	ARTIST OR GROUP
2002	Don't Know Why	Norah Jones
2001	Walk On	U2
2000	Beautiful Day	U2
1999	Smooth	Santana featuring Rob Thomas
1998	My Heart Will Go On	Celine Dion
1997	Sunny Came Home	Shawn Colvin
1996	Change the World	Eric Clapton
1995	Kiss from a Rose	Seal
1994	All I Wanna Do	Sheryl Crow
1993	I Will Always Love You	Whitney Houston

The Grammys are awarded retrospectively. Thus the 45th awards were presented in 2003 in recognition of musical accomplishment during 2002.

THE 10 · LATEST WINNERS OF THE BRIT AWARD FOR BEST BRITISH ALBUM*

YEAR	ALBUM	ARTIST OR GROUP
2003	A Rush of Blood to the Head	Coldplay
2002	No Angel	Dido
2001	Parachutes	Coldplay
2000	The Man Who	Travis
1999	This is My Truth, Tell Me Yours	Manic Street Preachers
1998	Urban Hymns	The Verve
1997	Everything Must Go	Manic Street Preachers
1996	(What's The Story) Morning Glory?	Oasis
1995	Parklife	Blur
1994	Connected	Stereo MCs

* *Previously "Best Album"*

A precursor of the Brit Awards was held in 1977, but it did not become an annual event until 1982, when Adam and The Ants won in this category for their album *Kings of the Wild Frontier*. Prior to the narrowing of the definition to British albums, winners included Barbra Streisand and Michael Jackson.

THE 10 · LATEST WINNERS OF THE BRIT AWARD FOR BEST BRITISH BREAKTHROUGH ARTIST

YEAR	ARTIST OR GROUP
2003	Will Young
2002	Blue
2001	A1
2000	S Club 7
1999	Belle and Sebastian
1998	Stereophonics
1997	Kula Shaker
1996	Supergrass
1995	Oasis
1994	Gabrielle

* *Best British Newcomer until 2002*

Until 1994, only members of the British Phonographic Industry were eligible to cast votes for Brit Awards, but that has since been extended, first to include representatives of the press, retailers, and others in the music business, and then – latterly by online voting – to members of the public.

THE 10 · LATEST WINNERS OF THE BRIT AWARD FOR BEST BRITISH FEMALE SOLO ARTIST

YEAR	ARTIST
2003	Ms. Dynamite
2002	Dido
2001	Sonique
2000	Beth Orton
1999	Des'ree
1998	Shola Ama
1997	Gabrielle
1996	Annie Lennox
1995	Eddie Reader
1994	Dina Carroll

In its inaugural year, 1982, this award was won by Randy Crawford. In subsequent years, Annie Lennox won it on a record six occasions, as well as receiving awards as a member of the Eurythmics. Both Lisa Stansfield and Alison Moyet won the solo award twice.

TOP 10 BEST-PAID ROCK AND POP STARS

	STAR	EST. EARNINGS (2001–02*) ($)
1	U2	69,000,000
2	Mariah Carey	58,000,000
3	Dave Matthews Band	50,000,000
4	Madonna	43,000,000
5	*NSYNC	42,300,000
6	Britney Spears	39,200,000
7	Jennifer Lopez	37,000,000
8	Backstreet Boys	36,800,000
9	Elton John	30,000,000
10	Aerosmith	25,000,000

For the period June 2001–June 2002

Source: Forbes

THE 10 LATEST WINNERS OF THE BRIT AWARD FOR BEST BRITISH MALE SOLO ARTIST

YEAR	ARTIST
2003	Robbie Williams
2002	Robbie Williams
2001	Robbie Williams
2000	Tom Jones
1999	Robbie Williams
1998	Finlay Quaye
1997	George Michael
1996	Paul Weller
1995	Paul Weller
1994	Sting

▶ **Pro Bono**
The combined revenue from record sales and concert tours have propelled U2 to the head of the rock star earnings league.

Gold & Platinum

TOP 10 GROUPS WITH THE MOST PLATINUM ALBUMS IN THE UK

	GROUP	AWARDS
1	Simply Red	38
2	Queen	35
3	U2	33
4	Oasis	29
5	Dire Straits	27
6	Fleetwood Mac	23
7	Abba	21
8 =	Boyzone	17
=	R.E.M.	17
=	UB40	17
=	Westlife	17
=	Wet Wet Wet	17

Source: BPI

▶ **They just keep rolling along**
The Rolling Stones' tally of gold albums spans the period from 1973, when they were first awarded in the UK, to 2002.

TOP 10 GROUPS WITH THE MOST GOLD ALBUMS IN THE UK

	GROUP	AWARDS
1	Queen	23
2	The Rolling Stones	20
3	Status Quo	19
4 =	Abba	15
=	The Beatles	15
=	Genesis	15
7	UB40	14
8 =	Roxy Music	13
=	U2	13
10	Pink Floyd	12

Source: BPI

Gold discs have been awarded since 1 April 1973 in the UK for sales of 400,000 singles or 100,000 albums, cassettes, or CDs (200,000 for budget-priced products). Two duos have received sufficient multiple gold albums to qualify them for a place in this list: the Carpenters (15) and Foster and Allen (12).

TOP 10 MALE ARTISTS WITH THE MOST GOLD ALBUMS IN THE UK

	ARTIST	AWARDS
1	Rod Stewart	24
2	Elton John	23
3	Cliff Richard*	21
4	Paul McCartney#	19
5	Neil Diamond	18
6 =	David Bowie	17
=	Elvis Presley	17
8	Mike Oldfield	16
9	James Last	15
10	Prince†	14

* Including two with the Shadows
# Including eight with Wings
† Including one with New Power Generation
Source: BPI

TOP 10 FEMALE ARTISTS WITH THE MOST GOLD ALBUMS IN THE UK

	ARTIST	AWARDS
1	Diana Ross*	17
2	Barbra Streisand#	14
3	Madonna	13
4 =	Mariah Carey	9
=	Donna Summer	9
6 =	Cher	8
=	Celine Dion	8
=	Tina Turner	8
9 =	Kate Bush	7
=	Janet Jackson	7
=	Kylie Minogue	7

* Including one with Marvin Gaye
# Including one with Kris Kristofferson
Source: BPI

MALE ARTISTS WITH THE MOST PLATINUM ALBUMS IN THE UK

	ARTIST	AWARDS
1	Michael Jackson	39
2	Robbie Williams	34
3	Phil Collins	31
4 =	Elton John	23
=	George Michael	23
6	Meat Loaf	17
7	Rod Stewart	15
8 =	Bon Jovi	14
=	Chris Rea	14
=	Cliff Richard	14

Source: *BPI*

Platinum albums in the UK are those that have achieved sales of 300,000. Relative to the population of the UK, where it represents approximately one sale per 196 inhabitants, this is a greater attainment than a US platinum award, where the ratio is one per 285. Multi-platinum albums are those that have sold multiples of 300,000; thus a quadruple platinum album denotes sales of 1.2 million units.

FEMALE ARTISTS WITH THE MOST PLATINUM ALBUMS IN THE UK

	ARTIST	AWARDS
1	Madonna	44
2 =	Celine Dion	21
=	Tina Turner	21
4 =	Whitney Houston*	18
=	Kylie Minogue	18
6 =	Enya	12
=	Shania Twain	12
8 =	Cher	11
=	Alanis Morissette	11
10 =	Kate Bush	10
–	Mariah Carey	10

* *Not including the compilation album* The Bodyguard

Source: *BPI*

Winning Whitney
Whitney Houston's album *Whitney* has gained six platinum awards in the UK, while *Whitney Houston* and *Whitney – The Greatest Hits* each earned four.

Music Genres

TOP 10 RAP SINGLES IN THE UK, 2002

	TITLE	ARTIST OR GROUP
1	Without Me	Eminem
2	Me Julie	Ali G & Shaggy
3	Hot in Herre	Nelly
4	Lose Yourself	Eminem
5	4 My People	Missy Elliott
6	Always on Time	Ja Rule featuring Ashanti
7	Black Suits Comin' (Nod Ya Head)	Will Smith featuring Tra-Knox
8	What's Luv	Fat Joe featuring Ashanti
9	I Need a Girl	P. Diddy featuring Usher & Loon
10	Cleanin' Out My Closet	Eminem

Source: *The Official UK Charts Company*

The UK's first rap singles chart was published in 1990. While the personnel have changed, the popularity of the genre has increased, elevating it from the marginal to the mainstream.

▼ Always first

Taken from his *Pain is Love* album, Ja Rule with Ashanti's hit single *Always on Time* was a global chart-topper in 2002.

TOP 10 DANCE SINGLES IN THE UK

	TITLE/ARTIST OR GROUP	YEAR
1	**Relax,** Frankie Goes to Hollywood	1983
2	**Barbie Girl,** Aqua	1997
3	**Believe,** Cher	1998
4	**Two Tribes,** Frankie Goes to Hollywood	1984
5	**Don't You Want Me,** Human League	1981
6	**Y.M.C.A.,** Village People	1978
7	**Heart of Glass,** Blondie	1979
8	**It's Like That,** Run D.M.C. vs. Jason Nevins	1998
9	**Saturday Night,** Whigfield	1994
10	**Can't Get You Out of My Head,** Kylie Minogue	2001

Source: *Music Information Database*

Despite being banned, initially by DJ Mike Reid and later by the entire BBC, Frankie Goes to Hollywood's *Relax* spent five weeks at No. 1 and went on to become the UK's bestselling dance single of all time, in 2000 ironically topping the BBC's Top of the Pops all-time poll.

TOP 10 BOY BAND ALBUMS IN THE UK

	TITLE/GROUP	YEAR
1	**By Request,** Boyzone	1999
2	**Coast to Coast,** Westlife	2000
3	**Where We Belong,** Boyzone	1998
4	**Everything Changes,** Take That	1993
5	**Westlife,** Westlife	1999
6	**All Rise,** Blue	2001
7	**Push,** Bros	1988
8	**World of Our Own,** Westlife	2001
9	**One Love,** Blue	2002
10	**Said and Done,** Boyzone	1995

Source: *Music Information Database*

Although they had isolated precursors, boy bands began in earnest in the USA in 1989 with the successes of New Kids on the Block, followed in the UK with Take That. They, along with Irish counterparts Boyzone, and, latterly, Blue, have extended what was viewed as a short-life phenomenon.

SINGLES MUSIC GENRES IN THE UK

	GENRE	MARKET SHARE (2002) %
1	Teen pop	28.0
2	Pop	23.4
3	Dance	15.4
4	Hip-hop	10.0
5	R&B	7.6
6	Contemporary rock	6.7
7	Rock (excluding contemporary and AOR)	5.3
8	AOR (adult oriented rock)	1.4
9	MOR (middle of the road)	0.9
10	Country	0.5

Source: *BPI*

In the singles market, the two sub-genres of pop, together with children's pop (0.4 per cent) comprise a cumulative total of 51.8 per cent. The only other category that is separately identified is reggae, with a mere 0.2 per cent of overall singles sales.

ROCK ALBUMS IN THE UK

	TITLE/ARTIST OR GROUP	YEAR OF ENTRY
1	(What's The Story) Morning Glory?, Oasis	1995
2	Brothers In Arms, Dire Straits	1985
3	Greatest Hits, Queen	1981
4	Rumours, Fleetwood Mac	1977
5	Urban Hymns, Verve	1997
6	The Man Who, Travis	1999
7	The Dark Side of The Moon, Pink Floyd	1973
8	Tango in the Night, Fleetwood Mac	1987
9	1, The Beatles	2000
10	The Joshua Tree, U2	1987

Source: *Music Information Database*

▶ **High-profile J-Lo**
Jennifer Lopez confirmed her singer/actress/celebrity status in 2002 with a pair of UK bestselling albums.

R&B ALBUMS IN THE UK, 2002

	TITLE	ARTIST OR GROUP
1	Songs In A Minor	Alicia Keys
2	Ashanti	Ashanti
3	J To Tha L-o – The Remixes	Jennifer Lopez
4	No More Drama	Mary J. Blige
5	A Little Deeper	Ms. Dynamite
6	This is Me ... Then	Jennifer Lopez
7	Encore	Lionel Richie
8	Legacy – The Greatest Hits Collection	Boyz II Men
9	Dreams Can Come True – Greatest Hits	Gabrielle
10	Slicker Than Your Average	Craig David

Source: *The Official UK Charts Company*

As well as releases by contemporary artists, ex-Commodores singer Lionel Richie scored a notable success with *Encore*, which featured tracks from a solo R&B career dating back over 20 years.

125

Broadcast Music

LATEST RECIPIENTS OF THE MTV VMA "BEST VIDEO" AWARD

	ARTIST OR GROUP	TITLE
2002	Eminem	Without Me
2001	Christina Aguilera, Lil' Kim, Mya, Pink, featuring Missy "Misdeameanor" Elliott	Lady Marmalade
2000	Eminem	The Real Slim Shady
1999	Lauryn Hill	Doo Wop (That Thing)
1998	Madonna	Ray of Light
1997	Jamiroquai	Virtual Insanity
1996	The Smashing Pumpkins	Tonight, Tonight
1995	TLC	Waterfalls
1994	Aerosmith	Cryin'
1993	Pearl Jam	Jeremy

LATEST RECIPIENTS OF THE MTV VMA "BEST GROUP VIDEO" AWARD

	ARTIST OR GROUP	TITLE
2002	No Doubt (featuring Bounty Killer)	Hey Baby
2001	*NSYNC	POP
2000	Blink 182	All the Small Things
1999	TLC	No Scrubs
1998	Backstreet Boys	Everybody (Backstreet's Back)
1997	No Doubt	Don't Speak
1996	Foo Fighters	Big Me
1995	TLC	Waterfalls
1994	Aerosmith	Cryin'
1993	Pearl Jam	Jeremy

MUSIC PROGRAMMES ON TELEVISION IN THE UK, 2002

	PROGRAMME	CHANNEL	AUDIENCE
1	Pop Idol: Live Final	ITV1	13,338,000
2	Party at the Palace	BBC1	12,539,000
3	Pop Idol: Result	ITV1	12,518,000
4	Pop Idol*	ITV1	10,281,000
5	Popstars: The Rivals	ITV1	8,905,000
6	Fame Academy#	BBC1	7,858,000
7	The Record of the Year Result 2002	ITV1	6,863,000
8	The Record of the Year 2002	ITV1	6,671,000
9	Jubilee 2002: Prom at the Palace	BBC1	5,449,000
10	Elton John's Greatest Hits Live	ITV1	5,190,000

* Highest audience viewing figure only, 2 February

\# Higest audience viewing figure only, 13 December

Source: *BARB/SPC*

The 3 June *Party at the Palace* concert celebrating the Queen's Golden Jubilee attracted a record audience for a live music show.

▶ **No Doubt about it**
The video of *Hey Baby*, co-written by Dave Stewart and performed by Gwen Stefani of No Doubt, received the accolade as MTV's "Best Group Video".

BBC RADIO 1 PROGRAMMES, 2002

	SHOW	LISTENERS
1	Sara Cox	7,020,000
2	Chris Moyles	6,420,000
3	Jo Whiley	5,310,000
4	Mark and Lard	4,960,000
5	Dave Pearce	3,820,000
6	UK Top 40	2,600,000
7	Jamie Theakston/Scott Mills	2,200,000
8 =	Scott Mills (Early Breakfast Mon–Fri)	1,890,000
=	Pete Tong	1,890,000
10	KC (Sat Breakfast)	1,870,000

Sara Cox first presented the Radio 1 Breakfast Show on Friday, 31 March 2000, becoming only the second female presenter of the programme to do so after Zoë Ball, from whom she took over and whose peak audience figure she exceeded.

LATEST RECIPIENTS OF THE MTV VMA "BEST FEMALE VIDEO" AWARD

	ARTIST	TITLE
2002	Pink	Get the Party Started
2001	Eve (featuring Gwen Stefani)	Let Me Blow Ya Mind
2000	Aaliyah	Try Again
1999	Lauryn Hill	Doo Wop (That Thing)
1998	Madonna	Ray of Light
1997	Jewel	You Were Meant for Me
1996	Alanis Morissette	Ironic
1995	Madonna	Take a Bow
1994	Janet Jackson	If
1993	k.d. lang	Constant Crying

THE 10 | LATEST RECIPIENTS OF THE MTV VMA "BEST MALE VIDEO" AWARD

	ARTIST	TITLE
2002	Eminem	Without Me
2001	Moby (featuring Gwen Stefani)	South Side
2000	Eminem	The Real Slim Shady
1999	Will Smith	Miami
1998	Will Smith	Just the Two of Us
1997	Beck	The Devil's Haircut
1996	Beck	Where It's At
1995	Tom Petty and the Heartbreakers	You Don't Know How it Feels
1994	Tom Petty and the Heartbreakers	Mary Jane's Last Dance
1993	Lenny Kravitz	Are You Gonna Go My Way

▼ **The real Slim Shady**
Eminem's award-winning video of his single *Without Me* depicts the rap star both as himself and in a diverse range of provocative personae, from a fat Elvis to Osama bin Laden.

TOP 10 | MOST PLAYED TRACKS ON UK RADIO, 2002

	TITLE	ARTIST(S)	UK RADIO PLAYS (2002)
1	Love at First Sight	Kylie Minogue	48,486
2	Just a Little	Liberty X	48,241
3	In Your Eyes	Kylie Minogue	45,057
4	Whenever Wherever	Shakira	44,033
5	How You Remind Me	Nickelback	43,468
6	A Little Less Conversation	Elvis Presley vs. JXL	42,309
7	Fly By II	Blue	41,673
8	Get the Party Started	Pink	39,094
9	Dilemma	Nelly featuring Kelly Rowland	38,634
10	Round Round	Sugababes	38,566

Source: *Music Control UK/BPI*

Movie Music

TOP 10 MUSICAL FILMS

FILM	YEAR
1 Grease	1978
2 Saturday Night Fever	1977
3 The Sound of Music	1965
4 Evita	1996
5 The Rocky Horror Picture Show	1975
6 Staying Alive	1983
7 American Graffiti	1973
8 Mary Poppins	1964
9 Flashdance	1983
10 Fantasia 2000	2000

Traditional musicals (films in which the cast actually sing) and films in which a musical soundtrack is a major component of the film are included here. The era of the blockbuster musical film may be over, but in recent years animated films with an important musical content appear to have taken over from them – *Beauty and the Beast*, *Aladdin*, *The Lion King*, *Pocahontas*, *The Prince of Egypt*, and *Tarzan* all won "Best Original Song" Oscars – while the film soundtrack album of *Titanic* is the bestselling of all time.

TOP 10 ORIGINAL SOUNDTRACK ALBUMS IN THE UK

TITLE	YEAR
1 The Bodyguard	1992
2 Dirty Dancing	1998
3 Titanic	1997
4 Bridget Jones's Diary	2001
5 Trainspotting	1996
6 The Commitments	1991
7 The Full Monty	1997
8 Top Gun	1986
9 Evita	1996
10 Buster	1988

Source: *Music Information Database*

TOP 10 FILMS WITH TITLES DERIVED FROM SONG TITLES

FILM	SONG*	FILM
1 American Pie	1972	1999
2 Sweet Home Alabama	1976	2002
3 Bad Boys	1983	1995
4 Sea of Love	1959	1989
5 One Fine Day	1963	1996
6 My Girl	1965	1991
7 Something To Talk About	1991	1995
8 When a Man Loves a Woman	1966	1994
9 The Crying Game	1964	1992
10 Addicted to Love	1986	1997

* *Release of first hit version*

Remarkably, the first film with a title derived from a song title was *How Would You Like to Be the Ice Man?*, released on 21 April 1899!

Grease is the word
Although it has celebrated its 25th anniversary, *Grease*, starring John Travolta as Danny and Olivia Newton-John as Sandy, remains unbeaten as the highest-earning musical film.

THE 10 LATEST "BEST SONG" OSCAR WINNERS

YEAR	TITLE	FILM
2002	Lose Yourself	8 Mile
2001	If I Didn't Have You	Monsters, Inc.
2000	Things Have Changed	Wonder Boys
1999	You'll Be in My Heart	Tarzan
1998	When You Believe	The Prince of Egypt
1997	My Heart Will Go On	Titanic
1996	You Must Love Me	Evita
1995	Colors of the Wind	Pocahontas
1994	Can You Feel the Love Tonight	The Lion King
1993	Streets of Philadelphia	Philadelphia

The "Best Song" Oscar was instituted at the 1934 Academy Awards ceremony, when it was won by *The Continental* from the film *The Gay Divorcee*. Songs from animated Disney films have been especially successful, winning on eight occasions since 1940, when *When You Wish Upon a Star* from *Pinocchio* received the award. *Zip-a-Dee-Doo-Dah* from part-animated *Song of the South* (1947) and *Chim Chim Cher-ee* from *Mary Poppins* (1964), along with songs from live-action films, bring the overall Disney total to 12.

TOP 10 BESTSELLING "BEST SONG" OSCAR-WINNING SINGLES IN THE UK

TITLE/ARTIST OR GROUP/FILM (IF DIFFERENT)	YEAR
1 I Just Called to Say I Love You, Stevie Wonder, *The Woman in Red*	1984
2 Fame, Irene Cara, *Fame*	1980
3 Take My Breath Away, Berlin, *Top Gun*	1986
4 My Heart Will Go On, Celine Dion, *Titanic*	1997
5 Flashdance...What a Feeling, Irene Cara, *Flashdance*	1983
6 Evergreen, Barbra Streisand, *A Star is Born*	1976
7 Streets of Philadelphia, Bruce Springsteen, *Philadelphia*	1994
8 Moon River, Danny Williams, *Breakfast at Tiffany's*	1961
9 Whatever Will Be, Will Be, Doris Day, *The Man Who Knew Too Much*	1956
10 Raindrops Keep Fallin' on My Head, Sacha Distel, *Butch Cassidy and the Sundance Kid*	1969

Source: *Music Information Database*

Stevie Wonder's *I Just Called to Say I Love You* was his first solo single (his 1982 No. 1 *Ebony and Ivory* was shared with Paul McCartney) to top the UK chart, where it remained for six weeks, selling over one million copies.

TOP 10 FILM MUSICALS ADAPTED FROM STAGE VERSIONS

	FILM MUSICAL	THEATRE OPENING	FILM RELEASE
1	Grease	1972	1978
2	The Sound of Music	1959	1965
3	Evita	1978	1996
4	The Rocky Horror Picture Show	1973	1975
5	Chicago	1975	2002
6	Fiddler on the Roof	1964	1971
7	My Fair Lady	1956	1964
8	The Best Little Whorehouse in Texas	1978	1982
9	Annie	1977	1982
10	West Side Story	1957	1961

The adapting of stage musicals as films has a long history, with these the most successful cinematic versions of, in most instances, long-running theatrical productions. Some followed an even longer progress from stage to screen, having been non-musical theatrical productions before being adapted as stage musicals, among them the recent success *Chicago*, which started life in 1926 as a play by Maurine Dallas Watkins and was made into two films, *Chicago* (1927) and *Roxie Hart* (1942), before Bob Fosse wrote the 1975 musical.

TOP 10 POP STAR FILM DEBUTS

	POP STAR(S)	FILM	YEAR
1	Whitney Houston	The Bodyguard	1992
2	Eminem	8 Mile	2002
3	Meatloaf	Rocky Horror Picture Show	1975
4	Dolly Parton	Nine to Five	1980
5	The Spice Girls	Spice World	1998
6	Jennifer Lopez	Money Train	1995
7	Aaliyah	Romeo Must Die	2000
8	Britney Spears	Crossroads	2002
9	Ice Cube	Boyz N the Hood	1991
10	Barbra Streisand	Funny Girl	1968

Since Al Jolson's debut role in the pioneering talkie *The Jazz Singer* (1927), many popular vocalists have made the transition to films, with those listed representing the most successful (although some had minor parts, often uncredited, in films before starring in these). Since the 1930s this catalogue has included artists of the calibre of Bing Crosby, Marlene Dietrich, Elvis Presley, the Beatles, David Bowie, Sting, Madonna, and Björk.

STAGE &
SCREEN

The Play's the Thing

THE 10 LATEST WINNERS OF THE LAURENCE OLIVIER AWARD FOR BEST ACTRESS

YEAR	ACTRESS	PLAY
2002	Clare Higgins	Vincent in Brixton
2001	Lindsay Duncan	Private Lives
2000	Julie Walters	All My Sons
1999	Janie Dee	Comic Potential
1998	Eileen Atkins	The Unexpected Man
1997	Zoë Wanamaker	Electra
1996	Janet McTeer	A Doll's House
1995	Judi Dench	Absolute Hell
1994	Clare Higgins	Sweet Bird of Youth
1993	Fiona Shaw	Machinal

THE 10 LATEST WINNERS OF THE LAURENCE OLIVIER AWARD FOR BEST ACTOR

YEAR	ACTOR	PLAY
2002	Simon Russell Beale	Uncle Vanya
2001	Rober Allam	Privates on Parade
2000	Conleth Hill	Stones in his Pockets
1999	Henry Goodman	The Merchant of Venice
1998	Kevin Spacey	The Iceman Cometh
1997	Ian Holm	King Lear
1996	Anthony Sher	Stanley
1995	Alex Jennings	Peer Gynt
1994	David Bamber	My Night with Reg
1993	Mark Rylance	Much Ado About Nothing

THE 10 LATEST WINNERS OF THE LAURENCE OLIVIER AWARD FOR BEST DIRECTOR

YEAR	DIRECTOR	PLAY
2002	Sam Mendes	Twelfth Night and Uncle Vanya
2001	Michael Boyd	Henry VI Parts I, II and III and Richard III
2000	Howard Davies	All My Sons
1999	Trevor Nunn	Summerfolk, The Merchant of Venice, and Troilus and Cressida
1998	Howard Davies	The Iceman Cometh
1997	Richard Eyre	King Lear
1996	Des McAnuff	Tommy
1995	Sam Mendes	Company and The Glass Menagerie
1994	Declan Donnellan	As You Like It (for a play)
	Scott Ellis	She Loves Me (for a musical)
1993	Stephen Daldry	Machinal (for a play)
	Declan Donellan	Sweeney Todd (for a musical)

◀ **Class comedy**
Seen here with co-star Alan Rickman, actress Lindsay Duncan received the Laurence Olivier Award for her role in Noel Coward's *Private Lives*.

TOP 10 MOST PRODUCED SHAKESPEARE PLAYS, 1878–2002

	PLAY	PRODUCTIONS
1	Twelfth Night	76
2 =	As You Like It	75
=	Hamlet	75
=	The Taming of the Shrew	75
5 =	A Midsummer Night's Dream	71
=	Much Ado About Nothing	71
7	The Merchant of Venice	70
8	Macbeth	64
9	The Merry Wives of Windsor	59
10	Romeo and Juliet	58

Source: *Shakespeare Centre*

This list, based on an analysis of Shakespearean productions from 31 December 1878 to 31 December 2002 at Stratford-upon-Avon, and by the Royal Shakespeare Company in London and on tour, gives a reasonable picture of his most popular plays.

TOP 10 LONGEST-RUNNING NON-MUSICALS IN THE UK

	SHOW/RUN(S)	PERFORMANCES
1	The Mousetrap (1952–)	20,848*
2	No Sex, Please – We're British (1971–81; 1982–86; 1986–87)	6,761
3	The Woman in Black (1989–)	5,585*
4	Oh! Calcutta! (1970–74; 1974–80)	3,918
5	The Complete Works of William Shakespeare (Abridged) (1996–)	3,332*
6	Run for Your Wife (1983–91)	2,638
7	There's a Girl in My Soup (1966–69; 1969–72)	2,547
8	Pyjama Tops (1969–75)	2,498
9	Sleuth (1970; 1972; 1973–75)	2,359
10	Worm's Eye View (1945–51)	2,245

Still running; total as at 1 January 2003

Oh! Calcutta! is included here as it is regarded as a revue with music, rather than a musical.

THE 10 LATEST WINNERS OF THE EVENING STANDARD AWARD FOR BEST PLAY

YEAR*	PLAY	PLAYWRIGHT
2002	A Number	Caryl Churchill
2001	The Far Side of the Moon	Robert Lepage
2000	Blue/Orange	Joe Penhall
1998	Copenhagen	Michael Frayn
1997	The Invention of Love	by Tom Stoppard
1996	Stanley	Pam Gems
1995	Pentecost	David Edgar
1994	Three Tall Women	Edward Albee
1993	Arcadia	Tom Stoppard
1992	Angels in America	Tony Kushner

* No award in 1999

THE 10 LATEST WINNERS OF THE EVENING STANDARD AWARD FOR MOST PROMISING PLAYWRIGHT*

YEAR	PLAYWRIGHT	PLAY
2002	Vassily Sigarev	Plasticine
2001	Roy Williams	Clubland
2000	Gary Mitchell	The Force of Change
1999	Rebecca Gilman	The Glory of Living
1998	Mark Ravenhill	Handbag
1997	Conor McPherson	The Weir
1996	Martin McDonagh	The Beauty Queen of Leenane
1995	Jez Butterworth	Mojo
1994	Jonathan Harvey	Babies
1993	= Brad Fraser	Unidentified Human Remains
	= Simon Donald	The Life of Stuff

* The Charles Wintour Award

TOP 10 LONGEST-RUNNING MUSICALS IN THE UK

	SHOW/RUN	PERFORMANCES
1	Cats (1981–2002)	8,949
2	Starlight Express (1984–2002)	7,406
3	Les Misérables (1985–)	7,085*
4	The Phantom of the Opera (1986–)	6,744*
5	Miss Saigon (1989–99)	4,263
6	Oliver! (1960–69)	4,125
7	Jesus Christ, Superstar (1972–80)	3,357
8	Evita (1978–86)	2,900
9	The Sound of Music (1961–67)	2,386
10	Salad Days (1954–60)	2,283

Still running; total as at 1 January 2003

Cats closed on 12 May 2002, its 21st birthday, having held the record as the UK's longest-running musical since 12 May 1989.

▶ **The cats' whiskers**
Cats made theatre history by topping the long-running musicals chart on both sides of the Atlantic.

Blockbusters

TOP 10 HIGHEST-GROSSING FILMS WORLDWIDE

	FILM	YEAR	USA	NON-USA	WORLD TOTAL
				GROSS INCOME ($)	
1	Titanic*	1997	600,800,000	1,234,600,000	1,835,400,000
2	Harry Potter and the Philosopher's Stone	2001	317,600,000	649,400,000	967,000,000
3	Star Wars: Episode I – The Phantom Menace	1999	431,100,000	492,000,000	923,100,000
4	Jurassic Park	1993	334,800,000	547,000,000	881,800,000
5	The Lord of the Rings: The Two Towers	2002	333,600,000	533,000,000	866,600,000
6	Harry Potter and the Chamber of Secrets	2002	261,700,000	604,000,000	865,700,000
7	The Lord of the Rings: The Fellowship of the Ring	2001	313,400,000	547,200,000	860,600,000
8	Independence Day	1996	306,300,000	505,000,000	811,300,000
9	Spider-Man	2002	403,700,000	402,000,000	805,700,000
10	Star Wars: Episode IV – A New Hope	1977	461,000,000	337,000,000	798,000,000

* Winner of "Best Picture" Academy Award

In March 2003, *Harry Potter and the Chamber of Secrets* became only the third film ever (after *Titanic* and *Harry Potter and the Philosopher's Stone*) to make more than $600 million at the international box office – a remarkable feat, since only four films have ever made more than $500 million and three over $400 million outside the USA.

TOP 10 FILM BUDGETS

	FILM	YEAR	BUDGET ($)
1	Titanic	1997	200,000,000
2 =	Waterworld	1995	175,000,000
=	Wild, Wild West	1999	175,000,000
4	Terminator 3: Rise of the Machines	2003	170,000,000
5	Tarzan*	1999	145,000,000
6	Die Another Day	2002	142,000,000
7 =	Armageddon	1998	140,000,000
=	Lethal Weapon 4	1998	140,000,000
=	Men in Black II	2002	140,000,000
=	Pearl Harbor	2001	140,000,000
=	Treasure Planet	2002	140,000,000

* Animated

The two most expensive films ever made are water-based, with large-scale special effects being major factors in escalating budgets. The two blockbusters of 2001, *Harry Potter and the Sorcerer's Stone* and *Lord of the Rings: The Fellowship of the Ring*, had budgets of $125 million and $109 million, and their sequels, *Harry Potter and the Chamber of Secrets* and *The Lord of the Rings: The Two Towers*, $100 million and $94 million respectively, and so do not make the Top 10.

▼ **Star quality**
Queen Padmé Amidala, played by Natalie Portman in *Star Wars: Episode I – The Phantom Menace*, which was second only to *Titanic* as the highest-grossing film of the 20th century.

HIGHEST-GROSSING FILMS IN THE UK

	FILM	YEAR	TOTAL UK BOX OFFICE GROSS (£)
1	Titanic	1998	68,989,379
2	Harry Potter and the Philosopher's Stone	2001	66,039,425
3	The Lord of the Rings: The Fellowship of the Ring	2001	62,759,289
4	The Lord of the Rings: The Two Towers	2002	57,062,828
5	Harry Potter and the Chamber of Secrets	2002	54,036,560
6	The Full Monty	1997	52,232,058
7	Star Wars: Episode I – The Phantom Menace	1999	51,063,811
8	Jurassic Park	1993	47,886,423
9	Toy Story 2*	2000	44,306,070
10	Bridget Jones's Diary	2001	42,007,008

* Animated

Inevitably, bearing inflation in mind, the top-grossing films of all time are releases from recent years, although it is also true that UK cinema admissions rose sharply in recent years – from 97,370,000 in 1990 to 175,902,533 in 2002. From the nadir of the late 1960s and 1970s, today's films are both more widely viewed (even excluding video) than those of 15 to 25 years ago, as well as grossing considerably more at the box office.

FILM FRANCHISES

	FRANCHISE	FILMS	YEARS	TOTAL WORLD GROSS ($)*
1	James Bond	20	1963–2002	3,630,559,554
2	Star Wars	5	1977–2002	3,471,554,580
3	Jurassic Park	3	1993–2001	1,901,027,106
4	Harry Potter	2	2001–02	1,832,722,908
5	The Lord of the Rings	2	2001–02	1,742,399,971
6	Batman	4	1989–97	1,268,376,929
7	Indiana Jones	3	1981–89	1,211,716,531
8	Star Trek	10	1979–2002	1,053,666,245
9	Men in Black	2	1997–2002	1,013,409,342
10	Mission: Impossible	2	1996–2000	1,012,391,875

* Cumulative global earnings of the original film and all its sequels to 31 March 2003

A successful film does not guarantee a successful sequel: although their total income earns them a place just outside the Top 10. Each of the four *Superman* films actually earned less than the previous one, with *Superman IV* earning just one-tenth of the original. *Smokey and the Bandit Part III* earned just one-seventeenth of the original, and *Grease* 2 less than one-tenth of the original *Grease*. Sometimes the situation is reversed: *Terminator 2: Judgment Day* earned more than six times as much as its "prequel".

MOST PROFITABLE FILMS OF ALL TIME*

	FILM	YEAR	BUDGET ($)	WORLD GROSS ($)	PROFIT RATIO
1	The Blair Witch Project	1999	35,000	248,662,839	7,104.65
2	American Graffiti	1973	750,000	115,000,000	153.33
3	Snow White and the Seven Dwarfs#	1937	1,488,000	187,670,866	126.12
4	The Rocky Horror Picture Show	1975	1,200,000	139,876,417	116.56
5	Rocky†	1976	1,100,000	117,235,147	106.58
6	Gone With the Wind†	1939	3,900,000	390,555,278	100.14
7	The Full Monty	1997	3,500,000	256,950,122	73.41
8	Star Wars§	1977	11,000,000	797,998,007	72.55
9	E.T. the Extra-Terrestrial	1982	10,500,000	756,774,579	72.07
10	My Big Fat Greek Wedding	2002	5,000,000	353,906,779	70.78

* Minimum entry $100 million world gross

Animated

† Academy Award for "Best Picture"

§ Later retitled Star Wars: Episode IV – A New Hope

It should be noted that the budget for *The Blair Witch Project* represents only the cost of making the film: further post-production costs, for example to enhance the sound quality, were incurred prior to theatrical release.

FILMS IN THE UK, 2002

	FILM
1	Harry Potter and the Chamber of Secrets
2	The Lord of the Rings: The Two Towers
3	Monsters, Inc.
4	Star Wars: Episode II – Attack of the Clones
5	Die Another Day
6	Spider-Man
7	Ocean's Eleven
8	Austin Powers in Goldmember
9	Men in Black II
10	Scooby-Doo

Three of the films listed – *Harry Potter and the Chamber of Secrets*, *The Lord of the Rings: The Two Towers*, and *Die Another Day* – were still on general release as the year ended, and went on to earn well into 2003. The Top 10 contributed £320,346,127, or 40 per cent, to an all-time record year at the UK box office, with total revenue of £802,058,288.

World Cinema

FILMS IN INDIA

	FILM	YEAR	TOTAL INDIA GROSS (IRs)
1	Gadar	2001	650,000,000
2	Hum Aapke Hai Kaun	1994	600,000,000
3	Dilwale Dulhania Le Jayenge	1995	500,000,000
4	Raja Hindustani	1996	450,000,000
5	Kuch Kuch Hota Hai	1998	425,000,000
6	Kabhi Khushi Kabhie Gham	2001	380,500,000
7	Kaho Na Pyaar Hai	2000	350,000,000
8	Karan Arjun	1995	320,000,000
9 =	Border	1997	300,000,000
=	Lagaan	2001	300,000,000

▼ Bollywood blockbuster
Aditya Chopra's popular directorial debut, *Dilwale Dulhania Le Jayenge* (*The Brave-Hearted Will Take the Bride*), starring Shahrukh Khan and Kajol, was a huge hit.

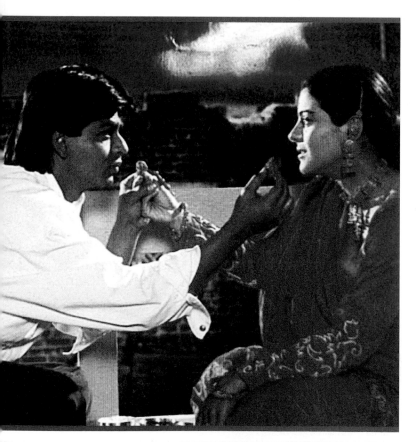

FILMS IN FRANCE

	FILM*	YEAR	TOTAL FRANCE GROSS (US$)
1	Titanic	1998	138,928,349
2	Astérix & Obélix: Mission Cleopatra (France)	2002	75,846,048
3	Taxi 2 (France)	2000	63,703,757
4	Astérix & Obélix contre César (France)	1999	59,154,242
5	Star Wars: Episode I – The Phantom Menace	1999	55,825,511
6	The Fifth Element	1997	54,080,230
7	Les Visiteurs II: Les couloirs du temps (France)	1998	53,898,537
8	Le Dîner de Cons (France)	1998	53,155,025
9	Harry Potter and the Chamber of Secrets	2002	53,141,000
10	Harry Potter and the Philosopher's Stone	2001	48,745,200

* All from USA unless otherwise specified

France's all-time Top 10 films mirrors the country's cosmopolitan cinematic tastes, with half the films among Hollywood blockbusters and half from the homegrown output.

FILMS IN AUSTRALIA

	FILM*	YEAR	TOTAL AUSTRALIA GROSS (AUS$)
1	Titanic	1997	57,642,943
2	Crocodile Dundee (Australia)	1986	47,707,045
3	The Lord of the Rings: The Fellowship of The Ring	2001	46,851,327
4	The Lord of the Rings: The Two Towers	2002	45,183,872
5	Harry Potter and the Philosopher's Stone	2001	42,310,037
6	Star Wars: Episode I – The Phantom Menace	1999	38,828,310
7	Harry Potter and the Chamber of Secrets	2002	37,009,842
8	Babe (Australia/USA)	1995	36,776,544
9	Star Wars: Episode II – Attack of the Clones	2002	33,811,334
10	Jurassic Park	1993	33,002,776

* All from USA unless otherwise specified

Australia's most popular films reflect the international box office, but with a distinct Antipodean bias: *Crocodile Dundee* is the most successful Australian film ever, earning over US$ 300 million worldwide, while *Babe* was an Australian/US co-production filmed in Australia with an Australian director (Chris Noonan). Australian films earned AUS$ 41.8 million, 4.9 per cent of the total, at the Australian box office in 2002.

TOP 10 FILMS IN JAPAN

	FILM*	YEAR	TOTAL JAPAN GROSS (US$)
1	Sen to Chihiro no Kamikakushi (Spirited Away)# (Japan)	2001	228,612,367
2	Harry Potter and the Chamber of Secrets	2002	142,786,414
3	Harry Potter and the Philosopher's Stone	2001	127,687,138
4	Titanic	1997	101,800,644
5	The Lord of the Rings: The Two Towers	2002	59,156,943
6	Star Wars: Episode I – The Phantom Menace	1999	50,812,345
7	Mononoke Hime (Princess Mononoke)# (Japan)	1997	49,959,609
8	Kindaichi Shonen no Jikenbo (The Case Book of Young Kindaichi)# (Japan)	1997	47,637,131
9	Armageddon	1998	45,533,387
10	Independence Day	1996	44,239,833

* All from USA unless otherwise specified

Animated

The Japanese Top 10 features a number of global successes while representing the local enthusiasm for *anime* – animation, often with a fantasy element, aimed to appeal to adults.

▶ **High spirits**
The popular Japanese *anime* production *Spirited Away* was the first film ever to earn more than $200 million before it opened in the USA and won the "Best Animated Feature" Oscar.

TOP 10 FOREIGN LANGUAGE FILMS IN THE UK

	FILM	YEAR	ORIGINAL LANGUAGE*	TOTAL UK GROSS (£)
1	Crouching Tiger, Hidden Dragon	2001	Mandarin	9,356,176
2	Amélie	2001	French	4,942,157
3	Life is Beautiful	1999	Italian	3,083,174
4	Kabhi Khushi Kabhie Gham	2001	Hindi	2,498,281
5	Cyrano de Bergerac	1991	French	2,458,175
6	Monsoon Wedding	2002	Hindi/Punjabi	2,059,552
7	Kuch Kuch Hota Hai	1998	Hindi	1,750,000
8	Devdas	2002	Hindi	1,663,692
9	Farewell My Concubine	1994	Mandarin	1,639,622
10	Il Postino	1994	Italian	1,292,525

* Some dubbed in English, others subtitled

TOP 10 FILMS IN SPAIN

	FILM*	YEAR	TOTAL SPAIN GROSS (US$)
1	Titanic	1997	43,672,525
2	The Lord of the Rings: The Two Towers	2002	32,840,128
3	The Lord of the Rings: The Fellowship of the Ring	2001	28,925,390
4	The Sixth Sense	1999	27,305,275
5	Harry Potter and the Chamber of Secrets	2002	25,890,767
6	Star Wars: Episode I – The Phantom Menace	1999	25,808,403
7	Harry Potter and the Philsopher's Stone	2001	24,685,592
8	The Others	2001	24,599,316
9	Mortadelo y Filemón (Spain)	2001	24,102,774
10	Spider-Man	2002	22,074,731

* All from USA unless otherwise specified

Film Genres

TOP 10 WAR FILMS

FILM	YEAR
1 Saving Private Ryan	1998
2 Pearl Harbor	2001
3 Schindler's List	1993
4 The English Patient	1996
5 Life Is Beautiful (La vita è bella)	1997
6 Braveheart	1995
7 Black Hawk Down	2001
8 U-571	2000
9 Three Kings	1999
10 Enemy at the Gates	2001

In recent years, until the hugely successful *Saving Private Ryan*, surprisingly few war films appeared in the high-earning bracket, which led some to consider that the days of big-budget films in this genre were over. However, excluding military-themed but non-war films, recent blockbusters, including "historical" war films such as Mel Gibson's two notable successes, *Braveheart* and *The Patriot*, and *Pearl Harbor*, appear to have disproved this prediction.

TOP 10 SUPERHERO FILMS

FILM	YEAR
1 Spider-Man	2002
2 Batman	1989
3 Batman Forever	1995
4 The Mask	1994
5 Superman	1978
6 X-Men	2000
7 Batman Returns	1992
8 Batman & Robin	1997
9 Teenage Mutant Ninja Turtles	1990
10 Blade II	2002

Superman makes a single showing in this Top 10, since it is in the unusual situation where the first film made a large amount (in excess of $300 million) at the world box office, while each of its three sequels made progressively less.

▼ World wide web
With global earnings of over $800 million, *Spider-Man* confirmed its place as the most successful superhero film ever.

TOP 10 SCIENCE-FICTION FILMS

FILM	YEAR
1 Star Wars: Episode I – The Phantom Menace	1999
2 Jurassic Park	1993
3 Independence Day	1996
4 Spider-Man	2002
5 Star Wars	1977
6 E.T. the Extra-Terrestrial	1982
7 Star Wars: Episode II – Attack of the Clones	2002
8 The Lost World: Jurassic Park	1997
9 Men in Black	1997
10 Star Wars: Episode VI – Return of the Jedi	1983

The first five films in this list are also in the all-time Top 10 films, and all 10 are among the 18 most successful films ever, having earned over $570 million each – a total of more than $7.4 billion at the worldwide box office.

TOP 10 MAGIC, WITCHES, AND WIZARDS FILMS

	FILM	YEAR
1	Harry Potter and the Philosopher's Stone	2001
2	The Lord of the Rings: The Two Towers	2002
3	The Lord of the Rings: The Fellowship of the Ring	2001
4	Harry Potter and the Chamber of Secrets	2002
5	Shrek*	2001
6	Beauty and the Beast*	1991
7	The Blair Witch Project	1999
8	Sleepy Hollow	1999
9	Snow White and the Seven Dwarfs*	1937
10	Fantasia/2000*	1999

Animated

▶ **Golden ring**

The second of the *Lord of the Rings* trilogy, *The Two Towers* has outearned its predecessor to become the fifth highest-earning film of all time.

TOP 10 DINOSAUR FILMS

	FILM	YEAR
1	Jurassic Park	1993
2	The Lost World: Jurassic Park	1997
3	Godzilla	1998
4	Jurassic Park III	2001
5	Dinosaur*	2000
6	Fantasia*#	1940
7	T-Rex: Back to the Cretaceous	1998
8	The Flintstones in Viva Rock Vegas	2000
9	The Land Before Time*	1988
10	Super Mario Bros.	1993

Animated; others live-action with mechanical or computer-generated animation sequences

Igor Stravinsky's "Rite of Spring" sequence

The animated *Gertie the Dinosaur* (1914) was the first notable example in a catalogue of well over 100 films featuring prehistoric monsters.

TOP 10 JAMES BOND FILMS

	FILM	BOND ACTOR	YEAR
1	Die Another Day	Pierce Brosnan	2002
2	The World Is Not Enough	Pierce Brosnan	1999
3	GoldenEye	Pierce Brosnan	1995
4	Tomorrow Never Dies	Pierce Brosnan	1997
5	Moonraker	Roger Moore	1979
6	The Living Daylights	Timothy Dalton	1987
7	For Your Eyes Only	Roger Moore	1981
8	The Spy Who Loved Me	Roger Moore	1977
9	Octopussy	Roger Moore	1983
10	Licence to Kill	Timothy Dalton	1990

Ian Fleming wrote 12 James Bond novels, only two of which, *Moonraker* (1955) and *The Spy Who Loved Me* (1962), figure in this Top 10. After his death in 1964, *For Your Eyes Only*, *Octopussy*, *The Living Daylights*, and *GoldenEye* were developed by other writers from his short stories, while subsequent releases were written without reference to Fleming's writings. *Casino Royale* (book 1953, film 1967), featuring 56-year-old David Niven as the retired spy Sir James Bond, is an oddity in that it was presented as a comedy. This and *Never Say Never Again* (1983), effectively a remake of *Thunderball*, are not considered "official" Bond films, making the 2002 release *Die Another Day* the 20th in the canonical series.

Leading Men

TOP 10 ACTORS AT THE US BOX OFFICE

	ACTOR	FILMS	TOTAL ($)
1	Harrison Ford	30	3,187,215,057
2	Samuel L. Jackson	56	2,832,308,762
3	Tom Hanks	30	2,805,563,647
4	Tom Cruise	25	2,389,498,678
5	James Earl Jones	36	2,326,924,965
6	Eddie Murphy	27	2,300,000,784
7	Mel Gibson	31	2,285,154,698
8	Robin Williams	41	2,230,226,135
9	Jim Cummings	24	2,193,119,817
10	Rance Howard	38	2,190,866,163

Although inevitably a volatile list, this Top 10 presents a snapshot of the actors who, to date, have appeared in the fims (or, in some instances, provided the voice for a character in an animated film) that cumulatively have earned the most in the USA. Such is the box office appeal of Harrison Ford that US distributors voted him "Star of the Century".

TOP 10 RUSSELL CROWE FILMS

	FILM	YEAR
1	Gladiator*	2000
2	A Beautiful Mind	2001
3	L.A. Confidential	1997
4	The Insider	1999
5	The Quick and the Dead	1995
6	Proof of Life	2000
7	Virtuosity	1995
8	Mystery, Alaska	1999
9	The Sum of Us	1994
10	Proof	1991

* Won Academy Award for "Best Actor"

After appearing in Australian TV series including Neighbours (1987), New Zealand-born Russell Crowe gained his first Hollywood role with The Quick and the Dead (1995).

TOP 10 PIERCE BROSNAN FILMS

	FILM	YEAR
1	Mrs. Doubtfire	1993
2	Die Another Day	2002
3	The World Is Not Enough	1999
4	GoldenEye	1995
5	Tomorrow Never Dies	1997
6	Dante's Peak	1997
7	The Thomas Crown Affair	1999
8	Mars Attacks!	1996
9	The Mirror Has Two Faces	1996
10	The Lawnmower Man	1992

Pierce Brosnan, now best known as James Bond, provided the voice of King Arthur in the animated Quest for Camelot (1998). If included, it would be ranked ninth. Each of the eight leading films in his Top 10 has earned in excess of $100 million worldwide.

TOP 10 BRAD PITT FILMS

	FILM	YEAR
1	Ocean's Eleven	2001
2	Se7en	1995
3	Interview with the Vampire: The Vampire Chronicles	1994
4	Sleepers	1996
5	Twelve Monkeys	1995
6	Legends of the Fall	1994
7	The Devil's Own	1997
8	Meet Joe Black	1998
9	Seven Years in Tibet	1997
10	Spy Game	2001

Brad Pitt is a member of an élite group of actors all of whose 10 highest-earning films have made more than $100 million in total at the world box office, with runners-up The Mexican (2001) and Fight Club (1999) also falling into this high-earning league.

FIRST $1M STAR

IN 1921 – after ironically appearing in a film called The Dollar a Year Man – silent film star Roscoe ("Fatty") Arbuckle (1887–1933) signed a three-year contract with Paramount that would have made him the first film star ever to earn $1 million a year. However, at a party to celebrate his success, a starlet called Virginia Rappe was injured and later died, and he was charged with her manslaughter. Although he was acquitted, the scandal meant Arbuckle became the first star to be banned from acting. He began working as a director under the pseudonym William Goodrich and in 1933 agreed a deal with Warner Bros. but died, aged 46, the day he signed the contract that would have enabled his return to the screen.

FIRST FACT

TOP 10 BRUCE WILLIS FILMS

	FILM	YEAR
1	The Sixth Sense	1999
2	Armageddon	1998
3	Die Hard: With a Vengeance	1995
4	The Fifth Element	1997
5	Unbreakable	2000
6	Die Hard 2	1990
7	Pulp Fiction	1994
8	Twelve Monkeys	1995
9	The Jackal	1997
10	Death Becomes Her	1992

Although discounted here, it is somewhat ironic to consider that the fourth most successful film role of an actor whose screen persona is of a tough guy would otherwise be that of a baby in Look Who's Talking (1989) – and that consisting only of Willis's dubbed voice.

TOP 10 LEONARDO DiCAPRIO FILMS

FILM	YEAR
1 Titanic	1997
2 Catch Me If You Can	2002
3 Gangs of New York	2002
4 The Man in the Iron Mask	1998
5 The Beach	2000
6 Romeo + Juliet	1996
7 The Quick and the Dead	1995
8 Marvin's Room	1996
9 What's Eating Gilbert Grape	1993
10 Celebrity	1998

A film career of less than 10 years has seen Leonardo DiCaprio star in six $100 million-plus earning films, including the biggest blockbuster of all time. His role in *What's Eating Gilbert Grape* also gained him an Oscar nomination.

TOP 10 TOM CRUISE FILMS

FILM	YEAR
1 Mission: Impossible II	2000
2 Mission: Impossible	1996
3 Rain Man	1988
4 Top Gun	1986
5 Minority Report	2002
6 Jerry Maguire	1996
7 The Firm	1993
8 A Few Good Men	1992
9 Interview with the Vampire: The Vampire Chronicles	1994
10 Vanilla Sky	2001

Few actors have matched Tom Cruise's commercial success: every one of his Top 10 films has earned more than $200 million worldwide, a total of $3.3 billion.

▼ **Leonardo masterpiece**
Leonardo DiCaprio stars as conman Frank Abagnale Jr. in *Catch Me If You Can*, which has netted over $300 million worldwide.

Leading Women

ACTRESSES AT THE US BOX OFFICE

	ACTRESS	FILMS	TOTAL ($)
1	Julia Roberts	27	1,889,883,547
2	Carrie Fisher	25	1,760,869,785
3	Whoopi Goldberg	41	1,683,352,258
4	Kathy Bates	31	1,447,092,182
5	Drew Barrymore	27	1,303,932,619
6	Cameron Diaz	21	1,289,627,290
7	Maggie Smith	20	1,286,055,060
8	Bonnie Hunt	16	1,270,837,762
9	Sally Field	20	1,237,398,519
10	Glenn Close	28	1,236,979,789

As with the actor counterpart list, these are the actresses whose films (and voice-only parts in animated films) have earned the most cumulatively in the USA. Julia Roberts has appeared in nine films that have made over $100 milion in the USA, and 13 that have netted more than that amount worldwide.

JULIANNE MOORE FILMS

	FILM	YEAR
1	The Lost World: Jurassic Park	1997
2	The Fugitive	1993
3	Hannibal	2001
4	Nine Months	1995
5	The Hand that Rocks the Cradle	1992
6	Evolution	2001
7	Assassins	1995
8	The Hours*	2002
9	Magnolia	1999

Nominated for Academy Award for "Best Actress"

Julianne Moore's early appearances were in TV series and TV films. Following her break into mainstream cinema, her relatively minor role in *The Fugitive* so impressed Steven Spielberg that he cast her in *The Lost World: Jurassic Park*, both of which top her personal Top 10.

MERYL STREEP FILMS

	FILM	YEAR
1	Out of Africa	1985
2	The Bridges of Madison County	1995
3	Death Becomes Her	1992
4	Kramer vs. Kramer	1979
5	The River Wild	1994
6	The Hours	2002
7	The Deer Hunter	1978
8	Manhattan	1979
9	Postcards from the Edge	1990
10	Silkwood	1983

Meryl Streep has been nominated for Academy Awards on a total of 13 occasions, winning for her supporting role in *Kramer vs. Kramer*, and "Best Actress" for *Sophie's Choice* (1982), which scores outside her personal Top 10. She provided the voice of the Blue Fairy in *A.I.: Artificial Intelligence* (2001), which, were it taken into account, would be in second place.

NICOLE KIDMAN FILMS

	FILM	YEAR
1	Batman Forever	1995
2	Moulin Rouge*	2001
3	The Others	2001
4	Days of Thunder	1990
5	Eyes Wide Shut	1999
6	The Peacemaker	1997
7	Practical Magic	1998
8	Far and Away	1992
9	The Hours#	2002
10	Malice	1993

Nominated for Academy Award for "Best Actress"
Winner of Academy Award for "Best Actress"

Honolulu-born Nicole Kidman was raised in Australia, where she acted on TV before her break into film, in which she has pursued a highly successful career: more than half her Top 10 films have earned over $100 million worldwide.

JUDI DENCH FILMS

	FILM	YEAR
1	Die Another Day	2002
2	The World is Not Enough	1999
3	GoldenEye	1995
4	Tomorrow Never Dies	1997
5	Shakespeare in Love	1998
6	Chocolat	2000
7	Tea with Mussolini	1999
8	A Room with a View	1986
9	Mrs. Brown	1997
10	The Shipping News	2001

After 40 years in the business, Dame Judi Dench's most successful pictures have been the last four James Bond films, in which she plays "M", the head of MI6. She has been nominated for Oscars on four occasions, winning for her eight-minute supporting role as Queen Elizabeth I in *Shakespeare in Love*.

CAMERON DIAZ FILMS

	FILM	YEAR
1	There's Something About Mary	1998
2	The Mask	1994
3	My Best Friend's Wedding	1997
4	Charlie's Angels	2000
5	Vanilla Sky	2001
6	Gangs of New York	2002
7	Any Given Sunday	1999
8	Being John Malkovich	1999
9	The Sweetest Thing	2002
10	A Life Less Ordinary	1997

Cameron Diaz's Top 10 films include several that are among the highest earning of recent years. She also provided the voice of Princess Fiona in *Shrek* (2001) – which has outearned all of them. Her uncredited cameo role as "woman on metro" in *Minority Report* (2002) has not been included, but would be in second place.

TOP 10 CATHERINE ZETA-JONES FILMS

	FILM	YEAR
1	The Mask of Zorro	1998
2	Entrapment	1999
3	Traffic	2000
4	Chicago	2002
5	The Haunting	1999
6	America's Sweethearts	2001
7	High Fidelity	2000
8	The Phantom	1996
9	Christopher Columbus: The Discovery	1992
10	Splitting Heirs	1993

After a debut as Sheherezade in the French film
Les Mille et Une Nuits (1990), Welsh-born Catherine
Zeta-Jones rose to prominence as Mariette Larkin in
the British TV series *The Darling Buds of May* before
her first Hollywood screen role in *Christopher
Columbus: The Discovery* (1992).

▶ Two Zed's
Catherine Zeta-Jones took the Oscar for "Best
Supporting Actress" as Velma Kelly in *Chicago*.
Actress Renee Zellweger was also nominated
for an award

TOP 10 RENEE ZELLWEGER FILMS

	FILM	YEAR
1	Bridget Jones's Diary	2001
2	Jerry Maguire	1996
3	Chicago	2002
4	Me, Myself & Irene	2000
5	Nurse Betty	2000
6	One True Thing	1998
7	The Bachelor	1999
8	Reality Bites	1994
9	8 Seconds	1994
10	White Oleander	2002

Apart from some unmemorable early parts in films
such as *The Return of the Texas Chainsaw Massacre*
(1994), Renée Zellweger has followed an ever-
upward trajectory in her film career. Her title role in
Bridget Jones's Diary and *Nurse Betty* earned her two
Golden Globe awards, and she was nominated for the
"Best Actress" Oscar for her performance in *Chicago*.

Oscar-Winning Films

THE 10 LATEST "BEST PICTURE" OSCAR WINNERS

YEAR	FILM	DIRECTOR
2002	Chicago	Rob Marshall*
2001	A Beautiful Mind	Ron Howard
2000	Gladiator	Ridley Scott*
1999	American Beauty	Sam Mendes
1998	Shakespeare in Love	John Madden*
1997	Titanic	James Cameron
1996	The English Patient	Anthony Minghella
1995	Braveheart	Mel Gibson
1994	Forrest Gump	Robert Zemeckis
1993	Schindler's List	Steven Spielberg

Did not also win "Best Director" Academy Award

The first picture to be honoured at the first ever Academy Awards ceremony, held on 16 May 1929, was *Wings*, a silent World War I epic.

TOP 10 HIGHEST-EARNING "BEST PICTURE" OSCAR WINNERS*

	FILM	YEAR#
1	Titanic	1997
2	Forrest Gump	1994
3	Gladiator	2000
4	Dances With Wolves	1990
5	Rain Man	1988
6	Gone With the Wind	1939
7	American Beauty	1999
8	Schindler's List	1993
9	A Beautiful Mind	2001
10	Shakespeare in Love	1998

* *Ranked by world box-office income*

Of release; Academy Awards are awarded the following year

THE 10 LATEST BLACK-AND-WHITE FILMS TO WIN "BEST PICTURE" OSCARS

	FILM	YEAR
1	Schindler's List	1993
2	The Apartment	1960
3	Marty	1955
4	On the Waterfront	1954
5	From Here to Eternity	1953
6	All About Eve	1950
7	All the King's Men	1949
8	Hamlet	1948
9	Gentleman's Agreement	1947
10	The Best Years of Our Lives	1946

TOP 10 STUDIOS WITH THE MOST "BEST PICTURE" OSCARS

	STUDIO	AWARDS
1 =	Columbia	12
=	United Artists	12
3	Paramount	11
4	MGM	9
5	20th Century Fox	7
6 =	Universal	6
=	Warner Bros.	6
8	Orion	4
9 =	DreamWorks	3
=	Miramax	3

In the 75 years of the Academy Awards up to the 2003 ceremony, these, along with RKO Radio Pictures with two wins (1931 and 1946), are the only studios to have won a "Best Picture" Oscar.

◀ Top Gere
Richard Gere as astute lawyer Billy Flynn in *Chicago*. The film, an adaptation of a stage musical, won "Best Picture" and five other Academy Awards.

TOP 10 FILMS TO WIN THE MOST OSCARS*

	FILM	YEAR	NOMINATIONS	AWARDS
1 =	Ben-Hur	1959	12	11
=	Titanic	1997	14	11
3	West Side Story	1961	11	10
4 =	Gigi	1958	9	9
=	The Last Emperor	1987	9	9
=	The English Patient	1996	12	9
7 =	Gone With the Wind	1939	13	8#
=	From Here to Eternity	1953	13	8
=	On the Waterfront	1954	12	8
=	My Fair Lady	1964	12	8
=	Cabaret	1972	10	8
=	Gandhi	1982	11	8
=	Amadeus	1984	11	8

* Oscar® is a Registered Trade Mark

Plus two special awards

Ten other films have won seven Academy Awards each: *Going My Way* (1944), *The Best Years of Our Lives* (1946), *The Bridge on the River Kwai* (1957), *Lawrence of Arabia* (1962), *Patton* (1970), *The Sting* (1973), *Out of Africa* (1985), *Dances With Wolves* (1991), *Schindler's List* (1993), and *Shakespeare in Love* (1998). *Titanic* (1997) matched the previous record of 14 nominations of *All About Eve* (1950), but outshone it by winning 11, compared with the latter's six.

TOP 10 FILMS WITH THE MOST NOMINATIONS WITHOUT A SINGLE WIN

	FILM	YEAR	NOMINATIONS
1 =	The Turning Point	1977	11
=	The Color Purple	1985	11
3 =	Gangs of New York	2002	10
4 =	The Little Foxes	1941	9
=	Peyton Place	1957	9
6 =	Quo Vadis	1951	8
=	The Nun's Story	1959	8
=	The Sand Pebbles	1966	8
=	The Elephant Man	1980	8
=	Ragtime	1981	8
=	The Remains of the Day	1993	8

Gangs of New York is the latest of a number of films to have received an impressive tally of nominations, but no wins in any category. *Mutiny on the Bounty* (1935) was the last to win "Best Picture" but no other awards.

TOP 10 FILMS NOMINATED FOR THE MOST OSCARS

	FILM	YEAR	AWARDS	NOMINATIONS
1 =	All About Eve	1950	6	14
=	Titanic	1997	11	14
3 =	Gone With the Wind	1939	8*	13
=	From Here to Eternity	1953	8	13
=	Mary Poppins#	1964	5	13
=	Who's Afraid of Virginia Woolf?#	1966	5	13
=	Forrest Gump	1994	6	13
=	Shakespeare in Love	1998	7	13
=	The Lord of the Rings: The Fellowship of the Ring	2001	4	13
=	Chicago	2002	6	13

* Plus two special awards

Did not win "Best Picture" Academy Award

Thirteen is clearly not unlucky where Oscar nominations are concerned, no fewer than nine films having received that number. They and the two with 14 are those that received the greatest share of votes from Academy members using a system that creates a shortlist of five nominees in each of 24 categories other than special, honorary, and technical awards. However, eliminating such specialist categories as "Best Foreign Language", "Live Action Short", and "Animated Feature" reduces the potential number of awards for which a film may be nominated, while those that are eligible may be nominated in one category but not another – screenplays, for example, are separately nominated according to whether they are based on material previously produced or published or written directly for the screen.

THE 10 LATEST "BEST FOREIGN LANGUAGE FILM" OSCAR WINNERS

YEAR	FILM	COUNTRY
2002	Nowhere in Africa (Nirgendwo in Afrika)	Germany
2001	No Man's Land (Nicija zemlja)	Bosnia and Herzegovina/ Slovenia/Italy/France/UK/Belgium
2000	Crouching Tiger, Hidden Dragon (Wo hu cang long)	Hong Kong/China/ Taiwan/USA
1999	All About My Mother (Todo sobre mi madre)	Spain/France
1998	Life Is Beautiful (La Vita è bella)	Italy
1997	Character (Karakter)	Belgium/Netherlands
1996	Kolya	Czech Republic
1995	Antonia's Line (Antonia)	Netherlands/Belgium/UK
1994	Burnt by the Sun (Utomlyonnye solntsem)	France/Russia
1993	The Age of Beauty (Belle époque)	Spain/Portugal/France

Prior to 1956, when *La Strada* won this award, foreign language films received awards in special or honorary categories.

Oscar-Winning Stars

THE 10 LATEST "BEST ACTRESS" OSCAR WINNERS

YEAR	ACTRESS	FILM
2002	Nicole Kidman	The Hours
2001	Halle Berry	Monster's Ball
2000	Julia Roberts	Erin Brockovich
1999	Hilary Swank	Boys Don't Cry
1998	Gwyneth Paltrow	Shakespeare in Love*
1997	Helen Hunt	As Good As It Gets
1996	Frances McDormand	Fargo
1995	Susan Sarandon	Dead Man Walking
1994	Jessica Lange	Blue Sky
1993	Holly Hunter	The Piano

* Won "Best Picture" Academy Award

Only one actress has ever won the "Best Actress in a Leading Role" Academy Award in consecutive years – Katharine Hepburn in 1967 and 1968 (shared with Barbra Streisand), with further wins in 1933 and 1981. Just 10 other actresses have won twice: Ingrid Bergman, Bette Davis, Olivia De Havilland, Sally Field, Jane Fonda, Jodie Foster, Glenda Jackson, Vivien Leigh, Luise Rainer, and Elizabeth Taylor.

► Unafraid of Virginia Woolf
Nicole Kidman gained her first "Best Actress" Oscar nomination for *Moulin Rouge!* (2001), winning with her role as Virginia Woolf in *The Hours* (2002).

THE 10 LATEST "BEST ACTOR" OSCAR WINNERS

YEAR	ACTOR	FILM
2002	Adrien Brody	The Pianist
2001	Denzel Washington	Training Day
2000	Russell Crowe	Gladiator*
1999	Kevin Spacey	American Beauty*
1998	Roberto Benigni	Life Is Beautiful
1997	Jack Nicholson	As Good As It Gets
1996	Geoffrey Rush	Shine
1995	Nicolas Cage	Leaving Las Vegas
1994	Tom Hanks	Forrest Gump*
1993	Tom Hanks	Philadelphia

* Won "Best Picture" Academy Award

Tom Hanks shares the honour of two consecutive wins with Spencer Tracy (1937: *Captains Courageous*, and 1938: *Boys Town*). Only four other actors have ever won twice: Marlon Brando (1954; 1972), Gary Cooper (1941; 1952), Dustin Hoffman (1977; 1988), and Jack Nicholson (1975; 1997).

THE 10 LATEST WINNERS OF AN OSCAR FOR THEIR DEBUT FILM*

	ACTOR/ACTRESS	FILM	FILM YEAR
1	Anna Paquin#	The Piano	1993
2	Marlee Matlin†	Children of a Lesser God	1986
3	Haing S. Ngor#	The Killing Fields	1984
4	Timothy Hutton#	Ordinary People	1980
5	Tatum O'Neal#	Paper Moon	1973
6	Barbra Streisand†	Funny Girl	1968
7 =	Julie Andrews†	Mary Poppins	1964
=	Lila Kedrova#	Zorba the Greek	1964
9	Miyoshi Umeki#	Sayonara	1957
10	Anna Magnani†	The Rose Tatoo	1955

* In a film eligible for a "Best" or "Best Supporting Actor/Actress" Academy Award win (hence excluding previous TV movies, etc)

\# "Best Actor/Actress in a Supporting Role"

† "Best Actor/Actress in a Leading Role"

TOP 10 ACTRESSES WITH THE MOST OSCAR NOMINATIONS*

	ACTRESS	WINS SUPPORTING	BEST	NOMINATIONS
1	Meryl Streep	1	1	13
2	Katharine Hepburn	0	4	12
3	Bette Davis	0	2	10
4	Geraldine Page	0	1	8
5 =	Ingrid Bergman	1	2	7
=	Jane Fonda	0	2	7
=	Greer Garson	0	1	7
8 =	Ellen Burstyn	0	1	6
=	Deborah Kerr	0	0	6
=	Jessica Lange	1	1	6
=	Vanessa Redgrave	1	0	6
=	Thelma Ritter	0	0	6
=	Norma Shearer	0	0	6
=	Maggie Smith	1	1	6
=	Sissy Spacek	0	1	6

* In all acting categories

TOP 10 ACTORS WITH THE MOST OSCAR NOMINATIONS*

	ACTOR	WINS SUPPORTING	BEST	NOMINATIONS
1	Jack Nicholson	1	3	12
2	Laurence Olivier	0	1	10
3 =	Paul Newman	0	1	9
=	Spencer Tracy	0	2	9
5 =	Marlon Brando	0	2	8
=	Jack Lemmon	1	1	8
=	Al Pacino	0	1	8
8 =	Richard Burton	0	0	7
=	Dustin Hoffman	0	2	7
=	Peter O'Toole	0	0	7

* In all acting categories

Several of the actors listed here were also nominated for and won awards in non-acting categories: Laurence Olivier won "Best Actor" for his leading role but also "Best Picture" as the producer of *Hamlet* (1948), for which he was also nominated as "Best Director", while Paul Newman was nominated as producer of "Best Picture" nominee *Rachel, Rachel* (1968). In 2003, Peter O'Toole initially declined an honorary award on the ground that, as his career was not yet over, he retained hopes of winning one for an acting role.

THE 10 LATEST ACTORS AND ACTRESSES TO RECEIVE THREE OR MORE CONSECUTIVE NOMINATIONS

	ACTOR/ACTRESS	NOMINATIONS	YEARS
1	Russell Crowe	3	1999–2001
2	William Hurt	3	1985–87
3	Glenn Close	3	1982–84
4	Meryl Streep	3	1981–83
5	Jane Fonda	3	1977–79
6 =	Jack Nicholson	3	1973–75
=	Al Pacino	4	1972–75
8	Richard Burton	3	1964–66
9	Elizabeth Taylor	4	1957–60
10	Deborah Kerr	3	1956–58

In the earlier years of the Academy Awards two actresses were nominated for "Best Actress" Oscars on a record five consecutive occasions: Bette Davis (1938–52), with wins in 1935 and 1939, and Greer Garson (1941–45), who never won.

THE 10 LATEST NOMINATIONS FOR ACTORS AND ACTRESSES FOR NON-ENGLISH LANGUAGE PERFORMANCES

	ACTOR/ACTRESS	FILM	LANGUAGE	YEAR
1	Javier Bardem	Before Night Falls	Spanish	2000
2 =	Roberto Benigni*	Life is Beautiful	Italian	1998
=	Fernanda Montenegro	Central Station	Portuguese	1998
4	Massimo Troisi	Il Postino	Italian	1995
5	Catherine Deneuve	Indochine	French	1992
6	Gérard Depardieu	Cyrano de Bergerac	French	1990
7	Isabelle Adjani	Camille Claudel	French	1989
8	Max von Sydow	Pelle the Conqueror	Swedish	1988
9	Marcello Mastroianni	Dark Eyes	Italian	1987
10	Marlee Matlin*	Children of a Lesser God	American sign language	1986

* Won Academy Award

And the Winner Is...

▲ Palme winner
Adrien Brody, in the title role in *The Pianist,* the latest winner of the prestigious Cannes Film Festival Palme d'Or.

THE10 LATEST WINNERS OF THE CANNES PALME D'OR FOR BEST FILM

YEAR	FILM	COUNTRY
2002	The Pianist	UK/France/Germany/Netherlands/Poland
2001	The Son's Room (La Stanza del figlio)	Italy/France
2000	Dancer in the Dark	Denmark/etc.
1999	Rosetta	France
1998	Eternity and a Day (Mia aioniotita kai mia mera)	Greece/France/Italy
1997	= The Eel (Unagi)	Japan
	= The Taste of Cherry (Ta`m e guilass)	Iran
1996	Secrets and Lies	UK
1995	Underground (Bila jednom jedna zemlja)	Yugoslavia/France/Germany/Hungary
1994	Pulp Fiction	USA

In its early years, there was no single "Best Film" award at the Cannes Film Festival, several films being honoured jointly. A "Grand Prize", first awarded in 1949, has been known since 1955 as the "Palme d'Or".

THE10 LATEST WINNERS OF THE EUROPEAN FILM ACADEMY "BEST EUROPEAN FILM" AWARD

YEAR	FILM	COUNTRY
2002	Talk to Her (Hable con Ella)	Spain
2001	Amélie	France/Germany
2000	Dancer in the Dark	Denmark/etc.
1999	All About My Mother (Todo sobre mi madre)	Spain/France
1998	Life Is Beautiful (La Vita è bella)	Italy
1997	The Full Monty	UK
1996	Breaking the Waves	France/Norway/Denmark/Sweden/Netherlands
1995	Land and Freedom	UK/Spain/Germany/Italy
1994	Lamerica	France/Italy
1993	Close to Eden (Urga)	France/Russia

THE10 LATEST WINNERS OF THE BAFTA "BEST FILM" AWARD

YEAR	FILM	COUNTRY
2002	The Pianist	UK/France/Germany/Netherlands/Poland
2001	The Lord of the Rings: The Fellowship of the Ring	New Zealand/USA
2000	Gladiator	USA/UK
1999	American Beauty	USA
1998	Shakespeare in Love	USA/UK
1997	The Full Monty	UK
1996	The English Patient	USA
1995	Sense and Sensibility	USA/UK
1994	Four Weddings and a Funeral	UK
1993	Schindler's List	USA

THE 10 LATEST WINNERS OF THE BAFTA "BEST ACTRESS" AWARD

YEAR	ACTRESS	FILM/COUNTRY
2002	Nicole Kidman	The Hours (USA)
2001	Judi Dench	Iris (UK/USA)
2000	Julia Roberts	Erin Brockovich (USA)
1999	Annette Bening	American Beauty (USA)
1998	Cate Blanchett	Elizabeth (UK)
1997	Judi Dench	Mrs. Brown (UK/USA/Ireland)
1996	Brenda Blethyn	Secrets and Lies (UK/France)
1995	Emma Thompson	Sense and Sensibility (UK)
1994	Susan Sarandon	The Client (USA)
1993	Holly Hunter	The Piano (Australia/New Zealand/France)

The British Film Academy – BAFTA (the British Academy of Film and Television Arts) since 1959 – first presented to actors and actresses at its 1953 ceremony, when Vivien Leigh won as "Best British Actress" for *A Streetcar Named Desire*.

THE 10 LATEST WINNERS OF THE BAFTA "BEST DIRECTOR" AWARD

YEAR	DIRECTOR	FILM/COUNTRY
2002	Roman Polanski	The Pianist (UK/France/Germany/Netherlands/Poland)
2001	Peter Jackson	The Lord of the Rings: The Fellowship of the Ring (New Zealand/USA)
2000	Ang Lee	Crouching Tiger, Hidden Dragon (Wo hu cang long) (Hong Kong/China/Taiwan/USA)
1999	Pedro Almodovar	All About My Mother (Todo sobre mi madre) (Spain/France)
1998	Peter Weir	The Truman Show (USA)
1997	Baz Luhrmann	Romeo + Juliet (USA)
1996	Joel Cohen	Fargo (USA)
1995	Michael Radford	The Postman (Il Postino) (France/Italy/Belgium)
1994	Mike Newell	Four Weddings and a Funeral (UK)
1993	Steven Spielberg	Schindler's List (USA)

THE 10 LATEST WINNERS OF THE BAFTA "BEST NON-ENGLISH LANGUAGE FILM" AWARD

YEAR	FILM	COUNTRY
2002	Talk to Her (Hable con ella)	Spain
2001	Love's a Bitch (Amores perros)	Mexico
2000	Crouching Tiger, Hidden Dragon (Wo hu cang long)	Hong Kong/USA/Taiwan/China
1999	All About My Mother (Todo sobre mi madre)	Spain/France
1998	Central Station (Central do Brasil)	Brazil/France
1997	The Apartment (L'Appartement)	France/Spain/Italy
1996	Ridicule	France
1995	The Postman (Il Postino)	France/Italy/Belgium
1994 =	The Age of Beauty (Belle époque)	Spain/Portugal/France
=	To Live (Huozhe)	China/Hong Kong

THE 10 LATEST WINNERS OF THE BAFTA "BEST ACTOR" AWARD

YEAR	ACTOR	FILM/COUNTRY
2002	Daniel Day-Lewis	Gangs of New York (USA)
2001	Russell Crowe	A Beautiful Mind (USA)
2000	Jamie Bell	Billy Elliot (UK)
1999	Kevin Spacey	American Beauty (USA)
1998	Roberto Benigni	Life Is Beautiful (La Vita è Bella) (Italy)
1997	Robert Carlyle	The Full Monty (UK)
1996	Geoffrey Rush	Shine (Australia)
1995	Nigel Hawthorne	The Madness of King George (UK)
1994	Hugh Grant	Four Weddings and a Funeral (UK)
1993	Anthony Hopkins	The Remains of the Day (UK/USA)

Ralph Richardson won the first "Best British Actor" BAFTA, for *Breaking the Sound Barrier* (1952); Marlon Brando won "Best Foreign Actor" for *Viva Zapata!* (1952).

THE 10 LATEST WINNERS OF THE BAFTA/ALEXANDER KORDA AWARD FOR AN "OUTSTANDING BRITISH FILM"

YEAR	FILM
2002	The Warrior
2001	Gosford Park
2000	Billy Elliott
1999	East Is East
1998	Elizabeth
1997	Nil By Mouth
1996	Secrets and Lies
1995	The Madness of King George
1994	Shallow Grave
1993	Shadowlands

This award, presented in the name of the distinguished Hungarian-born director Alexander Korda (1893–1956), is given to films that have received a minimum of 70 per cent of their finance from the UK.

FIRST FILM AWARDS

FIRST FACT

PRE-DATING THE ACADEMY AWARDS by almost a decade and the Golden Globes by more than two, the Photoplay Medal of Honor was the first ever annual film award. Presented by the US film magazine *Photoplay*, which had been founded in 1911, it was initially based on a poll of its readers, who in its debut year voted for *Humoresque*, a drama directed by Frank Borzage, later the winner of two Academy Awards. After 1930, when *All Quiet on the Western Front* won both the *Photoplay* Medal and the "Best Picture" Academy Award, the winners often coincided. "Most Popular Star" and other categories were later added to the *Photoplay* awards, the last of which were presented in 1968.

Funny Business

TOP 10 COMEDY FILMS*

	FILM	YEAR
1	Forrest Gump	1994
2	Men in Black	1997
3	Home Alone	1990
4	Ghost	1990
5	Pretty Woman	1990
6	Men in Black II	2002
7	Mrs. Doubtfire	1993
8	Ocean's Eleven	2001
9	What Women Want	2001
10	Notting Hill	1999

* Excluding animated

▼ Sky-high pie

American Pie 2 figures among the recent wave of popular gross-out comedies designed to appeal to the young and repel older audiences.

TOP 10 GROSS-OUT COMEDY FILMS

	FILM	YEAR
1	There's Something About Mary	1998
2	Austin Powers: The Spy Who Shagged Me	1999
3	Austin Powers in Goldmember	2002
4	Scary Movie	2000
5	American Pie 2	2001
6	Dumb & Dumber	1994
7	Big Daddy	1999
8	American Pie	1999
9	The Waterboy	1998
10	Nutty Professor II: The Klumps	2000

"Gross-out" films represent a new wave of films featuring outrageous and extreme juvenile comedy for teenagers and young adults, generally revolving round disgusting behaviour and often involving bodily functions.

THE 10 LATEST WINNERS OF THE BAFTA TELEVISION COMEDY SERIES AWARD

YEAR	PROGRAMME
2003	Alistair McGowan's Big Impression
2002	The Sketch Show
2001	Da Ali G Show
2000	The League of Gentlemen
1999	Father Ted
1998	I'm Alan Partridge
1997	Only Fools and Horses
1996	Father Ted
1995	Three Fights, Two Weddings and a Funeral
1994	Drop the Dead Donkey

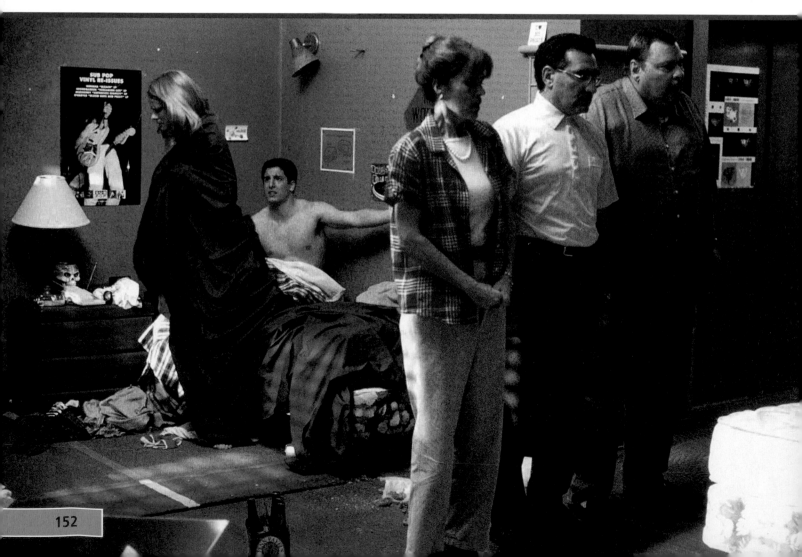

TOP 10 | LONGEST-RUNNING STAGE COMEDIES OF ALL TIME IN THE UK

	COMEDY/YEARS RUNNING	PERFORMANCES
1	**No Sex, Please – We're British** (1971–81; 1982–86; 1986–87)	6,761
2	**The Complete Works of William Shakespeare (Abridged)** (1996–)	3,332*
3	**Run for Your Wife** (1983–91)	2,638
4	**There's a Girl in My Soup** (1966–69; 1969–72)	2,547
5	**Pyjama Tops** (1969–75)	2,498
6	**Worm's Eye View** (1945–51)	2,245
7	**Boeing Boeing** (1962–65; 1965–67)	2,035
8	**Blithe Spirit** (1941–42; 1942; 1942–46)	1,997
9	**Dirty Linen** (1976–80)	1,667
10	**Reluctant Heroes** (1950–54)	1,610

* *Still running; total as at 1 January 2003*

No Sex Please – We're British is the world's longest-running comedy. It opened at the Strand Theatre, London, on 3 June 1971 and after transfers to the Garrick and Duchess Theatres finally closed on 5 September 1987.

THE 10 | LATEST WINNERS OF THE LAURENCE OLIVIER AWARD FOR BEST NEW COMEDY*

YEAR	PLAY	PLAYWRIGHT
2002	**The Lieutenant of Inishmore**	Martin McDonagh
2001	**The Play What I Wrote**	Hamish McColl, Sean Foley, and Eddie Braben
2000	**Stones in His Pockets**	Marie Jones
1999	**The Memory of Water**	Shelagh Stephenson
1998	**Cleo, Camping, Emmanuelle and Dick**	Terry Johnson
1997	**Popcorn**	Ben Elton
1996	**Art**	Yasmina Reza
1995	**Mojo**	Jez Butterworth
1994	**My Night with Reg**	Kevin Elyot
1993	**Hysteria**	Terry Johnson

* *Prior to 1996, award is for Best Comedy*

Presented by The Society of London Theatre since 1976, when Michael Frayn's *Donkey's Years* won in the Comedy category, the awards were named in honour of Lord Olivier in 1984.

TOP 10 | HORROR SPOOF FILMS

	FILM	YEAR
1	**Scary Movie**	2000
2	**Scream**	1996
3	**Scream 2**	1997
4	**Scream 3**	2000
5	**Scary Movie 2**	2001
6	**Young Frankenstein**	1974
7	**Love at First Bite**	1979
8	**An American Werewolf in London**	1981
9	**An American Werewolf in Paris**	1997
10	**Fright Night**	1985

While many films combine comedy and horror elements – among them *Ghoulies* (1985), the two *Gremlins* films (1984 and 1990), *Little Shop of Horrors* (1986), and *Arachnophobia* (1990) – those in this Top 10 represent the most successful of a species of parodies of classic horror films that began more than half a century ago with such examples as *Abbott and Costello Meet Frankenstein* (1948). Such has been the success of the most recent crop that each film in the *Scream* and *Scary Movie* franchise has earned more than $100 million globally.

THE 10 | LATEST WINNERS OF THE SONY RADIO COMEDY AWARD

YEAR	PROGRAMME	PRODUCERS
2003	**Just a Minute**	BBC Radio Entertainment for Radio 4
2002	**I'm Sorry I Haven't a Clue**	BBC Radio Entertainment for Radio 4
2001	**Dead Ringers**	BBC Radio Entertainment for Radio 4
2000	**Blue Jam**	TalkBack Productions for BBC Radio 1
1999	**Old Harry's Game**	BBC Radio 4
1998	**Blue Jam**	TalkBack Productions for BBC Radio 1
1997	**Goodness Gracious Me!**	BBC Radio 4
1996	**People Like Us**	BBC Radio 4
1995	**I'm Sorry I Haven't a Clue**	BBC Radio 4
1994	**A Look Back at the Nineties**	BBC Radio 4

Britain's prestigious Sony Radio Awards have been presented since 1983, with gold, silver, and bronze awards in several categories. Long-running show *I'm Sorry I Haven't a Clue* won the latest gold with the accompanying comment, "Despite its many years on air, this still stands out as a very funny programme – risky, rude, brilliantly written and superbly performed. Humphrey Lyttleton's comic timing is genius!", while previous winner *Dead Ringers* received the accolade "The team have clearly scored a huge hit with their target audience with a searingly accurate understanding of what makes the Radio 4 audience tick and what will make them laugh."

Animation

TOP 10 ANIMATED FILMS

	FILM	US RELEASE	WORLWIDE TOTAL GROSS ($)
1	The Lion King*	1994	771,900,000
2	Monsters, Inc.*	2001	529,000,000
3	Aladdin*	1992	502,400,000
4	Toy Story 2*	1999	485,800,000
5	Shrek	2001	477,000,000
6	Tarzan*	1999	449,400,000
7	Ice Age	2002	366,300,000
8	A Bug's Life*	1998	363,400,000
9	Toy Story*	1995	361,500,000
10	Dinosaur*	2000	356,100,000

* Disney

TOP 10 BUDGETS FOR ANIMATED FILMS

	FILM	DATE	BUDGET ($)
1 =	Tarzan	1999	150,000,000
=	The Polar Express	2004	150,000,000
3	Treasure Planet	2002	140,000,000
4	Final Fantasy: The Spirits Within	2001	137,000,000
5	Dinosaur	2000	128,000,000
6	Monsters, Inc.	2001	115,000,000
7	The Emperor's New Groove	2000	100,000,000
8	The Road to El Dorado	2000	95,000,000
9	Finding Nemo	2003	94,000,000
10	The Incredibles	2004	92,000,000

Animated film budgets have come a long way since *Snow White and the Seven Dwarfs* (1937) established a then record of $1.49 million. The $2.6 million budget for *Pinocchio* (1940), and $2.28 million for the original *Fantasia* (1940) were the two biggest of the 1940s, while *Sleeping Beauty* (1959) at $6 million was the highest of the 1950s. *Robin Hood* (1973) had a budget of $15 million, a record that remained unbroken until 1985 when *The Black Cauldron* (1985) became the first to break the $25 million barrier. Since the 1990s budgets of $50 million to $100 million or more have become commonplace.

▼ Towering success
One of the most successful films derived from a TV series, *Rugrats in Paris,* the $30 million budget sequel to *The Rugrats Movie* (1988), has made over $100 million worldwide.

PART ANIMATION/PART LIVE-ACTION FILMS

	FILM	YEAR
1	Who Framed Roger Rabbit	1988
2	Casper	1995
3	Space Jam	1996
4	9 to 5	1980
5	Mary Poppins	1964
6	Fantasia/2000	2000
7	Small Soldiers	1998
8	Song of the South	1946
9	James and the Giant Peach	1996
10	Pete's Dragon	1977

Many films now contain computer-generated images alongside live action, but these are the highest earning that combine traditional animation and live action as a key element. *Fantasia* (1940) may arguably warrant a place in the list, but the only combination sequence is a brief encounter between Mickey Mouse and the conductor Leopold Stokowski in what is otherwise an animated film. *The Adventures of Rocky and Bullwinkle* (2000) fails to make the grade, since it earned no more than a fraction of its reputed $76 million budget.

LATEST OSCAR-WINNING ANIMATED FILMS*

YEAR	FILM	DIRECTOR/COUNTRY
2002	The ChubbChubbs!	Eric Armstrong, Canada
2001	For the Birds	Ralph Eggleston, USA
2000	Father and Daughter	Michael Dudok de Wit, Netherlands
1999	The Old Man and the Sea	Aleksandr Petrov, USA
1998	Bunny	Chris Wedge, USA
1997	Geri's Game	Jan Pinkava, USA
1996	Quest	Tyron Montgomery, UK
1995	Wallace & Gromit: A Close Shave	Nick Park, UK
1994	Bob's Birthday	David Fine and Alison Snowden, UK
1993	Wallace & Gromit: The Wrong Trousers	Nick Park, UK

* In the category "Short Films (Animated)"

Oscars were first awarded in the category "Short Subjects (Cartoons)" – later "Short Subjects (Animated Films)" and "Short Films (Animated)" – in 1932. During the award's first decade, and with few exceptions up to 1968, it was won annually by Walt Disney. The new category "Best Animated Feature" has existed only since 2001 (when it was won by *Shrek*); prior to this, films such as *Snow White and the Seven Dwarfs* (1937) and *Fantasia* (1940) received honorary Oscars.

ANIMATED FILMS BASED ON TV SERIES

	FILM	TV SERIES*	YEAR
1	Pokémon: The First Movie	1997	1999
2	The Rugrats Movie	1991	1998
3	Rugrats in Paris: The Movie – Rugrats II	1991	2000
4	Beavis and Butt-head Do America	1993	1996
5	South Park: Bigger, Longer & Uncut	1997	1999
6	Pokémon: The Movie 2000	1997	2000
7	Recess: School's Out	1997	2001
8	Jetsons: The Movie	1962	1990
9	Doug's 1st Movie	1991	1999
10	The Smurfs and the Magic Flute	1981	1983

* Launched on TV in USA

Such is the fan following of many TV animated series that when they reach the big screen they attract huge audiences: the first three films in this list each earned in excess of $100 million, and the others have all made respectable eight-figure sums.

LATEST BAFTA-WINNING ANIMATED FILMS*

YEAR	FILM	DIRECTOR/COUNTRY
2002	Fish Never Sleep	Gaëlle Denis, UK
2001	Dog	Suzie Templeton, UK
2000	Father and Daughter	Michael Dudok de Wit, Netherlands
1999	The Man with Beautiful Eyes	Jonathan Hodgson, UK
1998	The Canterbury Tales	Jonathan Myerson, UK
1997	Stage Fright	Steve Box, UK
1996	La vieille dame et les pigeons	Sylvin Chomet, France
1995	Wallace & Gromit: A Close Shave	Nick Park, UK
1994	The Big Story	David Stoten and Tim Watts, USA
1993	Wallace & Gromit: The Wrong Trousers	Nick Park, UK

* In the category "Short Animation"

The first BAFTA award for "Best Animated Film" (now "Short Animation") was for *The Hill Farm* (1999). In the following year, Nick Park won the first of his three awards, for *Wallace & Gromit: A Grand Day Out*. There is no separate award for animated feature films, and *Shrek* (2001) was nominated for "Best Film" alongside live action films, although some have won specialist awards in special effects and musical categories.

Kids' Stuff

	ACTOR/ACTRESS	AWARD	AWARD YEAR	AGE (YRS)	(MTHS)	(DAYS)
1	**Shirley Temple**	Special Award (outstanding contribution during 1934)	1934	6	10	4
2	**Vincent Winter**	Special Award (*The Little Kidnappers*)	1954	7	3	1
3	**Margaret O'Brien**	Special Award (outstanding child actress of 1944)	1944	8	2	0
4	**Jon Whiteley**	Special Award (*The Little Kidnappers*)	1954	10	1	11
5	**Tatum O'Neal**	Best Supporting Actress (*Paper Moon*)	1973	10	4	27
6	**Anna Paquin**	Best Supporting Actress (*The Piano*)	1993	11	7	28
7	**Ivan Jandl**	Special Award (*The Search*)	1948	12	0	27
8	**Claude Jarman Jr.**	Special Award (*The Yearling*)	1946	12	5	16
9	**Bobby Driscoll**	Special Award (outstanding juvenile actor)	1949	13	0	20
10	**Hayley Mills**	Special Award (outstanding juvenile performance)	1960	13	11	29

The Academy Awards ceremony usually takes place in March the year after the film was released, so winners are generally at least a year older when they receive their Oscars than when they acted in their films. Hayley Mills, the 12th and last winner of the "Special Award" miniature Oscar (presented to her by its first winner, Shirley Temple), won her award one day before her 14th birthday. Subsequent winners have had to compete on the same basis as adult actors and actresses for the major awards. Tatum O'Neal is the youngest winner of – as well as the youngest ever nominee for – an "adult" Oscar. The youngest winner of the "Best Actor" award is Richard Dreyfuss (for *The Goodbye Girl* in the 1977 Awards). The youngest winner in the "Best Supporting Actor" category is Timothy Hutton, who was aged 20 when he won in the 1980 Awards for his role in *Ordinary People*.

▲ **The price of fame**
Youngest-ever Oscar winner Shirley Temple said, "I stopped believing in Santa Claus when my mother took me to see him in a department store and he asked for my autograph".

TOP 10 | BESTSELLING CHILDREN'S VIDEOS IN THE UK*

	VIDEO
1	The Jungle Book
2	Snow White and the Seven Dwarfs
3	Toy Story
4	The Lion King
5	Shrek
6	Beauty and the Beast
7	Fantasia
8	One Hundred and One Dalmatians#
9	Lady and The Tramp
10	Cinderella

* To 1 January 2003

\# Animated version

TOP 10 | CARTOONS ON UK TELEVISION MOST WATCHED BY CHILDREN, 2002

	CARTOON*	DATE	CHANNEL	AUDIENCE#
1	**The Simpsons**	10 Dec	BBC2	1,379,000
2	**Snow White and the Seven Dwarfs** (film)	24 Dec	Channel 4	893,000
3	**Mona the Vampire**	9 Dec	BBC1	865,000
4	**The Proud Family**	9 Feb	ITV1	857,000
5	**Mr. Bean** (animated series)	9 Mar	ITV1	837,000
6	**Bob the Builder**	23 Dec	BBC1	829,000
7	**The Cramp Twins**	22 Jan	BBC1	824,000
8	**Legend of the Lost Tribe**	25 Dec	BBC1	809,000
9	**The Scooby Doo Show**	24 Dec	BBC1	797,000
10	**The Wild Thornberrys**	21 Nov	BBC1	794,000

* Top rated episode only listed

\# Children only

Source: *BARB/TNS*

Matt Groening's enormously successful animated series *The Simpsons* originally appeared in 1987 as short episodes screened on the *Tracey Ullman Show*. It was developed – along with enhancements to its graphics – into longer weekly episodes that have been broadcast for more than a decade, attracting ever-wider audiences internationally and becoming the longest-running comedy series ever, passing its 300th episode in 2003.

TOP 10 | FILMS WITH CHILD STARS

	FILM	YEAR
1	Harry Potter and the Philsopher's Stone	2001
2	Star Wars: Episode I – The Phantom Menace	1999
3	Jurassic Park	1993
4	Harry Potter and the Chamber of Secrets	2002
5	E.T. the Extra-Terrestrial	1982
6	The Sixth Sense	1999
7	Home Alone	1990
8	Mrs. Doubtfire	1993
9	Signs	2002
10	Jurassic Park III	2001

Family films, especially those with child stars, are among the highest-earning of all time: all those in the Top 10 have earned upwards of $365 million each worldwide. Several of those appearing here featured children early in careers, with Drew Barrymore's one of the most notable. Having appeared in *Altered States* (1980) at the age of four, she took the role of Gertie in *E.T. the Extra-Terrestrial* while still only six, going on to pursue a successful adult career in such films as *Batman Forever* (1995) and *Charlie's Angels* (2000).

▲ **Secret success**
Child stars Ron and Harry take to the air in a flying Ford Anglia in box-office smash *Harry Potter and the Chamber of Secrets*.

TOP 10 | FILMS ON UK TELEVISION MOST WATCHED BY CHILDREN, 2002

	FILM	CHANNEL	AUDIENCE*
1	A Bug's Life	BBC1	1,942,000
2	The Mummy	BBC1	1,919,000
3	Chicken Run	BBC1	1,628,000
4	George of the Jungle	BBC1	1,593,000
5	Indiana Jones and the Temple of Doom	BBC1	1,447,000
6	Small Soldiers	BBC1	1,411,000
7	Indiana Jones and the Last Crusade	BBC1	1,351,000
8	Men in Black	BBC1	1,278,000
9	Bean: The Ultimate Disaster Movie	ITV1	1,228,000
10	Dragonheart	ITV1	1,221,000

* Children only

Source: *BARB/S.P. Consultants*

With the exception of *Small Soldiers*, which was only a modest success at the world box office, the viewing taste of British children mirrors that of the public at large, with all their most watched films appearing among the most successful family films of the past decade.

TOP 10 | CHILDREN'S TELEVISION PROGRAMMES IN THE UK, 2002

	PROGRAMME*	DATE	CHANNEL	AUDIENCE#
1	Newsround	10 Dec	BBC1	1,007,000
2	Smart on the Road	10 Dec	BBC1	989,000
3	All About Me	5 Apr	BBC1	976,000
4	Christmas at the Club Blue Peter	23 Dec	BBC1	958,000
5	CBBC at the Fame Academy	10 Dec	BBC1	949,000
6	Blue Peter	4 Feb	BBC1	915,000
7	Grange Hill	31 Jan	BBC1	894,000
8	Snow White and the Seven Dwarfs (film)	24 Dec	Channel 4	893,000
9	Viva S Club	10 Dec	BBC1	885,000
10	Mona the Vampire	9 Dec	BBC1	865,000

* Top rated episode only listed

 # Children only

Source: *BARB/S.P. Consultants*

Even with today's multiplicity of choices, the most popular children's programmes include several long-established regulars, among them *Newsround* (originally *John Craven's Newsround*), which was launched on 4 April 1972, *Blue Peter* (16 October 1958), and *Grange Hill* (8 February 1978).

DVD & Video

TOP 10 VIDEO COUNTRIES

	COUNTRY	DVD %	TOTAL SPENDING (2001) ($)
1	USA	34	20,549,000,000
2	Japan	35	4,768,000,000
3	UK	36	2,857,000,000
4	France	41	1,681,000,000
5	Canada	34	1,666,000,000
6	Germany	39	1,027,000,000
7	Australia	29	595,000,000
8	South Korea	3	556,000,000
9	Italy	23	540,000,000
10	Spain	31	405,000,000

Source: Screen Digest

The availability of comparative international statistics lags behind the rapidly moving video (VHS and DVD) business, but figures for the USA for 2002 revealed that the home-video industry in the USA – DVD and VHS rentals and sales – was worth $20.3 billion, more than double the $9.37 billion generated by domestic movie releases.

THE 10 WORST COUNTRIES FOR VIDEO PIRACY

	COUNTRY	PIRACY RATE (%)	EST. LOSSES (2002)* ($)
1	Russia	80	250,000,000
2	China	91	168,000,000
3	Italy	20	140,000,000
4	Brazil	35	120,000,000
5	India	60	75,000,000
6	Turkey	45	50,000,000
7 =	Malaysia	75	42,000,000
=	Taiwan	44	42,000,000
9 =	Colombia	90	40,000,000
=	Saudi Arabia	35	40,000,000
=	Ukraine	90	40,000,000

* Preliminary figures

Source: International Intellectual Property Alliance (IIPA)

Despite international attempts to curb video piracy by both legal and technological means, it has reached epidemic proportions in many territories.

TOP 10 VIDEOS RENTED IN THE UK*

	TITLE
1	Four Weddings and a Funeral
2	Dirty Dancing
3	Basic Instinct
4	Crocodile Dundee
5	Gladiator
6	Sister Act
7	Forrest Gump
8	The Sixth Sense
9	Home Alone
10	Ghost

* To 1 January 2003

Source: MRIB

Following its international box-office success, the British comedy Four Weddings and a Funeral was a consistently huge UK renter on video when it wrested the all-time champion slot from the long-resident Dirty Dancing. The latter and Crocodile Dundee are the only pre-1990 films to have maintained a place in this list.

TOP 10 VIDEOS RENTED IN THE UK, 2002

	TITLE
1	The Others
2	Swordfish
3	American Pie 2
4	Legally Blonde
5	Jurassic Park III
6	The 51st State
7	A Knight's Tale
8	The Fast and the Furious
9	Moulin Rouge!
10	Shallow Hal

Source: MRIB

Chart-topping The Others (Los Otros), starring Nicole Kidman, was a part-Spanish co-production that, on its cinema release, became Spain's highest-earning non-US film of all time. After making over $170 million worldwide, it repeated its success internationally with its video release.

TOP 10 BESTSELLING VIDEOS IN THE UK*

	TITLE	YEAR OF RELEASE
1	The Jungle Book	1993
2	Titanic	1998
3	Snow White and the Seven Dwarfs	1992
4	The Lord of the Rings: The Fellowship of the Ring	2002
5	Toy Story	1999
6	The Lion King	1995
7	Shrek	2001
8	Gladiator	2000
9	Harry Potter and the Philosopher's Stone	2002
10	Beauty and the Beast	1991

* To 1 January 2003

Source: British Video Association/Official UK Charts

Earning more than $200 million worldwide on its release in 1967, The Jungle Book's subsequent video release further enhanced its income internationally.

TOP 10 BESTSELLING DVDs IN THE UK*

	TITLE	YEAR OF RELEASE
1	The Lord of the Rings: The Fellowship of the Ring	2002
2	Gladiator	2000
3	Harry Potter and the Philosopher's Stone	2002
4	The Matrix	1999
5	Star Wars: Episode II – Attack of the Clones	2002
6	Shrek	2001
7	The Mummy	2000
8	Monsters, Inc.	2002
9	Bridget Jones's Diary	2001
10	The Mummy Returns	2001

* To 1 January 2003

Source: British Video Association

BESTSELLING DVDs IN THE UK, 2002

TITLE

1 The Lord of the Rings: The Fellowship of the Ring

2 Harry Potter and the Philosopher's Stone

3 Star Wars: Episode II – Attack of the Clones

4 Monsters, Inc.

5 Ocean's Eleven

6 Spider-Man

7 The Fast and the Furious

8 Scooby Doo – The Movie

9 Ice Age

10 Minority Report

Source: *British Video Association/Official UK Charts Company*

In 2002, the UK video market grew by 26 per cent, with total DVD and VHS shop sales (excluding mail order) of 154 million units, and DVD sales increasing by a remarkable 111 per cent.

DVDs RENTED IN THE UK, 2002

TITLE

1 The Others

2 Swordfish

3 The 51st State

4 American Pie 2

5 Shallow Hal

6 Black Hawk Down

7 The Fast and the Furious

8 A.I.: Artificial Intelligence

9 Panic Room

10 Jurassic Park III

Source: *MRIB*

The total value of the UK's video rental and retail business rose to £2.55 billion in 2002, with 169 million DVD and VHS sales and 176 million rentals. While the VHS format remains popular, it is steadily being eclipsed by DVD in rentals and especially in sales.

DVDs RENTED IN THE UK

TITLE

1 The Others

2 Minority Report

3 Swordfish

4 About a Boy

5 The 51st State

6 Panic Room

7 Shallow Hal

8 Black Hawk Down

9 American Pie 2

10 The Fast and the Furious

Source: *MRIB*

▼ Ocean wave
Recent releases such as *Ocean's Eleven* have gained from the rapid rise of DVD as today's format of choice.

Top TV

THE 10 LATEST WINNERS OF THE BAFTA "BEST ACTRESS" AWARD

YEAR	ACTRES	/PROGRAMME
2003	Julie Walters	Murder
2002	Julie Walters	My Beautiful Son
2001	Judi Dench	Last of the Blonde Bombshells
2000	Thora Hird	Lost for Words
1999	Thora Hird	Talking Heads: Waiting for the Telegram
1998	Daniela Nardini	This Life
1997	Gina McKee	Our Friends in the North
1996	Jennifer Ehle	Pride and Prejudice
1995	Juliet Aubrey	Middlemarch
1994	Helen Mirren	Prime Suspect 3

In 1959 the Society of Film and Television Arts was formed by the amalgamation of the British Film Academy (founded 1948) and the Guild of Television Producers and Directors (1954), changing its name to BAFTA (the British Academy of Film and Television Arts) in 1975. Past winners of the "Best Actress" award have included such stars as Vanessa Redgrave and Emma Thompson.

▼ TV age
The proliferation of terrestrial and satellite television in recent years has transformed both the industry and the skylines of today's cities.

THE 10 LATEST WINNERS OF THE BAFTA "BEST ACTOR" AWARD

YEAR	ACTOR	PROGRAMME
2003	Albert Finney	Gathering Storm
2002	Michael Gambon	Perfect Strangers
2001	Michael Gambon	Longitude
2000	Michael Gambon	Wives & Daughters
1999	Tom Courtenay	A Rather English Marriage
1998	Simon Russell-Beale	A Dance to the Music of Time
1997	Nigel Hawthorne	The Fragile Heart
1996	Robbie Coltrane	Cracker
1995	Robbie Coltrane	Cracker
1994	Robbie Coltrane	Cracker

FIRST TV BROADCASTS

FIRST FACT

ALTHOUGH THERE HAD BEEN earlier low-definition experimental transmissions, the world's first daily high-definition public broadcasting television service was launched by the BBC on 2 November 1936. Television's debut in the USA dates from 30 April 1939, when NBC showed an outside broadcast of the opening of the New York World's Fair by Franklin D. Roosevelt – who thereby became the first US President ever to appear on television.

TOP 10 SATELLITE TELEVISION COUNTRIES

	COUNTRY	HOME SATELLITE ANTENNAE (2000)
1	USA	16,000,000
2	Germany	12,900,000
3	Japan	10,620,000
4	UK	5,200,000
5	France	4,300,000
6	Indonesia	3,900,000
7	Algeria	3,500,000
8	Poland	2,500,000
9	Saudi Arabia	1,914,000
10	Spain	1,840,000

Source: *International Telecommunication Union*, World Telecommunication Development Report, 2002

TOP 10 TELEVISION-OWNING COUNTRIES

	COUNTRY	TVs PER 1,000 POPULATION (2000)
1	Qatar	869
2	USA	854
3	Denmark	807
4	Latvia	789
5	Australia	738
6	Japan	725
7	Canada	715
8	Finland	692
9	Norway	669
10	UK	653
	World	270

Source: *International Telecommunication Union*, World Telecommunication Development Report, 2002

TOP 10 TELEVISION AUDIENCES OF ALL TIME IN THE UK

	PROGRAMME	DATE	AUDIENCE
1	Royal Wedding of HRH Prince Charles to Lady Diana Spencer	29 July 1981	39,000,000
2	1970 World Cup: Brazil v England	10 June 1970	32,500,000
3	= 1966 World Cup Final: England v West Germany	30 July 1966	32,000,000
	= Cup Final Replay: Chelsea v Leeds	28 Apr 1970	32,000,000
5	Funeral of Diana, Princess of Wales	6 Sept 1997	31,000,000
6	EastEnders Christmas episode	26 Dec 1987	30,000,000
7	Morecambe and Wise Christmas Show	25 Dec 1977	28,000,000
8	= World Heavyweight Boxing Championship: Joe Frazier v Muhammad Ali	8 Mar 1971	27,000,000
	= Dallas	22 Nov 1980	27,000,000
10	Only Fools and Horses	29 Dec 1996	24,350,000

The funeral of Princess Diana is thought to have been seen by 2.5 billion people worldwide, the largest audience in television history. The 22 November 1980 screening of *Dallas* was the most-watched because it was the episode that revealed who shot J. R. Ewing.

TOP 10 LIGHT ENTERTAINMENT PROGRAMMES ON UK TELEVISION, 2002

	PROGRAMME*	CHANNEL	DATE	AUDIENCE
1	Only Fools and Horses	BBC1	25 Dec	17,403,000
2	Who Wants to be a Millionaire	ITV1	3 Feb	11,607,000
3	Who Wants to be a Millionaire: Celebrity Special	ITV1	3 Mar	11,204,000
4	I'm a Celebrity – Get Me Out of Here!	ITV1	8 Sept	10,949,000
5	Outtake TV	BBC1	27 Dec	10,112,000
6	Big Brother	Channel 4	26 July	10,008,000
7	Test the Nation: The National IQ Test	BBC1	11 May	9,211,000
8	The Best Ever You've Been Framed	ITV1	8 Sept	8,866,000
9	Home Alone	ITV1	9 Feb	8,845,000
10	It Shouldn't Happen to...	ITV1	2 Feb	8,744,000

* The highest-rated episode only of series shown

Source: *BARB/S.P. Consultants*

TOP 10 DRAMAS ON UK TELEVISION, 2002

	PROGRAMME*	CHANNEL	DATE	AUDIENCE
1	EastEnders	BBC1	25 Dec	16,966,000
2	Coronation Street	ITV1	17 Nov	15,014,000
3	Auf Wiedersehen, Pet	BBC1	28 Apr	12,415,000
4	A Touch of Frost	ITV1	27 Jan	12,374,000
5	Heartbeat	ITV1	17 Nov	12,096,000
6	Emmerdale	ITV1	27 Dec	11,786,000
7	EastEnders: Ricky and Bianca	BBC1	13 May	11,045,000
8	Foyle's War	ITV1	17 Nov	10,039,000
9	Blood Strangers	ITV1	4 Feb	9,676,000
10	The Bill	ITV1	23 Oct	9,625,000

* The highest-rated episode only of series shown

Source: *BARB/S.P. Consultants*

TOP 10 FACTUAL PROGRAMMES ON UK TELEVISION, 2002

	PROGRAMME*	CHANNEL	DATE	AUDIENCE
1	The Story of Only Fools and Horses	BBC1	20 Dec	9,192,000
2	Pyramid	BBC1	28 Oct	9,049,000
3	Being Victoria Beckham	ITV1	4 Mar	8,827,000
4	The Queen's Story	ITV1	5 June	8,627,000
5	Facelifts from Hell	ITV1	13 Feb	8,574,000
6	The Sahara with Michael Palin	BBC1	13 Oct	8,494,000
7	Holiday Airport: Lanzarote	ITV1	23 July	8,466,000
8	Airline	ITV1	29 July	8,393,000
9	Cruise Ship	ITV1	14 Oct	8,100,000
10	Neighbours from Hell	ITV1	6 Aug	8,058,000

* The highest-rated episode only of series shown

Source: *BARB/S.P. Consultants*

Radio Days

RADIO-OWNING COUNTRIES

COUNTRY	RADIOS PER 1,000 POPULATION (2000)
1 USA	2,118
2 Australia	1,908
3 Finland	1,623
4 UK	1,432
5 Denmark	1,349
6 Estonia	1,096
7 Canada	1,047
8 South Korea	1,033
9 Switzerland	1,002
10 New Zealand	997
World	419

Source: *World Bank, World Development Indicators 2002/UNESCO*

TOP 10 **RADIO STATIONS IN THE UK**

STATION	AVERAGE WEEKLY LISTENER HOURS*
1 BBC Radio 2	160,447,000
2 BBC Radio 4	124,322,000
3 BBC Radio 1	92,574,000
4 Classic FM	47,353,000
5 BBC Radio 5 Live	45,389,000
6 95.8 Capital FM	19,338,000
7 talkSPORT (Talk Radio)	17,860,000
8 Heart 106.2 FM	13,875,000
9 BBC Radio 3	13,871,000
10 Virgin Radio (AM)	11,278,000
All UK radio	1,055,338,000

* Total number of hours spent by all adults (over 15) listening to the station in an average week, July to September 2002

Source: *RAJAR*

THE 10 **LATEST RECIPIENTS OF THE SONY RADIO GOLD AWARD***

YEAR	RECIPIENT
2003	John Humphrys
2002	John Peel
2001	Chris Tarrant
2000	Ralph Bernard
1999	Zoë Ball
1998	Chris Evans
1997	Jimmy Young
1996	Richard Baker
1995	Alistair Cooke
1994	Kenny Everett

* The Gold Award is presented for "Outstanding Contribution to Radio Over the Years"

THE 10 LATEST WINNERS OF THE SONY RADIO NEWS COVERAGE AWARD*

YEAR	PROGRAMME	PRODUCERS
2003	Ethiopian Famine	BBC Radio News for Radio 4
2002	Holy Cross Girls School Dispute	BBC Radio Current Affairs for BBC Radio Ulster
2001	The Jon Gaunt Breakfast Show	BBC Three Counties Radio
2000	Late Night Live: Soho Bomb	BBC Current Affairs News for BBC Radio 5 Live
1999	Farming Today	BBC Radio 4
1998	The Death of the Princess of Wales	BBC Radio 4 and BBC Radio 5 Live
1997	Drumcree	BBC Radio Ulster
1996	Dallyn on Saturday	BBC Radio 5 Live
1995	The Magazine: IRA Ceasefire	BBC Radio 5 Live
1994	Today: The Moscow White House Siege	BBC Radio 4

Previously the "Best Response to a News Event" award

THE 10 LATEST WINNERS OF THE SONY RADIO COMMUNITY AWARD*

YEAR	PROGRAMME	PRODUCERS
2003	Altogether Now	BBC Radio Leeds
2002	Pillars of Faith	BBC Radio 1
2001	Floodwatch 2000	BBC Radio York
2000	Out of the Red, Chemical Beats, Sunday Surgery	BBC Music Entertainment for Radio 1
1999	Omagh	BBC Radio Ulster for BBC Northern Ireland
1998	Breast Cancer Awareness Week	BBC Radio Ulster
1997	Dunblane	BBC Radio Scotland
1996	Affairs of the Heart	BBC Radio 2
1995	Man Matters	BBC Radio 2
1994	Shout it Out	BBC Radio Devon

Previously the Public Service award

As with other Sony Radio Awards, gold, silver and bronze Community Awards are presented for programmes that, in the opinion of the judges, "recognise any campaign, programme or series through which radio has been used to affect the lives of the listening public in a positive, practical way".

TOP 10 MOST POPULAR PROGRAMMES ON BBC RADIO 4

	PROGRAMME
1	Today
2	The Archers
3	PM
4	Six o'clock News
5	You and Yours
6	The World at One
7	Woman's Hour
8	Daily Service
9	Afternoon Play
10	Front Row

Source: *RAJAR/BBC*

In addition to the *Daily Service*, one of the longest-running programmes on radio, several of the most popular Radio 4 programmes have a long pedigree: *Today* was first broadcast on 28 October 1957, and *Woman's Hour* dates from 7 October 1946.

◄ **Radio head**
Radio listeners maintain loyalty for their favourite stations, ensuring multi-million audiences for the leading broadcasters.

TOP 10 LONGEST-RUNNING PROGRAMMES ON BBC RADIO

	PROGRAMME	FIRST BROADCAST
1	The Week's Good Cause	24 Jan 1926
2	The Shipping Forecast	26 Jan 1926
3	Choral Evensong	7 Oct 1926
4	Daily Service	2 Jan 1928*
5	The Week in Westminster	6 Nov 1929
6	Sunday Half Hour	14 July 1940
7	Desert Island Discs	29 Jan 1942
8	Saturday Night Theatre	3 Apr 1943
9	Composer of the Week#	2 Aug 1943
10	Letter From America†	24 Mar 1946

Experimental broadcast; national transmission began December 1929

Formerly This Week's Composer

† Formerly American Letter

As well as these 10 long-running programmes, several others that date from the 1940s are still on the air, among them *From Our Own Correspondent*, which was first broadcast on 4 October 1946.

RADIO BROADCAST

ALTHOUGH WIRELESS MESSAGES had been broadcast earlier using Morse code, the first ever to transmit sound and music took place on Christmas Eve 1906. Canadian physicist and inventor Reginald Fessenden (1866–1932) set up a radio station and 128-m (420-ft) mast at Brant Rock Station in Massachusetts, USA. He opened the broadcast with an explanation of what he proposed to do, followed by a phonograph recording of Handel's *Largo*, after which he sang and played violin. This first radio show was repeated on New Year's Eve and received as far afield as Norfolk, Virginia, the West Indies, and by ships at sea. Over the years, radio continued as a means of telecommunications between ships, but did not become established as a popular medium until the 1920s.

FIRST FACT

COMMERCIAL
WORLD

World Finance

GLOBAL INDUSTRIAL COMPANIES

COMPANY/LOCATION	SECTOR	REVENUE (2001) ($)
1 **Wal-Mart Stores, Inc.,** USA	Retailing	219,812,000,000
2 **Exxon Mobil,** USA	Oil, gas, and fuel	191,581,000,000
3 **General Motors Corp.,** USA	Motor vehicles	177,260,000,000
4 **BP plc,** UK	Oil, gas	174,218,000,000
5 **Ford Motor Co.,** USA	Transport	162,412,000,000
6 **Enron Corp.*,** USA	Gas, electricity	138,718,000,000
7 **DaimlerChrysler AG,** Germany	Motor vehicles	136,897,300,000
8 **Royal Dutch/Shell Group,** Netherlands/UK	Oil, gas, chemicals	135,211,000,000
9 **General Electric,** USA	Electronics, electrical equipment	125,913,000,000
10 **Toyota Motor,** Japan	Motor vehicles	120,814,400,000

* Revenue for 9 months Jan–Sept 2001; filed for bankruptcy 2 December 2001

Source: Fortune *magazine,* The 2002 Global 500, 22 July 2002

Sam Walton opened his first Wal-Mart store in Rogers, Arkansas, in 1962. It has undergone phenomenal growth in the past 40 years, to become the world's No. 1 company. On the day after Thanksgiving, 2001, it achieved the largest single day's sales in retail history, taking $1.25 billion.

▼ **Retail giant**
Wal-Mart was founded in 1962. By 1979 it was achieving sales of over $1 billion a year; by 1993 it did so in a week, and can now sell that amount in a single day.

RICHEST COUNTRIES

COUNTRY	GDP* PER CAPITA (2000) ($)
1 **Luxembourg**	50,061
2 **USA**	34,142
3 **Norway**	29,918
4 **Ireland**	29,866
5 **Iceland**	29,581
6 **Switzerland**	28,769
7 **Canada**	27,840
8 **Denmark**	27,627
9 **Belgium**	27,178
10 **Austria**	26,765
World	7,446
UK	23,509

* Gross Domestic Product

Source: *United Nations,* Human Development Report, 2002

MOST EXPENSIVE COUNTRIES IN WHICH TO BUY A BIG MAC

	COUNTRY	COST OF A BIG MAC ($)*
1	Iceland	5.51
2	Switzerland	4.56
3	Sweden	3.46
4	UK	3.19
5	Malta	3.03
6	Euro area	2.87
7	South Korea	2.73
8	USA	2.65
9	United Arab Emirates	2.45
10	Saudi Arabia	2.40

As at 16 Jan 2003; of those countries surveyed

Source: *The Economist/McDonald's price data*

The Economist's Big Mac index assesses the value of countries' currencies against the standard US price of a Big Mac, by assuming that an identical amount of goods and services should cost the same in all countries. By this reckoning, all of the countries in the Top 10 are above the USA, which means that they have over-valued currencies. Conversely, all those below the USA (in Argentina a Big Mac costs just $1.18) are under-valued.

FASTEST-GROWING ECONOMIES

	COUNTRY	GDP* PER CAPITA (2000) ($)	GROWTH RATE (1990–2000) (%)
1	Equatorial Guinea	15,073	18.9
2	China	3,976	9.2
3	Ireland	29,866	6.5
4	Vietnam	1,996	6.0
5	Sudan	1,797	5.6
6	Maldives	4,485	5.4
7	Chile	9,417	5.2
8	Guyana	3,963	5.0
9	Myanmar	1,500	4.8
10 =	St. Kitts and Nevis	12,510	4.7
=	Singapore	23,356	4.7
=	South Korea	17,380	4.7
	World	7,446	1.2
	UK	23,509	2.2

Gross Domestic Product

Source: *United Nations*, Human Development Report, 2002

POOREST COUNTRIES

	COUNTRY	GDP* PER CAPITA (2000) ($)
1	Sierra Leone	490
2	Tanzania	523
3	Burundi	591
4	Malawi	615
5	Ethiopia	668
6	Niger	746
7	Guinea-Bissau	755
8	Dem. Rep. of Congo	765
9	Mali	797
10	Congo	825

Gross Domestic Product

Source: *United Nations*, Human Development Report, 2002

GDP is an indicator of a country's comparative economic performance, but the scale of extreme poverty is graphically revealed in statistics that show the proportion of the population with an income of under $1 a day: a figure as high as 72.8 per cent in Mali, while the figure for people earning less than $2 a day rises to 90.6 per cent.

COUNTRIES MOST IN DEBT

	COUNTRY	TOTAL EXTERNAL DEBT (2000) ($)
1	Brazil	237,953,000,000
2	Russia	160,300,000,000
3	Mexico	150,288,000,000
4	China	149,800,000,000
5	Argentina	146,172,000,000
6	Indonesia	141,803,000,000
7	South Korea	134,417,000,000
8	Turkey	116,209,000,000
9	India	100,367,000,000
10	Thailand	79,675,000,000

Source: *World Bank*, World Development Indicators 2002

BIGGEST EXPORTERS

	COUNTRY	EXPORTS (2000) ($)
1	USA	1,065,740,000,000
2	Germany	633,052,000,000
3	Japan	528,751,000,000
4	UK	401,385,000,000
5	France	377,274,000,000
6	Canada	321,693,000,000
7	Italy	294,852,000,000
8	China	279,562,000,000
9	Netherlands	258,951,000,000
10	Hong Kong (China)	244,004,000,000

Source: *World Bank*, World Development Indicators 2002

NOBEL ECONOMIC SCIENCES PRIZE-WINNING COUNTRIES

	COUNTRY	ECONOMIC SCIENCES PRIZES
1	USA	32
2	UK	7
3 =	Canada	2
=	Norway	2
=	Sweden	2
6 =	France	1
=	Germany	1
=	India	1
=	Israel	1
=	Netherlands	1
=	USSR	1

Workers of the World

COUNTRIES WITH THE HIGHEST PROPORTION OF CHILD WORKERS

	COUNTRY	10–14 YEAR OLDS AT WORK (2000) TOTAL	PERCENTAGE*
1	Mali	726,000	51.14
2	Bhutan	136,000	51.10
3	Burundi	445,000	48.50
4	Uganda	1,343,000	43.79
5	Niger	609,000	43.62
6	Burkina Faso	686,000	43.45
7	Ethiopia	3,277,000	42.45
8	Nepal	1,154,000	42.05
9	Rwanda	413,000	41.35
10	Kenya	1,699,000	39.15

* Excludes unpaid work

Source: *International Labour Organization*

It is estimated that there are some 21 million children aged from five to 14 working around the world, including as many as 111 million who are involved in tasks that are hazardous.

COUNTRIES WITH THE HIGHEST PROPORTION OF ELDERLY PEOPLE AT WORK

	COUNTRY	EST. PERCENTAGE OF OVER-64 YEAR OLDS ECONOMICALLY ACTIVE* (2000)
1	Mozambique	77.24
2	Malawi	74.85
3	Ghana	71.30
4	Central African Republic	70.91
5	Tanzania	69.80
6	Gambia	61.60
7	Uganda	61.01
8	Congo	60.07
9	Madagascar	57.92
10	Solomon Islands	57.91

* Excludes unpaid work

Source: *International Labour Organization*

The concept of retirement is a Western phenomenon that is unavailable to many, especially subsistence farmers in Africa.

COUNTRIES WITH THE LOWEST PROPORTION OF ELDERLY PEOPLE AT WORK

	COUNTRY	EST. PERCENTAGE OF OVER-64 YEAR OLDS ECONOMICALLY ACTIVE* (2000)
1	Hungary	0.46
2	Belgium	0.93
3	Netherlands	1.14
4	Luxembourg	1.16
5	Austria	1.26
6	France	1.52
7	Spain	2.04
8	Germany	2.30
9	Finland	2.35
10	Martinique	3.00
	World	18.77
	UK	4.42

* Excludes unpaid work

Source: *International Labour Organization*

COUNTRIES WITH THE MOST STRIKES AND LOCKOUTS, 2000

	COUNTRY	WORKERS INVOLVED	DAYS LOST	STRIKES AND LOCKOUTS
1	Denmark	75,656	124,800	1,081
2	Italy	687,000	884,100	966
3	Russia	31,000	236,400	817
4	Spain	2,067,287	3,616,907	750
5	Australia	325,400	469,100	698
6	India	689,592	16,720,762	656
7	Morocco	43,619	395,703	484
8	Tunisia	35,886	47,549	411
9	Canada	143,570	1,661,620	377
10	Guyana	no data	56,175	268
	UK	183,200	498,800	212

Source: *International Labour Organization*

Strikes are temporary work stoppages precipitated by workers attempting, for example, to enforce their demands, while lockouts involve the closure of workplaces.

COUNTRIES WITH THE HIGHEST PROPORTION OF FARMERS

	COUNTRY	WORKERS IN AGRICULTURE (2000) TOTAL	PERCENTAGE OF WORK FORCE
1	Bhutan	942,000	93
2 =	Burkina Faso	5,062,000	92
=	Nepal	10,109,000	92
4 =	Burundi	3,022,000	90
=	Rwanda	3,734,000	90
6	Niger	4,388,000	87
7 =	Ethiopia	22,891,000	82
=	Guinea Bissau	454,000	82
9 =	Mali	4,500,000	80
=	Uganda	9,130,000	80

Source: *Food and Agriculture Organization of the United Nations*

Despite a global trend towards urbanization, a very high proportion of the populations of many Asian and African countries depend on farming for their livelihoods.

TOP 10 COUNTRIES WITH THE HIGHEST PROPORTION OF WOMEN WORKING IN SERVICE INDUSTRIES

	COUNTRY	% FEMALE LABOUR FORCE IN SERVICES* (1998–2000)
1	Argentina	89
2	= Hong Kong (China)	88
	= Norway	88
	= Panama	88
5	= Canada	87
	= Sweden	87
	= UK	87
8	= Australia	86
	= Belgium	86
	= France	86
	= Israel	86
	= Peru	86
	= USA	86

* Service industries include wholesale and retail trade, restaurants and hotels; transport, storage, and communications; financing, insurance, real estate, and business services; and community, social, and personal services

Source: *World Bank*, World Development Indicators 2002

TOP 10 COUNTRIES WITH THE HIGHEST PROPORTION OF MEN WORKING IN SERVICE INDUSTRIES

	COUNTRY	% MALE LABOUR FORCE IN SERVICES* (1998–2000)
1	= Columbia	71
	= Hong Kong (China)	71
3	= Peru	67
	= Singapore	67
5	Argentina	65
6	= Australia	64
	= USA	64
8	= Canada	63
	= Ecuador	63
	= France	63
	= Morocco	63
	= Netherlands	63

* Service industries include wholesale and retail trade, restaurants and hotels; transport, storage, and communications; financing, insurance, real estate, and business services; and community, social, and personal services

Source: *World Bank*, World Development Indicators 2002

▶ **Leading the field**
The Himalayan kingdom of Bhutan tops the list of countries with the highest percentage of its people involved in agriculture, mainly growing rice, vegetables, and fruit.

THE 10 COUNTRIES WITH THE HIGHEST UNEMPLOYMENT

	COUNTRY	EST. % LABOUR FORCE UNEMPLOYED (2001*)
1	Liberia	70
2	Zimbabwe	60
3	= Djibouti	50
	= East Timor	50
	= Zambia	50
6	Senegal	48
7	Nepal	47
8	Lesotho	45
9	= Bosnia and Herzegovina	40
	= Botswana	40
	= Kenya	40
	UK	*5.1*

* Or latest year/those countries for which data available

Source: *CIA*, The World Factbook 2002

Hazards at Home & Work

THE 10 MOST COMMON CAUSES OF DOMESTIC FIRES IN THE UK

	CAUSE	% DOMESTIC FIRES
1	Pan of fat/oil catching fire	24
2	Grill pan	13
3	Leaving something in the oven/ on the hob for too long	7
4	Arson	6
5	= Candles	5
	= Chimney fires	5
	= Leaving something too close to the cooker	5
8	Toaster	4
9	Electric wiring worn out or faulty	3
10	= Microwave	2
	= Cigarette/cigar smoking	2

Source: 2000 British Crime Survey

THE 10 MOST COMMON ACCIDENTS IN UK HOMES

	ACCIDENT	ACCIDENTS (1999)*
1	Tripping over	419,372
2	Contact with static object	292,823
3	Falls on or from stairs or steps	290,536
4	Cut or tear from sharp object	273,161
5	Struck by moving object	156,947
6	Foreign body	134,377
7	Thermal effect	100,010
8	Pinched or crushed by blunt object	95,565
9	Acute overexertion	88,633
10	Bite/sting	74,806

* National estimates based on actual Home Accident Surveillance System figures for sample population

◄ **Flash in the pan**
Notoriously easy to start and equally hard to quench, more than one household in every hundred experiences an annual chip pan fire.

170

THE 10 COUNTRIES WITH THE MOST FATAL INJURIES AT WORK

	COUNTRY	FATAL INJURIES PER 100,000 WORKERS (2000)
1	Austria	39.0
2	Canada	31.2
3	India	31.0
4	Turkey	24.6
5	Argentina	18.6
6	Tunisia	15.1
7 =	Chile	14.0
=	Mexico	14.0*
9	Togo	11.7
10	Brazil	11.5
	UK	0.9

* Partial data

Source: International Labour Organization

THE 10 WORST INDUSTRIAL DISASTERS*

	LOCATION/DATE	INCIDENT	NO. KILLED
1	**Bhopal,** India, 3 December 1984	Methyl isocyanate gas escape at Union Carbide plant	up to 3,849
2	**Jesse,** Nigeria, 17 October 1998	Oil pipeline explosion	more than 700
3	**Oppau,** Germany, 21 September 1921	Chemical plant explosion	561
4	**San Juanico,** Mexico, 19 November 1984	Explosion at a PEMEX liquified petroleum gas plant	540
5	**Cubatão,** Brazil, 25 February 1984	Oil pipeline explosion	508
6	**Durunkah,** Egypt, 2 November 1994	Fuel storage depot fire	more than 500
7	**Novosibirsk,** USSR, precise date unknown, April 1979	Anthrax infection following an accident at a biological and chemical warfare plant	up to 300
8	**Adeje,** Nigeria, 10 July 2000	Oil pipeline explosion	250
9	**Guadalajara,** Mexico, 22 April 1992	Explosions caused by a gas leak into sewers	230
10	**Ludwigshafen,** Germany, 28 July 1948	Dimethyl ether explosion in a lacquer plant	184

* Including industrial sites, factories, and fuel depots and pipelines; excluding military, munitions, bombs, mining, marine and other transport disasters, dam failures, and mass poisonings

THE 10 COUNTRIES WITH THE MOST INJURIES AT WORK

	COUNTRY	NON-FATAL INJURIES PER 100,000 WORKERS (2000)
1	Costa Rica	15,994
2	Chile	7,964
3	Argentina	7,747
4	Spain	7,549
5	Portugal	5,471
6	Slovenia	5,091
7	Nicaragua	4,150
8	Italy	4,030
9	Germany	4,001
10	Tunisia	3,962
	UK	645

Source: International Labour Organization

Work injuries are those sustained during the course of employment, including acts of violence, but excluding long-term occupational diseases or accidents while travelling to and from work.

THE 10 MOST DANGEROUS INDUSTRIES FOR EMPLOYEES IN GREAT BRITAIN

	INDUSTRY	FATAL AND MAJOR INJURIES PER 100,000 EMPLOYEES (2000–01*)
1	Transport, storage, and communication#	557.3
2	Mining and quarrying	431.8
3	Manufacturing: wood and wood products	406.3
4	Construction	384.8
5	Manufacturing: non-metallic mineral products	301.1
6	Manufacturing: basic metals and fabricated metal products	294.5
7	Manufacturing: food products, beverages, and tobacco	278.0
8	Manufacturing: rubber and plastic products	272.9
9	Agriculture, hunting, forestry, and fishing	211.6
10	Manufacturing: transport equipment	186.9
	Average for all industries	108.1

* Provisional

Shore-based only

Source: Health and Safety Executive

In the period 2000–01, there were 156,104 workplace injuries in Great Britain. Of these, 213 were fatal, 26,547 non-fatal major injuries, with a further 129,344 requiring more than three days off work. The industry recording the highest rate of fatal injuries to workers is the quarrying of stone, ore, and clay: of an estimated 87,000 workers, nine were killed, equivalent to 10.4 deaths per 100,000 employees.

Advertising & Brands

TOP 10 ADVERTISING CATEGORIES

	CATEGORY	EST. GLOBAL ADVERTISING EXPENDITURE (2001) ($)
1	Automotives	19,334,400,000
2	Food	11,220,700,000
3	Personal care	10,300,200,000
4	Electronics, computers	6,557,500,000
5	Media and entertainment	6,285,400,000
6	Pharmaceuticals	5,655,800,000
7	Fast food	2,989,400,000
8	Household cleaners	2,203,500,000
9	Telecommunications	1,733,000,000
10	Financial services, credit	1,156,300,000

Source: Ad Age Special Report, *11 November, 2002*

TOP 10 TYPES OF ADVERTISING IN THE UK

	TYPE OF ADVERTISING	AD SPEND (2001) (£)
1	Television	4,147,000,000
2	Regional newspapers	2,834,000,000
3	Direct mail	2,228,000,000
4	National newspapers	2,071,000,000
5	Business and professional journals	1,202,000,000
6	Directories	959,000,000
7	Outdoor and transport	788,000,000
8	Consumer magazines	779,000,000
9	Radio	541,000,000
10	Internet	166,000,000

Source: *The Advertising Association*

FIRST TV SOAP AD!

FIRST FACT

THE FIRST TELEVISION BROADCAST of a live Major League baseball match was also the occasion of the first screening of a soap advertisement. The two events took place on 21 August 1939, when the Brooklyn Dodgers met the Cincinnati Reds at Ebbets Field, Brooklyn, New York. TV station W2XBS broadcast the event, but since television was in its infancy, barely 400 people, all in New York, were able to tune in. Those who did saw an advertisement for Procter & Gamble's Ivory Soap.

TOP 10 GLOBAL MARKETERS

	COMPANY/BASE	MEASURED MEDIA SPEND* (2001) ($)
1	Procter & Gamble Company, USA	3,820,100,000
2	General Motors Corporation, USA	3,028,900,000
3	Unilever, Netherlands/UK	3,005,500,000
4	Ford Motor Company, USA	2,309,000,000
5	Toyota Motor Corporation, Japan	2,213,300,000
6	AOL Time Warner, USA	2,099,800,000
7	Philip Morris Companies, USA	1,934,600,000
8	DaimlerChrysler, Germany/USA	1,835,300,000
9	Nestlé, Switzerland	1,798,500,000
10	Volkswagen, Germany	1,574,100,000

* Includes magazines, newspapers, outdoor, television, radio, internet, and Yellow Pages

Source: Ad Age Global

◄ **Car production**
With cars being one of the costliest of all items of consumer expenditure, advertising budgets for cars figure prominently among the highest for any products.

TOP 10 — MOST ADVERTISED GROCERY BRANDS IN THE UK

	BRAND	BRAND OWNER	AD SPEND (£)*
1	Coca-Cola	Coca-Cola GB	16,497,785
2	Guinness	Diageo	14,011,798
3	Budweiser	Anheuser-Busch	12,029,073
4	Carling	Coors Brewers	11,634,153
5	KitKat	Nestlé Rowntree	9,101,181
6	Nescafé	Nestlé	8,983,839
7	Red Bull	Red Bull	8,701,851
8	Stella Artois	Interbrew	8,158,371
9	Smirnoff	Diageo	7,399,756
10	Pantene Pro-V	Procter & Gamble	7,394,697

In year to August 2002

Source: Checkout/ACNielsen MMS

TOP 10 — MOST VALUABLE GLOBAL BRANDS

	BRAND NAME*	INDUSTRY	BRAND VALUE (2002) ($)
1	Coca-Cola	Beverages	69,637,000,000
2	Microsoft	Technology	64,091,000,000
3	IBM	Technology	51,188,000,000
4	General Electric	Diversified	41,311,000,000
5	Intel	Technology	30,861,000,000
6	Nokia, Finland	Technology	29,970,000,000
7	Disney	Leisure	29,256,000,000
8	McDonald's	Food retail	26,375,000,000
9	Marlboro	Tobacco	24,151,000,000
10	Mercedes, Germany	Automobiles	21,010,000,000

All US-owned unless otherwise stated

Source: Interbrand/Business Week

Brand consultants Interbrand use a method of estimating value that takes account of the profitability of individual brands within a business (rather than the companies that own them), as well as such factors as their potential for growth. Well over half of the 75 most valuable global brands surveyed by Interbrand are US-owned, with Europe accounting for another 30 per cent.

▶ **Things go better...**
The Coca-Cola brand stands alone as a symbol of American culture, the most valued international beverage and one of the bestselling products in the world.

Shopping Lists

TOP 10 GLOBAL RETAILERS

	COMPANY/COUNTRY	RETAIL SALES (2001*) ($)
1	**Wal-Mart,** USA	217,799,000,000
2	**Carrefour,** France	61,565,000,000
3	**Ahold,** Netherlands	57,976,000,000
4	**Home Depot,** USA	53,553,000,000
5	**Kroger Co.,** USA	50,098,000,000
6	**METRO AG,** Germany	43,357,000,000
7	**Target,** USA	39,455,000,000
8	**Albertson's,** USA	37,931,000,000
9	**Kmart,** USA	36,151,000,000
10	**Sears, Roebuck,** USA	35,843,000,000

* Financial year

Source: Stores *magazine* Top 200 Global Retailers

Formed in 1887, Sears Roebuck flourished to become the world's largest mail-order company, before opening its first stores in the 1920s.

TOP 10 SUPERMARKET COUNTRIES

	COUNTRY	SPENDING PER CAPITA (2000) ($)
1	**USA**	1,600.2
2	**UK**	1,366.5
3	**Sweden**	1,339.2
4	**Switzerland**	1,318.9
5	**Australia**	1,301.7
6	**Norway**	1,234.6
7	**Japan**	1,229.4
8	**Netherlands**	1,087.9
9	**Canada**	1,077.9
10	**Belgium**	1,051.0
	World	*244.6*

Source: *Euromonitor*

TOP 10 WORLD RETAIL SECTORS

	SECTOR	COMPANIES*
1	**Speciality**	96
2	**Supermarket**	81
3	**Department**	54
4	**Hypermarket**	42
5	**Discount**	39
6	**Convenience**	26
7	**Superstore**	24
8 =	**Mail order**	21
=	**DIY**	21
10	**Food service**	20

* Of those listed in Stores *magazine* Top 200 Global Retailers; *stores can operate in more than one area*

Source: Stores *magazine*

TOP 10 COUNTRIES WITH THE MOST SHOPS

	COUNTRY	SHOPS (2000)
1	**China**	19,306,800
2	**India**	10,537,080
3	**Brazil**	1,595,062
4	**Japan**	1,240,237
5	**Mexico**	1,087,995
6	**Spain**	780,247
7	**Vietnam**	727,268
8	**South Korea**	704,032
9	**Italy**	697,853
10	**USA**	685,367
	World	*44,443,840*
	UK	*311,844*

Source: *Euromonitor*

Less-developed countries tend to have a high ratio of small stores to population: China has 1 store per 67 people, whereas the ratio in the USA is 1 to 400.

► **Street trader**
India's tradition of entrepreneurship and trade has given rise to a culture in which small shops play a prominent part.

TOP 10 INTERNET RETAILERS

	COMPANY	WEBSITE	EST. US SALES ($)*
1	eBay	eBay.com	3,500–3,700,000,000
2	Amazon.com	amazon.com	1,700–1,900,000,000
3	Dell	dell.com	1,100–1,300,000,000
4	buy.com	buy.com	700–800,000,000
5 =	Egghead.com (formerly OnSale.com)	Egghead.com	500–600,000,000
=	Gateway	Gateway.com	500–600,000,000
7	Quixtar	Quixtar.com	400–450,000,000
8 =	Barnes & Noble	bn.com	275–325,000,000
=	uBid.com	uBid.com	275–325,000,000
10 =	Cyberian Outpost	Outpost.com	200–250,000,000
=	MicroWarehouse	MicroWarehouse.com	200–250,000,000
∞	Value America#	va.com	200–250,000,000

* In latest financial year surveyed   # Ceased retail operations

Source: Stores/*Verifone and Russell Reynold Associates'* Top 100 Internet Retailers, Sept 2001 © NRF Enterprises, Inc.

TOP 10 SPECIALITY RETAILERS

	COMPANY/HEADQUARTERS	SPECIALITY	RETAIL SALES (2001) ($)
1	Home Depot, Inc., USA	Home improvement supplies	53,553,000,000
2	Lowe's Companies, Inc., USA	Home improvement supplies	22,111,000,000
3	AutoNation, Inc., USA	Car dealers	19,989,000,000
4	Best Buy Co. Inc., USA	Consumer electronics	19,597,000,000
5	The Gap, Inc., USA	Clothing	13,848,000,000
6	Circuit City Stores, Inc., USA	Consumer electronics	12,791,000,000
7	TJX Companies, Inc., USA	Clothing and accessories	10,709,000,000
8	Toys "R" Us, Inc., USA	Toys	11,019,000,000
9	IKEA, Sweden	Home furnishing	10,359,000,000
10	Staples, Inc., USA	Office supplies	10,100,000,000

Source: Stores *magazine* Top 200 Global Retailers

TOP 10 MAIL-ORDER COUNTRIES

	COUNTRY	SPENDING PER CAPITA (2000) ($)
1	USA	520.6
2	Germany	228.6
3	UK	198.6
4	Denmark	171.7
5	Switzerland	149.1
6	Austria	137.4
7	France	111.7
8	Norway	109.2
9	Sweden	102.8
10	Finland	56.5

Source: *Euromonitor*

Despite a general global market slowdown, driven by new technologies such as the internet, the mail-order sector in many countries is growing: in the UK, for example, after dipping in 2000 (the latest year for which comparative country data are available), it expanded by 6.8 per cent in 2001 to reach a total value of almost £10.8 billion.

Rich Lists

TOP 10 RICHEST AMERICAN MEN

	NAME	SOURCE	NET WORTH ($)
1	William H. Gates III	Microsoft	40,700,000,000
2	Warren Edward Buffett	Berkshire Hathaway	30,500,000,000
3	Paul Gardner Allen	Microsoft	20,100,000,000
4	Lawrence Joseph Ellison	Oracle	16,600,000,000
5 =	Jim C. Walton	Wal-Mart	16,500,000,000
=	John T. Walton	Wal-Mart	16,500,000,000
=	S. Robson Walton	Wal-Mart	16,500,000,000
8	Steven Anthony Ballmer	Microsoft	11,100,000,000
9	John Werner Kluge	Metromedia	10,500,000,000
10 =	Forrest E. Mars Jr.	Mars Inc.	10,000,000,000
=	John F. Mars	Mars Inc.	10,000,000,000

Source: Forbes *magazine*, The World's Richest People, *27 February 2003*

TOP 10 RICHEST NON-AMERICAN MEN*

	NAME/COUNTRY	SOURCE	NET WORTH ($)
1	Karl and Theo Albrecht, Germany	Retail	25,600,000,000
2	Prince Alwaleed Bin Talal Alsaud, Saudi Arabia	Investments	17,700,000,000
3	Kenneth Thomson and family, Canada	Publishing	14,000,000,000
4	Ingvar Kamprad, Sweden	Ikea	13,000,000,000
5	Amancio Ortega, Spain	Clothing	10,300,000,000
6	Mikhail B. Khodorkovsky, Russia	Banking and oil	8,000,000,000
7	Li Ka-shing, Hong Kong	Diversified	7,800,000,000
8	Hans Rausing, Sweden	Packaging	7,700,000,000
9	Gerald Cavendish Grosvenor (Duke of Westminster), UK	Land and property	7,500,000,000
10	Carlos Slim Helu, Mexico	Telecom	7,400,000,000

* *Excluding rulers*

Source: Forbes *magazine*, The World's Richest People, *27 February 2003*

TOP 10 RICHEST UK CITIZENS

	NAME	SOURCE	NET WORTH (£)
1	Duke of Westminster	Land and property	7,500,000,000
2	Bernie and Slavica Ecclestone	Formula One motor racing	3,200,000,000
3	Lord Sainsbury and family	Retailing	3,000,000,000
4	Clive Calder	Music industry	2,300,000,000
5	Earl Cadogan and family	Property	2,100,000,000
6 =	Richard Branson	Travel, retailing, and entertainment	1,700,000,000
=	Kenneth Morrison and family	Supermarkets	1,700,000,000
8 =	Philip Green	Retailing	1,400,000,000
=	Adrian Swire and family	Trading	1,400,000,000
10	Bruno Schroder and family	Banking	1,200,000,000

Source: Forbes *magazine*, The World's Richest People, *27 February 2003*

◀ **World's richest**
Microsoft founder Bill Gates III has led both the list of the richest Americans and that of the world's richest people for the past 10 years.

TOP 10 RICHEST WOMEN*

	NAME/COUNTRY[#]	SOURCE	NET WORTH ($)
1 =	Alice L. Walton	Wal-Mart	16,500,000,000
=	Helen R. Walton	Wal-Mart	16,500,000,000
3	Liliane Bettencourt, France	L'Oreal	14,500,000,000
4	Birgit Rausing and family, Sweden	Inheritance/Packaging	12,900,000,000
5 =	Barbara Cox Anthony	Media	10,300,000,000
=	Anne Cox Chambers	Media	10,300,000,000
7	Jacqueline Mars	Mars Inc.	10,000,000,000
8	Abigail Johnson	Mutual funds	8,200,000,000
9	Susanne Klatten, Germany	Inheritance	5,300,000,000
10	Maria-Elisabeth and Georg Schaeffler (mother and son)	Roller bearings	3,800,000,000

* Excluding rulers

[#] All from USA unless otherwise specified

Source: Forbes magazine, The World's Richest People, 27 February 2003

TOP 10 BEST-PAID CELEBRITIES

	CELEBRITY	PROFESSION	EARNINGS (2001–02*) ($)
1	George Lucas	Film producer/director	200,000,000
2	Oprah Winfrey	TV host/producer	150,000,000
3	Steven Spielberg	Film producer/director	100,000,000
4 =	Tiger Woods	Golfer	69,000,000
=	U2	Rock band	69,000,000
6	Michael Schumacher	Racing driver	67,000,000
7	Mariah Carey	Pop singer	58,000,000
8	Stephen King	Writer/director	52,400,000
9	Dave Matthews Band	Rock band	50,000,000
10	Tom Clancy	Writer	47,800,000

* June 2001–June 2002

Source: Forbes magazine, The Celebrity 100

TOP 10 BEST-PAID PEOPLE IN THE UK

	NAME	SOURCE	EARNINGS (2001–02*) (£)
1	Philip Green	BHS	157,700,000
2	John Frieda	Hair products	153,000,000
3	Peter Prowting	Construction	88,500,000
4	Allen McClay	Pharmaceuticals	66,135,000
5	Chris Ingram	TV and media	64,934,000
6 =	Frank Brake	Food	63,705,000
=	Wanda Brake	Food	63,705,000
8	Stelios Haji-Ioannou	EasyJet	63,451,000
9	William Brake	Food	59,692,000
10	John Salmon	Technology	58,261,000

* 1 October 2001–30 September 2002

Source: The Sunday Times Magazine, 3 November 2002

▶ **Super celebrity**
Oprah Winfrey has consistently featured among – sometimes topping – the list of highest-earning celebrities since the 1980s.

Energy & Environment

TOP 10 PAPER-RECYCLING COUNTRIES

	COUNTRY	PRODUCTION PER 1,000 PEOPLE (2001) (TONNES)
1	Switzerland	167.36
2	Sweden	164.61
3	Austria	157.77
4	Netherlands	155.30
5	USA	144.14
6	Germany	140.55
7	Finland	134.80
8	Japan	116.55
9	Norway	98.26
10	France	93.62
	UK	89.77

Source: *Food and Agriculture Organization of the United Nations*

TOP 10 COUNTRIES WITH THE GREATEST CRUDE OIL RESERVES

	COUNTRY	2001 RESERVES (TONNES)
1	Saudi Arabia	36,000,000,000
2	Iraq	15,100,000,000
3	Kuwait	13,300,000,000
4	United Arab Emirates	13,000,000,000
5	Iran	12,300,000,000
6	Venezuela	11,200,000,000
7	Russia	6,700,000,000
8 =	Libya	3,800,000,000
=	Mexico	3,800,000,000
10	USA	3,700,000,000
	UK	700,000,000

Source: *BP Amoco Statistical Review of World Energy 2002*

TOP 10 CARBON DIOXIDE-EMITTING COUNTRIES

	COUNTRY	CO_2 EMISSIONS PER CAPITA (2001) (TONNES OF CARBON)
1	Qatar	13.66
2	United Arab Emirates	13.31
3	Bahrain	9.47
4	Kuwait	8.32
5	Singapore	7.57
6	Trinidad and Tobago	6.25
7	Luxembourg	5.61
8	USA	5.51
9	Canada	5.22
10	Guam	5.18
	UK	2.59

Source: *Energy Information Administration*

TOP 10 ENERGY-CONSUMING COUNTRIES

	COUNTRY	ENERGY CONSUMPTION (2001*)					
		OIL	GAS	COAL	NUCLEAR	HEP#	TOTAL
1	USA	895.6	554.6	555.7	183.2	48.3	2,237.3
2	China	231.9	24.9	520.6	4.0	58.3	839.7
3	Russia	122.3	335.4	114.6	30.9	39.8	643.0
4	Japan	247.2	71.1	103.0	72.7	20.4	514.5
5	Germany	131.6	74.6	84.4	38.7	5.8	335.2
6	India	71.1	23.7	173.5	4.4	16.1	314.7
7	Canada	88.0	65.4	28.9	17.4	75.0	274.6
8	France	95.8	36.6	10.9	94.9	18.1	256.4
9	UK	76.1	85.9	40.3	20.4	1.5	224.0
10	South Korea	103.1	20.8	45.7	25.4	0.9	195.9
	World	3,510.6	2,164.3	2,255.1	601.2	594.5	9,124.8

* *Millions of tonnes of oil equivalent*

\# *Hydroelectric power*

Source: *BP Amoco Statistical Review of World Energy 2002*

◄ **Paper chase**
Every tonne of recycled paper uses 64 per cent less energy and 50 per cent less water, causes 74 per cent less air pollution, and saves 17 trees compared with the same quantity derived from new wood pulp.

TOP 10 COUNTRIES WITH THE MOST RELIANCE ON NUCLEAR POWER

	COUNTRY	NUCLEAR ELECTRICITY AS PERCENTAGE OF TOTAL ELECTRICITY (2001)
1	Lithuania	78
2	France	77
3	Belgium	58
4	Slovakia	53
5	Ukraine	46
6	Sweden	44
7	Bulgaria	42
8 =	Hungary	39
=	Slovenia	39
=	South Korea	39
	UK	23

Source: *International Atomic Energy Agency*

TOP 10 ALTERNATIVE POWER*-CONSUMING COUNTRIES

	COUNTRY	KW/HR CONSUMPTION (2001)
1	USA	84,800,000,000
2	Germany	22,600,000,000
3	Japan	19,100,000,000
4	Brazil	14,800,000,000
5	Philippines	12,200,000,000
6	Spain	9,200,000,000
7	Finland	8,400,000,000
8 =	Italy	7,800,000,000
=	Luxembourg	7,800,000,000
10	Canada	7,200,000,000
	UK	5,700,000,000

* Includes geothermal, solar, wind, wood, and waste electric power

Source: *Energy Information Administration*

◄ **Wind power**
Some countries have taken the lead in the amount of electricity they generate by wind turbines: Germany's capacity is now double that of the USA.

Science & Technology

TOP 10 **INTERNATIONAL COMPANIES FOR RESEARCH AND DEVELOPMENT**

	COMPANY/COUNTRY	INDUSTRY	R&D SPENDING (2001) ($)
1	**Ford Motor,** USA	Automobiles and parts	7,400,000,000
2	**General Motors,** USA	Automobiles and parts	6,200,000,000
3	**Siemens,** Germany	Electronic and electrical	5,980,550,000
4	**DaimlerChrysler,** Germany	Automobiles and parts	5,231,880,000
5	**Pfizer,** USA	Pharmaceuticals	4,847,000,000
6	**IBM,** USA	Software and IT services	4,620,000,000
7	**Ericsson,** Sweden	IT hardware	4,410,410,000
8	**Microsoft,** USA	Software and IT services	4,379,000,000
9	**Motorola,** USA	IT hardware	4,318,000,000
10	**Matsushita Electric,** Japan	Electronic and electrical	4,310,440,000

Source: *The Financial Times Ltd, 2002*

The 300 international companies featured in the *Financial Times*' survey spent a total of $267.6 trillion on research and development. Of them, some 70 firms spent in excess of $1 billion a year, with motor manufacturers representing the most prominent among the world's biggest R&D spenders.

TOP 10 **INDUSTRIES FOR RESEARCH AND DEVELOPMENT**

	INDUSTRY	R&D SPENDING (2001) ($)
1	**IT hardware**	69,687,090,000
2	**Automobiles and parts**	47,877,160,000
3	**Pharmaceuticals**	46,553,340,000
4	**Electronic and electrical**	28,751,540,000
5	**Software and IT services**	15,925,250,000
6	**Chemicals**	11,725,580,000
7	**Aerospace and defence**	11,367,060,000
8	**Engineering and machinery**	5,941,040,000
9	**Telecommunications**	5,898,190,000
10	**Health**	4,727,640,000

Source: *The Financial Times Ltd, 2002*

▼ **Chips with everything**
With one computer for every 10 people in the world, the workplace has undergone a transformation, although the true "paperless office" remains a rarity.

THE 10 **FIRST PATENTS IN THE UK**

	PATENT	PATENTEE(S)	PATENT DATE
1	**Engraving and printing the king's head on documents**	Nicholas Hillyard	5 May 1617
2	**Locks, mills, and other river and canal improvements**	John Gason	1 July 1617
3	**Oil for suits of armour**	John Miller and John Jasper Wolfen	3 Nov 1617
4	**Tunnels and pumps**	Robert Crumpe	9 Jan 1618
5	**Making maps of English cities**	Aaron Rathburne and Roger Burges	11 Mar 1618
6	**River dredger**	John Gilbert	16 July 1618
7	**Water-powered engine for making nails**	Clement Dawbeney	11 Dec 1618
8	**Sword blades**	Thomas Murray	11 Jan 1619
9	**Ploughs, pumps, and ships' engines**	Thomas Wildgoose and David Ramsey	17 Jan 1619
10	**Smalt (glass) manufacture**	Abram Baker	16 Feb 1619

The first patent granted in England dates from 1449, when John of Utynam received a patent by Henry VI for making glass for the windows of Eton College. The system was not codified until 1617, and this list of the first 10 patents issued under this system gives some indication of the diverse range of inventions being developed even at this early date.

TOP 10 COUNTRIES WITH THE HIGHEST PROPORTION OF COMPUTER USERS

	COUNTRY	TOTAL	COMPUTERS (2001) PER 100 INHABITANTS
1	**USA**	178,000,000	62.25
2	**Sweden**	5,000,000	56.12
3	**Australia**	10,000,000	51.71
4	**Luxembourg**	230,000	51.45
5	**Singapore**	2,100,000	50.83
6	**Norway**	2,300,000	50.80
7	**Switzerland**	3,600,000	49.97
8	**Denmark**	2,300,000	43.15
9	**Netherlands**	6,900,000	42.85
10	**Finland**	2,200,000	42.35
	World	*455,366,000*	*7.74*
	UK	*22,000,000*	*36.62*

Source: *International Telecommunication Union,* World Telecommunication Development Report, 2002

TOP 10 COUNTRIES REGISTERING THE MOST PATENTS

	COUNTRY	PATENTS REGISTERED (2000)
1	**USA**	157,496
2	**Japan**	125,880
3	**Germany**	41,585
4	**France**	36,404
5	**South Korea**	34,956
6	**UK**	33,756
7	**Italy**	19,652
8	**Russia**	17,592
9	**Netherlands**	17,052
10	**Spain**	15,809

Source: *World Intellectual Property Organization*

This international list provides a yardstick of the state of each nation's technological development. A further 35,357 patents were granted by the European Patent Office, which has no national affiliation.

TOP 10 MOST VALUABLE TECHNOLOGY BRANDS*

	BRAND NAME/COUNTRY	BRAND VALUE (2002) ($)
1	**Microsoft,** USA	64,091,000,000
2	**IBM,** USA	51,188,000,000
3	**Intel,** USA	30,861,000,000
4	**Nokia,** Finland	29,970,000,000
5	**Hewlett-Packard,** USA	16,780,000,000
6	**Cisco,** USA	16,220,000,000
7	**AT&T,** USA	16,060,000,000
8	**Sony,** Japan	13,900,000,000
9	**Oracle,** USA	11,510,000,000
10	**Compaq,** USA	9,800,000,000

* *Includes computer, telecommunications, and consumer electronics brands*

Source: *Interbrand*/Business Week

Brand consultants Interbrand use a method of estimating value that takes account of the profitability of individual brands within a business (rather than the companies that own them), as well as such factors as their potential for growth.

TOP 10 NOBEL PHYSICS PRIZE-WINNING COUNTRIES

	COUNTRY	PHYSICS PRIZES
1	**USA**	73
2	= **Germany**	21
	= **UK**	21
4	**France**	12
5	**Netherlands**	8
6	**USSR**	7
7	= **Japan**	4
	= **Sweden**	4
9	= **Austria**	3
	= **Denmark**	3
	= **Italy**	3

World Wide Web

TOP 10 | MOST WIRED CITIES

	CITY/COUNTRY	COUNTRIES CONNECTED	INTERNATIONAL INTERNET BANDWIDTH (MBPS)(2001)
1	**London,** UK	61	237,389.2
2	**Paris,** France	48	179,064.8
3	**New York,** USA	71	173,098.6
4	**Amsterdam,** Netherlands	27	170,371.8
5	**Frankfurt,** Germany	28	160,459.0
6	**Brussels,** Belgium	17	76,246.4
7	**Stockholm,** Sweden	18	60,349.0
8	**Copenhagen,** Denmark	13	43,456.0
9	**Milan,** Italy	15	29,701.8
10	**Toronto,** Canada	6	24,942.3

Source: *TeleGeography*

These are the top cities in the world for connection to the internet. New York has direct connections with 71 countries, and has the highest bandwidth capacity of any city in the world

TOP 10 | INTERNET FRAUDS, 2002

	CATEGORY	% ALL COMPLAINTS*
1	**Online auctions**	90
2	**General merchandise**	5
3	**Nigerian money offers**	4
4	**Computer equipment/software**	0.5
5	**Internet access services**	0.4
6 =	**Work-at-home plans**	more than 0.1
=	**Information/adult services**	more than 0.1
=	**Advance-fee loans**	more than 0.1
=	**Travel/vacations**	more than 0.1
=	**Prizes/sweepstakes**	more than 0.1

Source: *National Fraud Information Center, National Consumers League*

The overall loss in the USA to internet fraud in 2002 was $14,647,933, with an average loss (per victim of internet fraud) of $468.

TOP 10 COUNTRIES WITH THE MOST INTERNET USERS

	COUNTRY	INTERNET USERS*
1	USA	168,600,000
2	Japan	56,000,000
3	China	45,800,000
4	Germany	41,800,000
5	UK	30,400,000
6	Italy	25,300,000
7	France	23,000,000
8	Brazil	19,700,000
9	Spain	17,000,000
10	Canada	16,840,000
	World	*580,000,000*

* Estimate, as at 14 March 2003

Source: *CyberAtlas/Nielsen/NetRatings*

◄ **Cyber café**
The arrival of internet cafés in 1984 heralded a new era of communications and information gathering for people on the move, those lacking personal internet access, or as a social activity.

TOP 10 COUNTRIES WITH THE HIGHEST DENSITY OF INTERNET HOSTS

	COUNTRY	INTERNET HOSTS PER 1,000 PEOPLE (2001)
1	USA	371.40
2	Tonga	209.00
3	Iceland	190.48
4	Finland	170.72
5	Netherlands	163.47
6	Australia	118.34
7	New Zealand	104.95
8	Denmark	104.53
9	Canada	93.19
10	Sweden	82.51
	UK	*37.13*

Source: *International Telecommunication Union*, World Telecommunciation Development Report, 2002

An internet host is a computer system connected to the internet – either a single terminal directly connected, or a computer that allows multiple users to access network services through it. The ratio of hosts to population is a crude measure of how "wired" a country is.

TOP 10 WEBSITES IN THE UK, 2002

	WEBSITE	ESTIMATED VISITS IN UK (2002)
1	msn.com	704,000,000
2	passport.com	449,000,000
3	yahoo.com	413,000,000
4	msn.co.uk	379,000,000
5	yahoo.co.uk	354,000,000
6	google.com	341,000,000
7	bbc.co.uk	318,000,000
8	btopenworld.com	317,000,000
9	aol.com	284,000,000
10	freeserve.com	276,000,000

Source: *Nielsen/NetRatings*

The UK's Top 10 domains by number of visits is based on estimates of the "unique audience" – individuals identified by their internet address – of each, factoring in the number of visits made per person, and multiplying this over the course of the whole year. Those providing search engines fared especially well.

WORLD WIDE WORDS

BOTH THE INTERNET AND ITS language have evolved over the past 40 years. "Hypertext" was first proposed as early as 1965 by Ted Nelson. Ray Tomlinson pioneered and named e-mail in 1971 and the following year advocated the use of the "@" sign. The first "smiley" [:-)]or emoticon was used by Scott E. Fahlman on a Carnegie Mellon University Bulletin Board in 1982, the same year that William Gibson invented the term "cyberspace" in his novel *Neuromancer*. The "World Wide Web", and its name, were devised by Tim Berners-Lee in 1990, and the description "surfing the internet" was coined in 1992 by Jean Armour Polly.

TOP 10 MOST SEARCHED TERMS OF ALL TIME ON LYCOS

	TERM	WEEKS ON LIST*
1	= Pamela Anderson	188
	= Britney Spears	188
	= Dragonball	188
	= Las Vegas	188
	= Tattoos	188
	= Jennifer Lopez	188
	= WWF	188
8	Final Fantasy	186
9	The Bible	185
10	Harry Potter	143

* Continuous runs only; as at 22 March 2003

Source: *Lycos 50*

TOP 10 SEARCH ENGINES

	SEARCH ENGINE	SEARCHES PER DAY*
1	Google	112,000,000
2	AOL Search	93,000,000
3	Yahoo	42,000,000
4	MSN Search	32,000,000
5	Ask Jeeves	14,000,000
6	InfoSpace	7,000,000
7	= AltaVista	5,000,000
	= Overture	5,000,000
9	Netscape	4,000,000
10	Earthlink	3,000,000

* As of Januaray 2003, US traffic only; estimated by dividing search hours per month by 30 to get the number of minutes per day, and assuming that a typical search takes 20 seconds

Source: SearchEngineWatch.com

Keep in Touch

▲ **Syncom IV (LEASAT) satellite**
Since the mid-1960s, satellites launched into geostationary orbit have enabled international telecommunications to become one of the fastest growing industries on Earth – and beyond.

TOP 10 COUNTRIES MAKING THE MOST INTERNATIONAL PHONE CALLS

	COUNTRY	MINUTES (2000) PER HEAD	TOTAL
1	USA	125.9	34,640,700,000
2	Germany	112.1	9,223,000,000
3	UK	133.5	7,981,000,000
4	Canada	234.9	7,224,000,000
5	France	84.1	4,952,000,000
6	Hong Kong	466.8	3,142,400,000
7	Netherlands	177.0	2,830,000,000
8	Italy	47.8	2,740,000,000
9	Japan	20.3	2,575,000,000
10	Spain	64.1	2,570,000,000

Source: *International Telecommunication Union, World Telecommunication Development Report, 2002*

Dividing international call minutes by the number of inhabitants provides a somewhat different picture, in which Bermuda leads the world with 944.1 minutes per capita, compared with the USA's 125.9.

TOP 10 INTERNATIONAL TELECOMMUNICATIONS CARRIERS

	COMPANY/ORIGIN COUNTRY	OUTGOING TRAFFIC (2001) (MINUTES)
1	**AT&T Corp,** USA	12,006,800,000
2	**WorldCom,** USA	11,454,700,000
3	**Sprint,** USA	5,384,400,000
4	**Deutsche Telekom,** Germany	5,025,100,000
5	**France Télécom,** France	4,592,000,000
6	**BT,** UK	4,233,500,000
7	**Cable & Wireless,** UK	3,113,800,000
8	**Telefónica,** Spain	3,084,800,000
9	**Telecom Italia,** Italy	3,042,000,000
10	**China Telecom,** China	2,600,000,000

Source: *TeleGeography*

In 2001, the Top 10 and other international telecommunications carriers handled an estimated total of 144 billion minutes of outgoing traffic – equivalent to more than 23 minutes for every person on the planet.

TOP 10 COUNTRIES WITH THE MOST POST OFFICES

	COUNTRY	AVERAGE NO. OF PEOPLE SERVED PER OFFICE	TOTAL NO. OF POST OFFICES (2001*)
1	India	6,568	154,919
2	China	22,490	57,135
3	Russia	3,546	41,052
4	USA	7,471	38,123
5	Japan	5,143	24,760
6	Indonesia	10,806	19,881
7	UK	3,377	17,633
8	France	3,469	17,067
9	Ukraine	3,282	14,963
10	Italy	4,203	13,788

* Or latest year for which data available

Source: *Universal Postal Union*

There are some 770,000 post offices worldwide, ranging from major city post offices offering a wide range of services to small establishments providing only basic facilities, such as the sale of stamps.

TOP 10 LETTER-POSTING COUNTRIES

	COUNTRY	AVERAGE NO. OF LETTER POST ITEMS POSTED PER INHABITANT (2001*)
1	Vatican City	6,500.00
2	USA	706.11
3	Norway	561.72
4	Liechtenstein	556.00
5	Austria	467.10
6	Luxembourg	449.21
7	France	447.57
8	Finland	344.58
9	Belgium	344.05
10	Slovenia	272.74

* Or latest year for which data available

Source: *Universal Postal Union*

The Vatican's statistics are partly explained by the number of official missives sent by the Holy See, and partly by the fact that mail posted within the Vatican, and bearing its stamps, is treated as a priority.

COUNTRIES WITH THE MOST TELEPHONES PER 100 PEOPLE

COUNTRY	TOTAL	TELEPHONE LINES (2001) PER 100 INHABITANTS
1 Guernsey	55,000	87.50
2 Bermuda	56,300	87.15
3 Jersey	73,000	84.79
4 Luxembourg	350,900	78.30
5 Sweden	6,585,000	73.91
6 Denmark	3,882,000	72.33
7 Norway	3,262,000	72.04
8 Switzerland	5,183,000	71.79
9 USA	190,000,000	66.45
10 Iceland	190,600	66.39
UK	34,710,000	57.78

Source: *International Telecommunications Union*, World Telecommunication Development Report, *2002*

COUNTRIES WITH THE HIGHEST RATIO OF MOBILE PHONE USERS

COUNTRY	SUBSCRIBERS	MOBILE PHONES (2001) PER 100 INHABITANTS
1 Luxembourg	432,400	96.73
2 Taiwan	21,633,000	96.55
3 Hong Kong	5,701,700	84.35
4 Italy	48,698,000	83.94
5 Norway	3,737,000	82.53
6 Iceland	235,400	82.02
7 Israel	5,260,000	80.82
8 Austria	6,565,900	80.66
9 UK	47,026,000	78.28
10 Finland	4,044,000	77.84

Source: *International Telecommunications Union*, World Telecommunication Development Report, *2002*

FIRST CITIES AND COUNTRIES TO ISSUE POSTAGE STAMPS

CITY OR COUNTRY	STAMPS ISSUED
1 Great Britain	May 1840
2 New York City, USA	Feb 1842
3 Zurich, Switzerland	Mar 1843
4 Brazil	Aug 1843
5 Geneva, Switzerland	Oct 1843
6 Basle, Switzerland	July 1845
7 USA	July 1847
8 Mauritius	Sept 1847
9 Bermuda	Unknown 1848
10 France	Jan 1849

The first adhesive postage stamps issued in Great Britain were the Penny Blacks, which went on sale on 1 May 1840. The first issued in the USA were designed for local delivery (as authorized by an 1836 Act of Congress) and produced by the City Despatch Post, New York City, inaugurated on 15 February 1842, and incorporated into the US Post Office Department later that year.

▶ **Phone home**
The adoption of mobile phones has revolutionized telecommunications worldwide, with Scandinavian countries standing out among those with the highest density of users.

Food Favourites

TOP 10 BAKED BEAN CONSUMERS

	COUNTRY	EST. CONSUMPTION PER CAPITA (2004)		
		(KG)	(LB)	(OZ)
1	Ireland	5.6	12	5
2	UK	4.8	10	9
3	New Zealand	2.3	5	1
4	USA	2.0	4	6
5	Australia	1.9	4	3
6 =	France	1.6	3	8
=	Saudi Arabia	1.6	3	8
8	Switzerland	1.5	3	5
9	Ukraine	1.3	2	13
10 =	Canada	1.2	2	10
=	Mexico	1.2	2	10

Source: *Euromonitor*

Canned baked beans originated in New England, USA. Brand leader Heinz's baked beans were test-marketed in the North of England in 1901. They were imported from the USA until 1928, when they were first canned in the UK.

TOP 10 FROZEN FOOD CONSUMERS

	COUNTRY	EST. CONSUMPTION PER CAPITA (2004)		
		(KG)	(LB)	(OZ)
1	Denmark	47.4	104	7
2	Norway	34.9	76	15
3	Sweden	24.7	54	7
4	Finland	23.5	51	12
5	UK	22.3	49	2
6	Ireland	20.5	45	3
7	Switzerland	16.6	36	9
8	Israel	16.4	36	2
9	New Zealand	15.6	34	6
10	USA	14.2	31	4

Source: *Euromonitor*

Having studied Eskimos' methods of preserving food by freezing, Clarence Birdseye established the first frozen food company in 1924 in Gloucester, Massachusetts. The Birds Eye company sold its first individual frozen meals – chicken fricassée and steak – in 1939.

TOP 10 CRISP CONSUMERS

	COUNTRY	EST. CONSUMPTION PER CAPITA (2004)		
		(KG)	(LB)	(OZ)
1	UK	3.0	6	9
2 =	Australia	2.7	5	15
=	Ireland	2.7	5	15
4	New Zealand	2.6	5	12
5 =	Norway	2.4	4	14
=	USA	2.4	4	14
7	Finland	2.1	4	10
8	Sweden	1.8	3	15
9	Israel	1.7	3	11
10	Canada	1.6	3	8

Source: *Euromonitor*

◀ **Full of beans**
Although baked beans originated in the USA, the British have adopted them as a staple dish to become the world's foremost consumers.

TOP 10 MEAT CONSUMERS

	COUNTRY	EST. CONSUMPTION PER CAPITA (2000)		
		(KG)	(LB)	(OZ)
1	USA	122.3	269	10
2	Denmark	114.8	253	1
3	Spain	113.8	250	14
4	Australia	110.4	243	6
5	New Zealand	106.8	235	7
6	Austria	106.6	235	0
7	Cyprus	106.2	234	2
8	Mongolia	103.7	228	9
9	France	99.9	220	3
10	Canada	99.8	220	0
	World	*38.1*	*83*	*15*
	UK	*76.8*	*169*	*5*

Source: *Food and Agriculture Organization of the United Nations*

Worldwide, meat consumption ranges from 100 kg or more for countries in the Top 10 to less than 5 kg per head in countries such as India.

TOP 10 FOOD ITEMS CONSUMED IN THE UK BY WEIGHT

FOOD	AVERAGE WEEKLY CONSUMPTION PER HEAD (G)	(LB)	(OZ)
1 Milk and cream	2,140	4	11
2 Meat and meat products	966	2	2
3 Flour and other cereals or cereal products (excluding bread)	788	1	11
4 Fresh fruit	745	1	10
5 Fresh vegetables (excluding potatoes)	732	1	9
6 Bread	720	1	9
7 Fresh potatoes	707	1	8
8 Processed vegetables (including processed potatoes)	546	1	2
9 Processed fruit and nuts	375	0	13
10 Fats	186	0	6

Source: *Department of Environment, Food and Rural Affairs (DEFRA)*, National Food Survey 2000

TOP 10 FAST FOOD COMPANIES

COMPANY/COUNTRY	FAST FOOD MARKET SHARE (1999) (%)
1 McDonald's Corporation, USA	21.9
2 Tricon Global Restaurants, Inc., USA	10.7
3 Diageo plc, UK	7.1
4 Wendy's International, Inc., USA	3.8
5 = Allied Domecq plc, UK	2.3
= Doctor's Associates, Inc., USA	2.3
7 CKE Restaurants, Inc.	2.0
8 Domino's Pizza, Inc., USA	1.8
9 Berkshire Hathaway, Inc., USA	1.5
10 Triarc Corporation, USA	1.3

Source: *Euromonitor*

The world's leading fast food company, McDonald's, began in Des Plaines, Illinois, in 1955, with the opening of Ray Kroc's first restaurant. Today more than 30,000 restaurants serve 46 million people a day in 121 countries; the one in Pushkin Square, Russia, is the busiest of all.

TOP 10 CANNED FOOD CONSUMERS

COUNTRY	EST. CONSUMPTION PER CAPITA (2004) (KG)	(LB)	(OZ)
1 Sweden	33.4	73	10
2 UK	23.5	51	12
3 Portugal	23.2	51	2
4 France	22.3	49	2
5 Belgium	21.4	47	2
6 USA	21.2	46	11
7 New Zealand	16.5	36	6
8 Norway	16.4	36	2
9 Czech Republic	16.2	35	11
10 Australia	16.0	35	4

Source: *Euromonitor*

Bryan Donkin and John Hall of Bermondsey, London, were the first to can food in tinplate cans, originally designed for military use during the Napoleonic wars, but sold to the public from 1814 onwards.

▶ Fruit and veg
Although apples and bananas remain the UK's favourite fruits, the modern shopping basket contains a far more diverse range of products than in the past.

Drink Up

TOP 10 | CARBONATED SOFT DRINK CONSUMERS

	COUNTRY	CONSUMPTION PER CAPITA (2000) (LITRES)	(PINTS)
1	USA	161.8	284.7
2	Mexico	114.2	200.9
3	Norway	102.0	179.4
4	Canada	85.6	150.6
5	Australia	82.3	144.8
6	Belgium	79.8	140.4
7	Chile	79.5	139.9
8	Argentina	72.8	128.1
9	UK	72.7	127.9
10	Saudi Arabia	72.2	127.0

Source: *Euromonitor*

◀ **Café society**
The world's most enthusiastic coffee drinkers are all Europeans – led by the Scandinavians, who each consume two or more cups a day.

TOP 10 | BOTTLED WATER CONSUMERS

	COUNTRY	CONSUMPTION PER CAPITA (2000) (LITRES)	(PINTS)
1	France	130.0	228.7
2	Italy	115.7	203.6
3	Spain	93.1	163.8
4	Belgium	84.8	149.2
5	Germany	74.7	131.4
6	Switzerland	68.0	119.6
7	Austria	61.2	107.6
8	Czech Republic	60.4	106.2
9	Slovakia	39.6	69.6
10	Poland	34.6	60.8
	UK	14.9	26.2

Source: *Euromonitor*

French bottled mineral water consumption began in the 19th century. Leading sources such as Evian, Perrier, and Vittel supply the domestic market as well as annually exporting billions of bottles to the rest of the world.

TOP 10 | BEER CONSUMERS

	COUNTRY	CONSUMPTION PER CAPITA (2001) (LITRES)	(PINTS)
1	Czech Republic	158.1	278.2
2	Ireland	150.8	265.4
3	Germany	123.1	216.6
4	Austria	106.9	188.1
5	Luxembourg	100.9	177.6
6	Denmark	98.6	173.5
7	Belgium	98.0	172.5
8	UK	97.1	170.9
9	Australia	93.0	163.7
10	Slovak Republic	86.4	152.0*

* Estimated from beer production data due to lack of consumption data

Source: *Commission for Distilled Spirits*

Whilst no African countries appear in this list – or even in the Top 50 countries – this does not mean that people in Africa do not drink beer. Bottled beer is often prohibitively expensive, so people tend to consume home-made beers sold in local markets – beers that are excluded from national statistics.

CARBONATED DRINKS

THE FIRST ARTIFICIAL MINERAL WATER – "soda water" – was made by English chemist Joseph Priestley in 1767. His process, which he called "Impregnating Water with Fixed Air", was improved by others. Various manufacturers, including Jacob Schweppe in Europe, began bottling water, while in Philadelphia, Pennsylvania, USA, Townsend Speakman supplied carbonated water to a local doctor, Philip Syng Physick, who administered it to his patients as a medicine. In 1807 Speakman mixed fruit juice with it to create the first flavoured fizzy drink, to which he gave the name "Nephite Julep".

FIRST FACT

TOP 10 | COFFEE CONSUMERS

	COUNTRY	CONSUMPTION PER CAPITA (2001) (KG)	(LB)	(OZ)	(CUPS*)
1	Finland	11.01	24	4	1,652
2	Denmark	9.79	21	9	1,469
3	Norway	9.46	20	13	1,419
4	Sweden	8.55	18	13	1,283
5	Austria	7.08	15	9	1,062
6	Germany	6.90	15	3	1,035
7	Switzerland	6.80	14	15	1,020
8	Netherlands	6.34	13	15	951
9	Belgium and Luxembourg	5.53	12	3	830
10	Italy	5.44	11	15	816
	UK	2.20	4	13	330

* Based on 150 cups per kg/2 lb 3 oz

Source: *International Coffee Organization*

TOP 10 | TEA CONSUMERS

	COUNTRY	ANNUAL CONSUMPTION PER CAPITA* (KG)	(LB)	(OZ)	(CUPS#)
1	Ireland	2.71	5	15	1,192
2	Libya	2.65	5	13	1,166
3	Kuwait	2.29	5	1	1,007
4	UK	2.28	5	0	1,003
5	Qatar	2.23	4	14	981
6	Iraq	2.20	4	13	968
7	Turkey	2.17	4	12	954
8	Iran	1.43	3	2	629
9	Hong Kong	1.36	3	0	598
10	Morocco	1.34	2	15	589

* 1999–2001

 # Based on 440 cups per kg/2 lb 3 oz

Source: *International Tea Committee Ltd., London*

TOP 10 | WINE PRODUCERS

	COUNTRY	PRODUCTION (1999) (LITRES)	(PINTS)
1	France	6,093,300,000	10,723,000,000
2	Italy	5,811,000,000	10,225,900,000
3	Spain	3,680,200,000	6,476,200,000
4	USA	2,069,100,000	3,641,100,000
5	Argentina	1,588,800,000	2,795,900,000
6	Germany	1,224,400,000	2,154,600,000
7	Australia	851,100,000	1,497,700,000
8	South Africa	796,800,000	1,402,100,000
9	Portugal	780,600,000	1,373,600,000
10	Romania	650,400,000	1,144,500,000

Source: *Commission for Distilled Spirits*

▶ **Wine lovers**
The world's vineyards produce a total of 26 billion litres (55 billion pints) of wine annually – more than five bottles for every inhabitant on the planet.

TRANSPORT & TOURISM

SPORT & LEISURE

Summer Olympics

THE 10 | FIRST INDIVIDUALS TO WIN GOLD IN THE SAME EVENT AT FOUR SUMMER OLYMPICS

	INDIVIDUAL/COUNTRY	SPORT	EVENT	YEARS
1 =	**Aladár Gerevich***, Hungary	Fencing	Team Sabre	1932–52
=	**Pál Kovács**, Hungary	Fencing	Team Sabre	1932–52
3 =	**Paul Elvstrøm**, Denmark	Sailing	Finn	1948–60
=	**Edoardo Mangiarotti**, Italy	Fencing	Team Epee	1936–60
=	**Rudolf Kárpáti**, Hungary	Fencing	Team Sabre	1948–60
6	**Al Oerter**, USA	Athletics	Discus	1956–68
7	**Hans–Günther Winkler**, Germany	Show jumping	Team	1956–72
8	**Reiner Klimke#**, West Germany	Dressage	Team	1964–84
9	**Carl Lewis**, USA	Athletics	Long Jump	1984–96
10	**Teresa Edwards**, USA	Basketball	Women's	1984–2000

* *Also won gold in the same event in 1956 and 1960*

Also won gold in the same event in 1988

Few Olympic competitors have succeeded in attaining gold over a span of 16 years or more. When, after becoming the first person to do so, 50-year-old Aladár Gerevich was refused a place in the Hungarian fencing squad at the 1960 Games, he promptly challenged the entire team, defeating them all.

TOP 10 | COUNTRIES WITH THE MOST SUMMER OLYMPICS MEDALS, 1896–2000

	COUNTRY	MEDALS			
		GOLD	SILVER	BRONZE	TOTAL
1	**USA**	872	659	581	2,112
2	**USSR***	485	395	354	1,234
3	**UK**	188	245	232	665
4	**France**	189	195	217	601
5	**Germany#**	165	198	210	573
6	**Italy**	179	144	155	478
7	**Sweden**	138	157	176	471
8	**Hungary**	150	134	158	442
9	**East Germany**	153	130	127	410
10	**Australia**	103	110	139	352

* *Includes Unified Team of 1992; does not include Russia since then*

Not including West/East Germany 1968–88

The host nations at the first two Modern Olympics – Greece in 1896 and France in 1900 – both led the medal table, with the USA achieving its first commanding total of 72 medals at the 1904 St. Louis Games. Other hosts, the USA and USSR, vied for first place in subsequent Olympics, with the USA the ultimate victor.

▶ **Record leap**
Carl Lewis's long jump victory at the 1996 Atlanta Olympics gained him his ninth gold at four consecutive Games.

TOP 10 MEDAL WINNERS IN A SUMMER OLYMPICS CAREER

	WINNER/COUNTRY	SPORT	YEARS	GOLD	MEDALS SILVER	BRONZE	TOTAL
1	**Larissa Latynlna**, USSR	Gymnastics	1956–64	9	5	4	18
2	**Nikolay Andrianov**, USSR	Gymnastics	1972–80	7	5	3	15
3 =	**Edoardo Mangiarotti**, Italy	Fencing	1936–60	6	5	2	13
=	**Takashi Ono**, Japan	Gymnastics	1952–64	5	4	4	13
=	**Boris Shakhlin**, USSR	Gymnastics	1956–64	7	4	2	13
6 =	**Sawao Kato**, Japan	Gymnastics	1968–76	8	3	1	12
=	**Paavo Nurmi**, Finland	Athletics	1920–28	9	3	0	12
8 =	**Viktor Chukarin**, USSR	Gymnastics	1952–56	7	3	1	11
=	**Vera Cáslavská**, Czechoslovakia	Gymnastics	1964–68	7	4	0	11
=	**Carl Osburn**, USA	Shooting	1912–24	5	4	2	11
=	**Mark Spitz**, USA	Swimming	1968–72	9	1	1	11
=	**Matt Biondi**, USA	Swimming	1984–92	8	2	1	11

Larissa Latynina won six medals at each of three Games between 1956 and 1964. The only discipline at which she did not win a medal was on the beam in 1956. An achievement that rivals those of the individuals represented by this Top 10 was that of Ray C. Ewry (USA), a competitor at the Games from 1900 to 1908, who won 10 medals, all in jumping events (and hence does not make this list) – but all of them were gold.

TOP 10 MEDAL-WINNING COUNTRIES AT THE SUMMER PARALYMPICS*

	COUNTRY	GOLD	MEDALS SILVER	BRONZE	TOTAL
1	USA	576	523	522	1,621
2	UK	389	401	387	1,177
3	Germany/ West Germany	404	385	361	1,150
4	Canada	311	250	262	823
5	France	279	264	241	784
6	Australia	240	248	228	716
7	Holland	219	179	153	551
8	Poland	194	184	148	526
9	Sweden	197	190	135	522
10	Spain	156	137	152	445

Excluding medals won at the 1960 Rome and 1968 Tel Aviv Games – the International Paralympic Committee has not kept records of medals won at these Games

The first international games for the disabled were at Stoke Mandeville, England, in 1952, when 130 athletes from the UK and the Netherlands competed.

TOP 10 MOST SUCCESSFUL COUNTRIES AT ONE SUMMER OLYMPICS

	COUNTRY	VENUE	YEAR	GOLD	MEDALS SILVER	BRONZE	TOTAL
1	USA	St. Louis	1904	80	84	76	242
2	USSR	Moscow	1980	80	69	46	195
3	USA	Los Angeles	1984	83	61	30	174
4	Great Britain	London	1908	56	50	39	145
5	USSR	Seoul	1988	55	31	46	132
6	East Germany	Moscow	1980	47	37	42	126
7	USSR	Montreal	1976	49	41	35	125
8	EUN*	Barcelona	1992	45	38	29	112
9	USA	Barcelona	1992	37	34	37	108
10	USA	Mexico City	1968	45	28	34	107

Unified Team, Commonwealth of Independent States, 1992

The Soviet Union's total at Seoul in 1988 is the highest by a country not competing on home soil. East Germany's 126 in 1980 is the highest total of a country not heading the medal list, although the USA boycotted the Games that year, enabling Eastern Bloc countries to achieve their greatest-ever medal haul. The only other nations with 100 medals at one Games are East Germany (1988, Seoul) with 102, and France (1900, Paris) with 100 exactly. The USA gained 97 medals (39 gold, 25 silver, and 33 bronze) at the 2000 Sydney Olympics, the most of any nation.

TOP 10 SPORTS AT WHICH THE MOST GOLD MEDALS HAVE BEEN WON AT THE OLYMPIC GAMES, 1896–2000

	SPORT	GOLD MEDALS
1	Athletics	818
2	Swimming/diving	527
3	Wrestling	340
4	Gymnastics	291
5	Shooting	229
6	Boxing	204
7	Rowing	203
8	Fencing	179
9	Cycling	166
10	Canoeing	161

Winter Olympics

▲ Salt Lake City celebration
Olympic medal-winning German, Norwegian, and Swiss ski teams celebrate their respective victories at Salt Lake City, 2002.

TOP 10 | MEDAL-WINNING COUNTRIES AT THE 2002 SALT LAKE WINTER OLYMPICS

	COUNTRY	GOLD	SILVER	BRONZE	TOTAL
			MEDALS		
1	Germany	12	16	7	35
2	USA	10	13	11	34
3	Norway	11	7	6	24
4	Canada	6	3	8	17
5	= Austria	2	4	10	16
	= Russia	6	6	4	16
7	Italy	4	4	4	12
8	= France	4	5	2	11
	= Switzerland	3	2	6	11
10	= China	2	2	4	8
	= Netherlands	3	5	0	8
	Great Britain	*1*	*-*	*2*	*3*

TOP 10 | GOLD MEDALLISTS AT THE WINTER OLYMPICS (MEN)

	MEDALLIST/COUNTRY	SPORT	GOLD MEDALS
1	**Bjørn Dählie,** Norway	Nordic skiing	8
2	= **Eric Heiden,** USA	Speed skating	5
	= **Clas Thunberg,** Norway	Speed skating	5
4	= **Ivar Ballangrud,** Norway	Speed skating	4
	= **Yevgeny Grishin,** Soviet Union	Speed skating	4
	= **Sixten Jernberg,** Sweden	Nordic skiing	4
	= **Johann Olav Koss,** Norway	Speed skating	4
	= **Matti Nykänen,** Finland	Ski jumping	4
	= **Alexander Tikhonov,** Soviet Union	Biathlon	4
	= **Thomas Wassberg,** Sweden	Nordic skiing	4
	= **Nikolai Zimyatov,** Soviet Union	Nordic skiing	4
	= **Gunde Svan,** Sweden	Nordic skiing	4

TOP 10 | GOLD MEDALLISTS AT THE WINTER OLYMPICS (WOMEN)

	MEDALLIST/COUNTRY	SPORT	GOLD MEDALS
1	= **Lydia Skoblikova,** Soviet Union	Speed skating	6
	= **Lyubov Egorova,** EUN*/Russia	Nordic skiing	6
3	= **Bonnie Blair,** USA	Speed skating	5
	= **Larissa Lazutina,** EUN*/Russia	Nordic skiing	5
5	= **Galina Kulakova,** Soviet Union	Nordic skiing	4
	= **Lee-Kyung Chun,** South Korea	Short track speed skating	4
	= **Claudia Pechstein,** Germany	Speed skating	4
	= **Raisa Smetanina,** EUN*/Russia	Nordic skiing	4
9	= **Claudia Boyarskikh,** Soviet Union	Nordic skiing	3
	= **Marja-Liisa Kirvesniemi** (née Hämäläinen), Finland	Nordic skiing	3
	= **Sonja Henie,** Norway	Figure skating	3
	= **Karin Kania** (née Enke), East Germany	Speed skating	3
	= **Gunda Niemann-Stirnemann,** Germany	Speed skating	3
	= **Anfisa Reztsova,** Soviet Union/EUN*	Nordic skiing/biathlon	3
	= **Irina Rodnina,** Soviet Union	Figure skating	3
	= **Vreni Schneider,** Switzerland	Alpine skiing	3
	= **Katja Seizinger,** Germany	Alpine skiing	3
	= **Elena Valbe,** EUN*/Russia	Nordic skiing	3
	= **Yvonne van Gennip,** Netherlands	Speed skating	3

* Unified Team, Commonwealth of Independent States, 1992

TOP10 WINTER OLYMPICS MEDAL-WINNING COUNTRIES, 1924–2002*

	COUNTRY	GOLD	SILVER	BRONZE	TOTAL
			MEDALS		
1	Soviet Union#	113	82	78	273
2	Norway	94	93	73	260
3	USA	70	70	51	191
4	Austria	41	57	65	163
5	Germany†	54	51	37	142
6	Finland	41	51	49	141
7	East Germany	39	37	35	111
8	Sweden	36	28	38	102
9	Switzerland	32	33	36	101
10	Canada	30	28	37	95

* Includes medals won at figure skating and ice hockey included in the Summer Games prior to the launch of the Winter Olympics in 1924

Includes Unified Team of 1992; excludes Russia since then

† Not including East/West Germany, 1968–88

The Winter Olympics have been staged on 19 occasions since the first, with the 20th scheduled for Turin, Italy, 10–26 February 2006. The Soviet Union first competed at the seventh Games at Cortina d'Ampezzo, Italy, where they succeeded in leading the medal table with seven gold, three silver, and six bronze medals

TOP10 COMPETITOR-ATTENDED WINTER OLYMPICS

	HOST CITY/COUNTRY	YEAR	COMPETITORS
1	Salt Lake City, USA	2002	2,399
2	Nagano, Japan	1998	2,177
3	Albertville, France	1992	1,801
4	Lillehammer, Norway	1994	1,736
5	Calgary, Canada	1988	1,425
6	Sarajevo, Yugoslavia	1984	1,274
7	Grenoble, France	1968	1,158
8	Innsbruck, Austria	1976	1,123
9	Innsbruck, Austria	1964	1,091
10	Lake Placid, USA	1980	1,072

The first Winter Games at Chamonix, France, in 1924 were attended by 258 competitors (of which 13 were women), representing 16 countries. The second Winter Games, held at St. Moritz, Switzerland, in 1928, saw the number of competitors and countries increase to 464 (including 26 women) and 25 respectively. The third Games in 1932, at Lake Placid, New York, USA, were affected by the Depression, which saw the numbers reduced to 252 competitors (with 21 women) from 17 countries. Since the fourth Games, in 1936 at Garmisch-Partenkirchen, Germany (668 competitors, with 80 women, from 28 countries), the number of competitors and countries represented have generally increased: a total of 2,399 competitors (886 women) from 77 countries took part in the 19th Games at Salt Lake City, Utah, USA.

▼ Red hot team
The German four-man bobsleigh hurtles to Olympic gold at the 2002 Winter Games.

Winter Sports

TOP 10 ALPINE SNOW-BOARDERS (MALE)

SNOWBOARDER/COUNTRY	TOTAL POINTS*
1 **Tony Albrecht,** Switzerland	2,221.48
2 **Gilles Jaquet,** Switzerland	2,213.60
3 **Cyrill Buehler,** Switzerland	2,194.53
4 **Urs Eiselin,** Switzerland	2,166.30
5 **Simon Schoch,** Switzerland	2,131.04
6 **Philippe Schoch,** Switzerland	2,080.01
7 **Martin Bolt,** Switzerland	1,888.93
8 **Nicolas Wolken,** Switzerland	1,815.41
9 **Roland Haldi,** Switzerland	1,792.86
10 **Antonin Cip,** Czech Republic	1,788,22

* Ranked by best four results in a 52-week period to 29 January 2003

Source: *World Snowboarding Federation*

Snowboarding was invented in 1965 by Sherman Poppen (USA), and the sport became an Olympic event in 1998.

TOP 10 ALPINE SNOW-BOARDERS (FEMALE)

SNOWBOARDER/COUNTRY	TOTAL POINTS*
1 **Daniela Meuli,** Switzerland	1,172.30
2 **Perrine Buehler,** Switzerland	1,064.44
3 **Ursula Bruhin,** Switzerland	1,049.06
4 **Blanka Isielonis,** Poland	986.82
5 **Malgorzata Kukcz,** Poland	985.68
6 **Nadia Livers,** Switzerland	913.33
7 **Petra Elsterova,** Czech Republic	911.72
8 **Milena Meisser,** Switzerland	828.13
9 **Fraenzi Kohli,** Switzerland	776.09
10 **Rebekka von Kaenel,** Switzerland	773.97

* Ranked by best four results in a 52-week period to 29 January 2003

Source: *World Snowboarding Federation*

The World Snowboarding Federation was constituted in Munich, Germany, in 2002 and is now the governing body for the sport internationally.

TOP 10 SKIERS IN THE 2002/03 ALPINE WORLD CUP (FEMALE)

SKIER/COUNTRY	OVERALL POINTS*
1 **Janica Kostelic,** Croatia	1,570
2 **Karen Putzer,** Italy	1,100
3 **Anja Paerson,** Sweden	1,042
4 **Michaela Dorfmeister,** Austria	972
5 **Martina Ertl,** Germany	922
6 **Carole Montillet,** France	869
7 **Renate Goetschl,** Austria	830
8 **Alexandra Meissnitzer,** Austria	776
9 **Kirsten L. Clark,** USA	661
10 **Nicole Hosp,** Austria	558

* Awarded for performances in slalom, giant slalom, super giant, downhill, and combination disciplines

Source: *International Ski Federation*

Downhill racer
Swiss snowboarder Gilles Jaquet is among the world's leading exponents, in a sport dominated by his countrymen.

SKI-JUMPERS IN THE 2002/03 SKI-JUMPING WORLD CUP

	SKIER/COUNTRY	OVERALL POINTS
1	**Adam Malysz**, Poland	1,357
2	**Sven Hannawald**, Germany	1,235
3	**Andreas Widhoelzl**, Austria	1,028
4	**Janne Ahonen**, Finland	1,016
5	**Florian Liegl**, Austria	986
6	**Martin Hoellwarth**, Austria	925
7	**Primoz Peterka**, Slovenia	805
8	**Matti Hautamaeki**, Finland	797
9	**Roar Ljoekelsoey**, Norway	757
10	**Sigurd Pettersen**, Norway	747

Source: *International Ski Federation*

▶ **A jump ahead**
German ski-jumper Sven Hannawald gained his fifth World Cup victory at Bad Mittendorf, Austria, but lost out to overall points leader Adam Malysz.

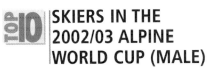

SKIERS IN THE 2002/03 ALPINE WORLD CUP (MALE)

	SKIER/COUNTRY	OVERALL POINTS*
1	**Stephen Eberharter**, Austria	1,333
2	**Bode Miller**, USA	1,100
3	**Kjetil Andre Aamodt**, Norway	940
4	**Kalle Palander**, Finland	718
5	**Didier Cuche**, Switzerland	709
6	**Daron Rahlves**, USA	647
7	**Ivica Kostelic**, Croatia	632
8	**Benjamin Raich**, Austria	622
9	**Michael Walchhofer**, Austria	600
10	**Hans Knauss**, Austria	596

* *Awarded for performances in slalom, giant slalom, super giant, downhill, and combination disciplines*

Source: *International Ski Federation*

FASTEST SPEED-SKATERS

	SKATER*/COUNTRY	LOCATION	DATE	TIME FOR 500 M (SECS)
1	**Hiroyasu Shimizu**, Japan	Salt Lake City, USA	10 Mar 2001	34.32
2	**Jeremy Wotherspoon**, Canada	Salt Lake City	11 Jan 2003	34.41
3	**Casey FitzRandolph**, USA	Salt Lake City	11 Feb 2002	34.42
4	**Gerard van Velde**, Netherlands	Calgary, Canada	18 Jan 2003	34.61
5	**Toyoki Takeda**, Japan	Calgary	9 Dec 2001	34.62
6	= **Joey Cheek**, USA	Salt Lake City	19 Dec 2001	34.66
	= **Michael Ireland**, Canada	Calgary	18 Mar 2000	34.66
8	**Kip Carpenter**, USA	Salt Lake City	11 Feb 2002	34.68
9	**Jan Bos**, Netherlands	Salt Lake City	12 Feb 2002	34.72
10	**Lee Kyu-Hyuk**, South Korea	Salt Lake City	11 Feb 2002	34.74

* *Skater's fastest time only included*

Source: *International Skating Union*

American Football

PLAYERS WITH THE MOST CAREER TOUCHDOWNS

PLAYER	TOUCHDOWNS
1 Jerry Rice*	192
2 Emmitt Smith*	164
3 Marcus Allen	145
4 Cris Carter*	130
5 Jim Brown	126
6 Walter Payton	125
7 Marshall Faulk*	120
8 John Riggins	116
9 Lenny Moore	113
10 Barry Sanders	109

* Still active at end of 2002 season

Source: *National Football League*

PLAYERS WITH THE MOST CAREER POINTS

PLAYER	POINTS
1 Gary Anderson*	2,223
2 Morten Andersen*	2,153
3 George Blanda	2,002
4 Norm Johnson	1,736
5 Nick Lowery	1,711
6 Jan Stenerud	1,699
7 Eddie Murray	1,594
8 Al Del Greco	1,584
9 Jim Carney*	1,541
10 Pat Leahy	1,470

* Still active at end of 2002 season

Source: *National Football League*

PLAYERS WITH THE MOST PASSING YARDS IN AN NFL CAREER

PLAYER	PASSING YARDS
1 Dan Marino	61,361
2 John Elway	51,475
3 Warren Moon	49,325
4 Fran Tarkenton	47,003
5 Dan Fouts	43,040
6 Brett Favre*	42,285
7 Joe Montana	40,551
8 Johnny Unitas	40,239
9 Vinny Testaverde*	39,558
10 Dave Krieg	38,147

* Still active at end of 2002 season

Source: *National Football League*

◄ **Rice records**

Wide receiver Jerry Rice, considered one of the greatest players of all time, has held numerous NFL career records during his time with the San Francisco 49ers (1985–2000) and Oakland Raiders (2001–).

COACHES WITH THE MOST CAREER WINS

COACH	GAMES WON
1 Don Shula	347
2 George Halas	324
3 Tom Landry	270
4 Curly Lambeau	229
5 Chuck Noll	209
6 Dan Reeves*	195
7 Chuck Knox	193
8 Paul Brown	170
9 Bud Grant	168
10 Marv Levy	154

* Still active at end of 2002 season

Source: *National Football League*

▲ **Giants Stadium**
The first game played at Giants Stadium was on 10 October 1976, when the New York Giants were beaten by the Dallas Cowboys 24–14.

TOP 10 | MOST SUCCESSFUL SUPER BOWL TEAMS

	TEAM	WINS	SUPER BOWL GAMES RUNNERS-UP	POINTS*
1	Dallas Cowboys	5	3	13
2	San Francisco 49ers	5	0	10
3	Pittsburgh Steelers	4	1	9
4 =	Oakland/Los Angeles Raiders	3	2	8
=	Washington Redskins	3	2	8
6	Denver Broncos	2	4	8
7	Green Bay Packers	3	1	7
8	Miami Dolphins	2	3	7
9	New York Giants	2	1	5
10 =	Buffalo Bills	0	4	4
=	Minnesota Vikings	0	4	4

* Based on two points for a Super Bowl win, and one for the runner-up; wins take precedence over runners-up in determining ranking

Source: *National Football League*

TOP 10 | LARGEST NFL STADIUMS

	STADIUM	HOME TEAM	CAPACITY
1	Giants Stadium	New York Giants/Jets	80,242
2	FedExField	Washington Redskins	80,116
3	Arrowhead Stadium	Kansas City Chiefs	79,451
4	Invesco Stadium	Denver Broncos	76,125
5	Pro Player Stadium	Miami Dolphins	75,540
6	Ralph Wilson Stadium	Buffalo Bills	73,967
7	Ericsson Stadium	Carolina Panthers	73,367
8	Sun Devil Stadium	Arizona Cardinals	73,273
9	Cleveland Browns Stadium	Cleveland Browns	73,200
10	Alltel Stadium	Jacksonville Jaguars	73,000

Source: *National Football League*

The seating capacity of most stadiums varies according to the event. The Giants Stadium reached a capacity of 82,948 on 5 October 1995 when Pope John Paul II celebrated Mass there.

217

Test Cricket

TOP 10 WICKET TAKERS IN TEST CRICKET

	PLAYER/COUNTRY	YEARS	TESTS	WICKETS
1	**Courtney Walsh,** West Indies	1984–2001	132	519
2	**Shane Warne,** Australia	1992–2003	107	491
3	**Muttiah Muralitharan,** Sri Lanka	1992–*	78	437
4	**Kapil Dev,** India	1978–94	131	434
5	**Richard Hadlee,** New Zealand	1973–90	86	431
6	**Glenn McGrath,** Australia	1993–*	91	422
7	**Wasim Akram,** Pakistan	1985–*	104	414
8	**Curtly Ambrose,** West Indies	1988–2000	98	405
9	**Ian Botham,** England	1977–92	102	383
10	**Malcolm Marshall,** West Indies	1978–91	81	376

* Still active in 2003

Courtney Walsh surpassed Kapil Dev's record on 27 March 2000, when he dismissed Zimbabwe's Henry Olonga in the 2nd Test at Courtney's home ground, Sabina Park, Kingston, Jamaica. His first Test victim was Australia's Graeme Wood, at Perth, in the second innings of the 1st Test in November 1984. And his 519th and last victim was South Africa's Allan Donald, also at Sabina Park, on 19 April 2001. His best Test haul was 7–37 in the first innings of the 2nd Test against New Zealand at Wellington in February 1995. He took 6–18 in the second innings.

TOP 10 RUN MAKERS IN A TEST INNINGS

	BATSMAN	MATCH	VENUE	YEARS	RUNS
1	**Brian Lara**	West Indies v England	St. John's	1993–94	375
2	**Gary Sobers**	West Indies v Pakistan	Kingston	1957–58	365*
3	**Len Hutton**	England v Australia	The Oval	1938	364
4	**Sanath Jayasuriya**	Sri Lanka v India	Colombo	1997–98	340
5	**Hanif Mohammad**	Pakistan v West Indies	Bridgetown	1957–58	337
6	**Walter Hammond**	England v New Zealand	Auckland	1932–33	336*
7 =	**Don Bradman**	Australia v England	Leeds	1930	334
=	**Mark Taylor**	Australia v Pakistan	Peshawar	1998–99	334*
9	**Graham Gooch**	England v India	Lord's	1990	333
10	**Inzamam-ul-Haq**	Pakistan v New Zealand	Lahore	2002	329

* Not out

After setting the new Test record against England, one of the first people to congratulate Brian Lara, the new star of West Indies cricket, was former record-holder Gary Sobers, who was in the crowd at Antigua. Sobers, who had held the record for 36 years, was only 21 years 216 days of age at the time of his achievement; Lara himself was just short of his 25th birthday. A few months after his record Test score, Lara became the first man to score 500 runs in a First Class Innings.

TOP 10 PARTNERSHIPS IN TEST CRICKET

	BATSMEN	MATCH	YEARS	RUNS
1	**Sanath Jayasuriya/ Roshan Mahanama**	Sri Lanka v India	1997–98	576
2	**Andrew Jones/ Martin Crowe**	New Zealand v Sri Lanka	1990–91	467
3 =	**Bill Ponsford/Don Bradman**	Australia v England	1934	451
=	**Mudassar Nazar/ Javed Miandad**	Pakistan v India	1982–83	451
5	**Conrad Hunte/Gary Sobers**	West Indies v Pakistan	1957–58	446
6	**Vinoo Mankad/Pankaj Roy**	India v New Zealand	1955–56	413
7	**Peter May/Colin Cowdrey**	England v West Indies	1957	411
8	**Sidney Barnes/Don Bradman**	Australia v England	1946–47	405
9	**Gary Sobers/Frank Worrell**	West Indies v England	1959–60	399
10	**Qasim Omar/Javed Miandad**	Pakistan v Sri Lanka	1985–86	397

Gundappa Viswanath, Yashpal Sharma, and Dilip Vengsarkar put on 415 runs for India's third wicket against England at Madras in 1981–82; Vengsarkar retired hurt when the partnership was on 99.

TOP 10 RUN MAKERS IN A TEST SERIES

	BATSMAN	SERIES/TESTS	YEARS	RUNS
1	**Don Bradman**	Australia v England (5)	1930	974
2	**Walter Hammond**	England v Australia (5)	1928–29	905
3	**Mark Taylor**	Australia v England (6)	1989	839
4	**Neil Harvey**	Australia v South Africa (5)	1952–53	834
5	**Viv Richards**	West Indies v England (4)	1976	829
6	**Clyde Walcott**	West Indies v Australia (5)	1954–55	827
7	**Gary Sobers**	West Indies v Pakistan (5)	1957–58	824
8	**Don Bradman**	Australia v England (5)	1936–37	810
9	**Don Bradman**	Australia v South Africa (5)	1931–32	806
10	**Brian Lara**	West Indies v England (5)	1993–94	798

Don Bradman's remarkable tally against England in 1930 came only a year after Walter Hammond had become the first man to score 900 runs in a series. Bradman, who was making his debut on English soil, scored his runs in just seven innings at an average of 139. He scored just eight runs in the first innings of the opening Test, but then came the first of his centuries when he went on to score 131 in the second innings. He scored 254 and one in the second Test, and at Headingley scored 309 on the first day before being dismissed for 334. He scored only 14 in the rain-affected Old Trafford Test, but in the final Test his 232 helped Australia to an innings victory.

TOP 10 HIGHEST COMPLETED INNINGS IN TEST CRICKET

	MATCH	VENUE	YEARS	SCORE
1	Sri Lanka v India	Colombo	1997–98	952–6 dec
2	England v Australia	The Oval	1938	903–7 dec
3	England v West Indies	Kingston	1929–30	849
4	West Indies v Pakistan	Kingston	1957–58	790–3 dec
5	Australia v West Indies	Kingston	1954–55	758–8 dec
6	Australia v England	Lord's	1930	729–6 dec
7	Pakistan v England	The Oval	1987	708
8	Australia v England	The Oval	1934	701
9	Pakistan v India	Lahore	1989–90	699–5
10	Australia v England	The Oval	1930	695

Despite their record-breaking total, Sri Lanka could only draw their match with India in 1997. India batted first and scored 537 before declaring their innings with eight wickets down. Remarkably, Sri Lanka had surpassed that total for the loss of just one wicket, that of Atapattu, as Jayasuriya and Mahanama put on 576 for the second wicket. Jayasuriya was the top scorer with 340. Spare a thought for the Indian bowler Rajesh Chauhan, he returned figures of one wicket for 276 runs. India's highest total is 676–7, v Sri Lanka at Kanpur in 1986–87.

TOP 10 LOWEST COMPLETED INNINGS IN TEST CRICKET

	MATCH	VENUE	YEARS	TOTAL
1	New Zealand v England	Auckland	1954–55	26
2 =	South Africa v England	Port Elizabeth	1895–96	30
=	South Africa v England	Edgbaston	1924	30
4	South Africa v England	Cape Town	1898–99	35
5 =	Australia v England	Edgbaston	1902	36
=	South Africa v Australia	Melbourne	1931–32	36
7 =	Australia v England	Sydney	1887–88	42
=	New Zealand v Australia	Wellington	1945–46	42
=	India* v England	Lord's	1974	42
10	South Africa v England	Cape Town	1888–89	43

* India batted one man short

The record low occurred at Eden Park, Auckland, on 28 March 1955, when the home side was dismissed in a total of 27 overs by the England team led by Len Hutton, playing his last Test. England's lowest total is 45, when dismissed by Australia at Sydney in 1886–87; West Indies' lowest total is 51, v Australia at Port of Spain in 1998–99.

TOP 10 RUN MAKERS IN TEST CRICKET

	BATSMAN/COUNTRY	YEARS	TESTS	RUNS
1	Allan Border, Australia	1978–94	156	11,174
2	Sunil Gavaskar, India	1971–87	125	10,122
3	Steve Waugh, Australia	1985–*	156	10,039
4	Graham Gooch, England	1975–95	118	8,900
5	Javed Miandad, Pakistan	1976–94	124	8,832
6	Sachin Tendulkar, India	1989–*	105	8,811
7	Viv Richards, West Indies	1974–91	121	8,540
8	David Gower, England	1978–92	117	8,231
9	Alec Stewart, England	1989–*	126	8,187
10	Geoff Boycott, England	1964–82	108	8,114

* Still active in 2003

Born in Sydney, New South Wales, Allan Border made his Test debut against England at Melbourne in the 3rd Test in 1978–79 and bowed out of Test cricket at Durban in the 3rd Test against South Africa in 1993–94. In 265 Test innings he averaged 50.56 runs. He made 63 50s, 27 centuries, and two double centuries. His best innings was 205 against New Zealand at Adelaide in 1987. In his 265 innings he was dismissed for a duck on only 11 occasions. The *Wisden* Cricketer of the Year in 1982, he played for New South Wales, Queensland, Gloucestershire, Essex, and Australia.

TOP 10 NARROWEST TEST WINS

	MATCH	VENUE	YEAR	WINNING MARGIN (RUNS)
1	West Indies v Australia	Adelaide	1993	1
2 =	Australia v England	Manchester	1902	3
=	England v Australia	Melbourne	1982	3
4	South Africa v Australia	Sydney	1994	5
5	Australia v England	Sydney	1885	6
6 =	Australia v England	The Oval	1882	7
=	South Africa v Sri Lanka	Kandy	2000	7
8	England v Australia	Sydney	1894	10
9	Australia v England	Adelaide	1925	11
10 =	England v Australia	Sydney	1929	12
=	England v Australia	Melbourne	1998	12
=	Pakistan v India	Chennai	1999	12

Source: *CricInfo*

Football UK

TOP 10 TRANSFER FEES BETWEEN ENGLISH CLUBS

	PLAYER	FROM	TO	YEAR	FEE (£)
1	Rio Ferdinand	Leeds United	Manchester United	2002	30,000,000
2	Rio Ferdinand	West Ham United	Leeds United	2000	18,000,000
3	Alan Shearer	Blackburn Rovers	Newcastle United	1996	15,000,000
4	Dwight Yorke	Aston Villa	Manchester United	1998	12,600,000
5 =	Emile Heskey	Leicester City	Liverpool	2000	11,000,000
=	Robbie Fowler	Liverpool	Leeds United	2001	11,000,000
=	Frank Lampard	West Ham United	Chelsea	2001	11,000,000
8	Chris Sutton	Blackburn Rovers	Chelsea	1999	10,000,000
9	Jonathan Woodgate	Leeds United	Newcastle United	2003	9,000,000
10	Stan Collymore	Nottingham Forest	Liverpool	1995	8,500,000

Transfer fees appear to have spiralled in recent years, but it was a similar story in 1979 when Trevor Francis became the UK's first million-pound footballer. In 1962, Manchester United made Denis Law the UK's first £100,000 player when they bought him from Italian club Torino. The first four-figure transfer fee came in 1905, when Middlesbrough paid Sunderland £1,000 for Alf Common, and the first £100 deal was clinched in 1892 when Aston Villa bought Willie Groves from West Bromwich. When Bill Nicholson signed Jimmy Greaves for Spurs from Milan in 1961 he paid £99,999, but would not pay the other £1 because he did not want Greaves to have to carry the burden of being "Britain's first £100,000 footballer".

TOP 10 LONGEST CONTINUOUS SPELLS IN THE "TOP FLIGHT"

	CLUB*	YEARS
1	Arsenal	83
2	Everton	48
3	Liverpool	40
4	Manchester United	27
5 =	Southampton	24
=	Tottenham Hotspur	24
7	Aston Villa	14
8	Chelsea	13
9	Leeds United	12
10 =	Newcastle United	9
=	West Ham United	9

* Current Premier League clubs only

"Top flight" refers to either the old 1st Division or, since 1992–93, the Premier League. Coventry City ended 34 years in the "top flight" in 2001 when they were relegated from the Premier League.

TOP 10 MOST-CAPPED ENGLAND PLAYERS

	PLAYER	YEARS	GOALS	INTERNATIONAL CAPS
1	Peter Shilton	1970–90	0	125
2	Bobby Moore	1962–73	2	108
3	Sir Bobby Charlton	1958–70	49	106
4	Billy Wright	1946–59	3	105
5	Bryan Robson	1980–91	26	90
6	Kenny Sansom	1979–88	1	86
7	Ray Wilkins	1976–86	3	84
8	Gary Lineker	1984–92	48	80
9	John Barnes	1983–95	11	79
10	Stuart Pearce	1987–2001	5	78

Ray Clemence vied with Peter Shilton in the 1970s for the position of England's first choice goalkeeper, and won 61 caps between 1975 and 1981. It is therefore much speculated how many caps Shilton might have finished his England career with, had the Liverpool and Tottenham Hotspur goalkeeper not been around at the same time.

TOP 10 ENGLAND GOALSCORERS IN FULL INTERNATIONALS

	PLAYER	YEARS	GOALS*
1	Sir Bobby Charlton	1958–70	49
2	Gary Lineker	1984–92	48
3	Jimmy Greaves	1959–67	44
4 =	Tom Finney	1946–58	30
=	Nat Lofthouse	1950–58	30
=	Alan Shearer	1991–2000	30
7	Vivian Woodward	1903–11	29
8	Steve Bloomer	1895–1907	28
9	David Platt	1989–96	27
10	Bryan Robson	1980–91	26

* At end of the 2002 World Cup

Had Gary Lineker not been substituted in his final game, against Sweden in 1992, he may well have gone on to equal or beat Bobby Charlton's record.

TOP 10 CLUBS WITH THE MOST FOOTBALL LEAGUE TITLES

	CLUB	PERIOD	FL TITLES
1	Liverpool	1894–1990	22
2	Manchester United	1908–2001	16
3	Arsenal	1931–2002	12
4 =	Aston Villa	1894–1981	10
=	Everton	1891–1987	10
=	Sunderland	1892–1999	10
7 =	Manchester City	1899–2002	9
=	Sheffield Wednesday	1900–59	9
9 =	Preston North End	1889–2000	8
=	Wolverhampton Wanderers	1889–1989	8

* Including the Premier League

The first of Liverpool's 22 titles was gained in 1893–94, when they won the old 2nd Division title. They won this four times and the 1st Division (now Premier League) a record 18 times between 1900–01 and 1989–90. They have never won the Premiership. Their best season was in 2001–02, when they finished second to champions Arsenal. In 1983–84 they became only the third team after Arsenal and Huddersfield Town to win three consecutive titles.

TOP 10 CLUBS WITH THE MOST FA CUP WINS

	CLUB	YEARS	WINS
1	Manchester United	1909–99	10
2 =	Arsenal	1930–2002	8
=	Tottenham Hotspur	1901–91	8
4	Aston Villa	1887–1957	7
5	Blackburn Rovers	1884–1928	6
=	Liverpool	1965–2001	6
=	Newcastle United	1910–55	6
8 =	Everton	1906–95	5
=	The Wanderers	1872–78	5
=	West Bromwich Albion	1888–1968	5

The first ever FA Cup Final was played in 1872 at the Kennington Oval cricket ground with a crowd of about 2,000, when Wanderers beat Royal Engineers 1–0. Matches were played at Wembley (except for the 1970 replay, which took place at Old Trafford) from 1923, when Bolton Wanderers met West Ham United in front of a record crowd of 126,047, until the ground's closure in 2001, when the Millennium Stadium in Cardiff became the new home of English football.

TOP 10 CLUBS TO SCORE THE MOST GOALS IN A FOOTBALL SEASON

	CLUB	SEASON	DIVISION	GOALS
1	Peterborough United	1960–61	4	134
2 =	Aston Villa	1930–31	1	128
=	Bradford City	1928–29	3(N)	128
4 =	Arsenal	1930–31	1	127
=	Millwall	1927–28	3(S)	127
6	Doncaster Rovers	1946–47	3(N)	123
7	Middlesbrough	1926–27	2	122
8 =	Everton	1927–28	1	121
=	Lincoln City	1951–52	3(N)	121
10	Chester	1964–65	4	119

In 1931–32 Coventry City scored 108 goals in Division 3 (South) yet finished in 12th place. In 1957–58 Manchester City scored 104 1st Division goals – and conceded 100. The last team to score 100 goals was Manchester City (108) in the 1st Division in 2001–02. Peterborough's record tally is even more remarkable because it was achieved in their first season in the Football League. Their top scorer was Terry Bly with 52 goals.

TOP 10 HIGHEST-SCORING FA CUP FINALS*

	MATCH/YEAR	SCORE(S)	GOALS
1 =	Manchester United v Brighton and Hove Albion (1983)	2–2, 4–0	8
=	Tottenham Hotspur v Sheffield United (1901)	2–2, 3–1	8
3 =	Blackburn Rovers v Sheffield Wednesday (1890)	6–1	7
=	Blackpool v Bolton Wanderers (1953)	4–3	7
=	Chelsea v Leeds United (1970)	2–2, 2–1	7
=	Manchester United v Crystal Palace (1990)	3–3, 1–0	7
=	Tottenham Hotspur v Manchester City (1981)	1–1, 3–2	7
8 =	Bury v Derby County (1903)	6–0	6
=	Manchester United v Blackpool (1948)	4–2	6
=	Sheffield Wednesday v West Bromwich Albion (1935)	4–2	6

* Including replays

International Football

TOP 10 TRANSFERS IN WORLD FOOTBALL

	PLAYER/COUNTRY	FROM	TO	YEAR	FEE (£)*
1	Zinedine Zidane, France	Juventus, Italy	Real Madrid, Spain	2001	47,700,000
2	Luis Figo, Portugal	Barcelona, Spain	Real Madrid, Spain	2000	37,400,000
3	Hernan Crespo, Argentina	Parma, Italy	Lazio, Italy	2000	35,700,000
4	Gianluigi Buffon, Italy	Parma, Italy	Juventus, Italy	2001	32,600,000
5	Rio Ferdinand, UK	Leeds United, England	Manchester United, England	2002	30,000,000
6	Gaizka Mendieta, Spain	Valencia, Spain	Lazio, Italy	2001	28,900,000
7	Juan Sebastian Veron, Argentina	Lazio, Italy	Manchester United, England	2001	28,100,000
8	Rui Costa, Portugal	Fiorentina, Italy	AC Milan, Italy	2001	28,000,000
9	Pavel Nedved, Czech Republic	Lazio, Italy	Juventus, Italy	2001	25,500,000
10	Christian Vieri, Italy	Lazio, Italy	Inter Milan, Italy	1999	24,000,000#

* Figures vary slightly from source to source, depending on whether local taxes, agent's fees, and player's commission are included

\# Vieri's transfer was part of a package deal with Nicola Ventola, who was valued at £7 million. Vieri was valued at £24 million

The world's first £100,000 player was Omar Sivori, when he moved to Juventus (Italy) from Río de la Plata (Argentina) in 1957; the world's first £1,000,000 player was Giuseppe Savoldi, when he moved from Bologna (Italy) to Napoli (Italy) in 1975; the world's first £10,000,000 player was Gianluigi Lentini, when he moved from Torino (Italy) to AC Milan (Italy) in June 1992, and the first to be transferred for £20,000,000 was the Brazilian Denilson, when he moved from São Paolo (Brazil) to Real Betis (Spain) in 1998.

TOP 10 COUNTRIES THAT HAVE PLAYED THE MOST MATCHES IN THE FINAL STAGES OF THE WORLD CUP

	COUNTRY	TOURNAMENTS	MATCHES PLAYED
1	Brazil	17	87
2	Germany/West Germany	15	85
3	Italy	15	70
4	Argentina	13	60
5	England	11	50
6	Spain	11	45
7	France	11	44
8	Sweden	10	41
9	Uruguay	10	40
10 =	Russia/USSR	9	37
=	Yugoslavia	9	37

Brazil is the only country to have appeared in the final stages of all 17 competitions.

TOP 10 GOALSCORERS IN INTERNATIONAL FOOTBALL

	PLAYER/COUNTRY	YEARS	GOALS
1	Ferenc Puskás, Hungary/Spain	1945–56	84
2 =	Ali Daei, Iran	1993–2002	77
=	Pelé, Brazil	1957–71	77
4	Sándor Kocsis, Hungary	1948–56	75
5	Gerd Müller, West Germany	1966–74	68
6	Majed Abdullah, Saudi Arabia	1978–94	67
7	Jassem Al-Houwaidi, Kuwait	1992–*	63
8 =	Hossam Hassan, Egypt	1985–*	60
=	Imre Schlosser, Hungary	1906–27	60
10	Kiatisuk Senamuang, Thailand	1993–*	59

* Still active in 2003

Source: Roberto Mamrud, Karel Stokkermans, and RSSSF 1998/2003

Puskás played for Hungary 84 times, and for Spain on four occasions. For all his exploits, his only international honour with Hungary came in 1952 when he captained his country to the Olympic title. He had made his international debut against Austria as an 18 year old in 1945, but rose to world prominence when his Hungary side demolished England 6–3 at Wembley in November 1953.

TOP 10 GOALSCORERS IN THE FINAL STAGES OF THE WORLD CUP

	PLAYER/COUNTRY	YEARS	GOALS
1	Gerd Müller, West Germany	1970–74	14
2	Just Fontaine, France	1958	13
3 =	Pelé, Brazil	1958–70	12
=	Ronaldo, Brazil	1998–2002	12
5 =	Jürgen Klinsman, Germany	1990–98	11
=	Sándor Kocsis, Hungary	1954	11
7 =	Gabriel Batistuta, Argentina	1994–2002	10
=	Teófilo Cubillas, Peru	1970–82	1
=	Grzegorz Lato, Poland	1974–82	10
=	Gary Lineker, England	1986–90	10
=	Helmut Rahn, West Germany	1954–58	100

Source: Jaroslaw Owsianski and RSSSF 2002

Gerd Müller scored his first goal in the World Cup finals at Leon, Mexico, on 3 June 1970 – just 12 minutes from time to save West Germany from embarrassment, beating Morocco 2–1 in their opening match. He had already scored ten goals in the qualifying tournament and added ten more in the 1970 final stages, including two hat-tricks. Just Fontaine's 13 goals in 1958 is a record for one tournament.

TOP 10 — RICHEST FOOTBALL CLUBS

	CLUB/COUNTRY	TURNOVER (£)
1	**Manchester United,** England	117,000,000
2	**Real Madrid,** Spain	103,700,000
3	**Bayern Munich,** Germany	91,600,000
4	**AC Milan,** Italy	89,700,000
5	**Juventus,** Italy	88,400,000
6	**SS Lazio,** Italy	79,400,000
7	**Chelsea,** England	76,700,000
8	**Barcelona,** Spain	75,200,000
9	**Inter Milan,** Italy	68,900,000
10	**AS Roma,** Italy	64,100,000

Source: *Deloitte & Touche Sport*

The latest Deloitte & Touche/SportBusiness International Rich List compares the incomes of the world's top football clubs during the 1999–2000 season. It reveals the extent to which soccer has become a major business enterprise, many clubs making considerably more revenue from commercial activities such as the sale of merchandise and income from TV rights than they do from match admissions.

TOP 10 — COUNTRIES WITH THE MOST REGISTERED FOOTBALL CLUBS

	COUNTRY	REGISTERED CLUBS*
1	**South Africa**	51,944
2	**Russia**	43,700
3	**England**	42,000
4	**Germany**	26,760
5	**France**	21,629
6	**Italy**	20,961
7	**Uzbekistan**	15,000
8	**Japan**	13,047
9	**Brazil**	12,987
10	**Spain**	10,240

* Registered with FIFA through national associations

◄ **World class**
One of the foremost World Cup goalscorers, Ronaldo is seen in action here during the 2002 World Cup tournament.

Rugby Highlights

BIGGEST WINS IN RUGBY UNION FULL INTERNATIONALS

	MATCH (WINNER FIRST)	COMPETITION	DATE	SCORE	WINNING MARGIN
1	Japan v Taiwan	World Cup Qualifier	7 July 2002	155–3	152
2	Hong Kong v Singapore	World Cup Qualifier	27 Oct 1994	164–13	151
3	England v Romania	International	17 Nov 2001	134–0	134
4	Japan v Thailand	International	4 Nov 1996	141–10	131
5 =	Japan v Taiwan	World Cup Qualifier	27 Oct 1998	134–6	128
=	New Zealand v Japan	World Cup	4 June 1995	145–17	128
7	Zimbabwe v Botswana	International	7 Sept 1996	130–10	120
8	Tonga v Korea	World Cup Qualifier	22 Mar 2003	119–0	119
9	Japan v Taiwan	World Cup Qualifier	21 July 2002	120–3	117
10 =	Japan v Sri Lanka	International	16 Dec 1998	116–0	116
=	Namibia v Madagascar	World Cup Qualifier	15 June 2002	116–0	116

In three consecutive World Cup qualifying matches between 30 June and 21 July 2002, Taiwan lost to Korea 119–7, and twice to Japan, 155–3 and 120–3. Toru Kurihara scored a total of 81 points in the latter two matches for Japan. Taiwan's only points in the record-breaking match were for a penalty from Chi-Chung Chen.

RANKED RUGBY UNION COUNTRIES

	COUNTRY	POINTS*
1	England	1,221
2	New Zealand	1,206
3	Australia	1,146
4	France	1,125
5	South Africa	1,045
6	Ireland	875
7	Scotland	793
8	Argentina	755
9	Wales	734
10	Samoa	680

As at 1 April 2003

Source: *Zurich World Rankings*

Zurich World Rankings take into account only the last 12 games played by a nation, as a greater number would give an unrealistic assessment of current form.

MOST-CAPPED RUGBY UNION PLAYERS

	PLAYER	COUNTRY	YEARS	CAPS
1	Philippe Sella	France	1982–95	111
2	Jason Leonard	England/British Lions	1990–2003	107
3	David Campese	Australia	1982–96	101
4	Serge Blanco	France	1980–91	93
5	Sean Fitzpatrick	New Zealand	1987–97	92
6 =	Neil Jenkins	Wales/British Lions	1991–2002	91
=	Rory Underwood	England/British Lions	1984–96	91
8	John Eales	Australia	1991–2001	86
9	George Gregan	Australia	1994–2002	82
10	Mike Gibson	Ireland/British Lions	1964–79	81

As at 1 April 2003

A world-class centre, Philippe Sella was born at Tonniens on Valentine's Day 1962. He started his senior career at Agen but crossed the Channel to play for Saracens, with whom he lifted the Tetley's Bitter Cup for the first time in the club's history, in 1998 – his last game at club level. He made his international debut at the age of 20 in a shock 13–9 defeat by Romania in Bucharest, bowing out 110 matches later in the French side that beat England in the 3rd place play-off match at Pretoria on 22 June 1995, France winning that game 19–9. Sella played on 72 winning French sides during his career. Described by former French coach Jacques Fouroux as "having the strength of a bull but the touch of a piano player", Sella's greatest try was probably at Twickenham against England in 1987, when he intercepted a pass and ran a full 70 yards before touching down.

HIGHEST SCORES IN THE SIX NATIONS CHAMPIONSHIP

	MATCH (WINNER FIRST)	VENUE	YEAR	SCORE
1	England v Italy	Twickenham	2001	80–23
2	Ireland v Italy	Dublin	2000	60–13
3	England v Wales	Twickenham	1998	60–26
4	England v Italy	Rome	2000	59–12
5	Ireland v Wales	Dublin	2002	54–10
6	France v Wales	Wembley	1998	51–0
7	France v Scotland	Murrayfield	1998	51–16
8	England v Wales	Twickenham	2002	50–10
9	England v Ireland	Twickenham	2000	50–18
10	Wales v France	Swansea	1910	49–14

This Top 10 is based on the winning team's scores, not the margin of victory. However, where two nations share the highest score, then margin of victory is used to separate them. The biggest victory by margin is England's 80–23 win over Italy at Twickenham in 2001.

TOP 10 POINTS-SCORERS IN MAJOR INTERNATIONALS*

	PLAYER/COUNTRY	YEARS	POINTS
1	**Neil Jenkins**, Wales/British Lions	1991–2002	1,090
2	**Diego Dominguez**, Italy/Argentina	1989–2003	1,010
3	**Andrew Mehrtens**, New Zealand	1995–2002	932
4	**Michael Lynagh**, Australia	1984–95	911
5	**Matthew Burke**, Australia	1993–2002	833
6	**Gavin Hastings**, Scotland/British Lions	1986–95	733
7	**Jonny Wilkinson**, England/British Lions	1998–2003	697
8	**Grant Fox**, New Zealand	1985–93	645
9	**Hugo Porta**, Argentina	1971–90	590
10	**Nicky Little**, Fiji	1976–2002	556

As at 1 April 2003

Nicknamed "The Ginger Monster", Neil Jenkins became Rugby Union's most prolific points-scorer in the World Cup match against Samoa at Cardiff's Millennium Stadium on 14 October 1999. He scored 16 points, taking his tally to 925, breaking the record of 911 set four years earlier by Australian Michael Lynagh. Sadly for Jenkins, who was also earning his 72nd cap, the game ended in a shock 38–31 defeat by the Samoans.

TOP 10 POINTS-SCORERS IN A BRITISH RUGBY LEAGUE MATCH

	PLAYER	MATCH	YEAR	POINTS
1	**George West**	Hull Kingston Rovers v Brookland Rovers	1905	53
2	**Jim Sullivan**	Wigan v Flimby and Fothergill	1925	44
3	**Sammy Lloyd**	Castleford v Millom	1973	43
4 =	**Darren Carter**	Barrow v Nottingham City	1994	42
=	**Lestyn Harris**	Leeds Rhinos v Huddersfield Giants	1999	42
=	**Dean Marwood**	Workington Town v Highfield	1992	42
=	**Dean Marwood**	Workington Town v Leigh	1995	42
8 =	**Lee Briers**	Warrington Wolves v York	2000	40
=	**Shaun Edwards**	Wigan v Swinton	1992	40
=	**Paul Loughlin**	St. Helens v Carlisle	1986	40
=	**Martin Offiah**	Wigan v Leeds	1992	40
=	**Martin Pearson**	Featherstone Rovers v Whitehaven	1995	40

George Henry West, known as "Titch" because he was only 1.63 m (5 ft 4 in) tall, joined Hull Kingston Rovers from local side Beverley Victoria in 1901. In his record-breaking game against Brookland on 4 March 1905, he also scored a club record 11 tries.

TOP 10 HIGHEST WINNING SCORES IN BRITISH RUGBY LEAGUE HISTORY

	MATCH (WINNER FIRST)	DATE	COMPETITION	SCORE
1	**Huddersfield v Blackpool Gladiators**	26 Nov 1994	Regal Trophy	142–4
2	**Barrow v Nottingham City**	27 Nov 1994	Regal Trophy	138–0
3	**Huddersfield v Swinton Park Rangers**	28 Feb 1914	Challenge Cup	119–2
4	**Wigan v Flimby and Fothergill**	14 Feb 1925	Challenge Cup	116–0
5	**St. Helens v Carlisle**	14 Sept 1986	Lancashire Cup	112–0
6	**Leeds Rhinos v Swinton Lions***	11 Feb 2001	Challenge Cup	106–10
7 =	**Keighley v Highfield#**	23 Apr 1995	Division 2	104–4
=	**St. Helens v Trafford Borough**	15 Sept 1991	Lancashire Cup	104–12
9	**Leeds v Coventry**	12 Apr 1913	League	102–0
10 =	**Hull Kingston Rovers v Nottingham City†**	19 Aug 1990	Yorkshire Cup	100–6
=	**Salford City Reds v Gateshead Thunder**	23 Mar 2003	Arriva Trains Cup	100–12

*At Swinton

At Rochdale, Highfield's home match

† At Doncaster, Nottingham's home match

The highest score in the top division is Leeds' 90–0 victory over Barrow on 11 February 1990. Huddersfield had held the record score in British Rugby League for more than 80 years until 1994, when they beat their own record by a full 23 points. Remarkably, Barrow also broke the old record the very next day when they notched up 138 points against Nottingham. Their winning margin, of 138 points, mirrors that of Huddersfield against Blackpool.

TOP 10 TRY-SCORERS IN THE 2002 BRITISH SUPER LEAGUE

	PLAYER/CLUB	TRIES*
1	**Dennis Moran**, London Broncos	22
2 =	**Darren Albert**, St. Helens	19
=	**Mark Calderwood**, Leeds Rhinos	19
=	**Tevita Vaikona**, Bradford Bulls	19
5 =	**Adam Hughes**, Widnes Vikings	18
=	**Graham Mackay**, Hull FC	18
=	**Tommy Martyn**, St. Helens	18
=	**Keith Senior**, Leeds Rhinos	18
9	**Michael Withers**, Bradford Bulls	17
10	**Darren Rogers**, Castleford Tigers	16

*League matches only

Sydney-born Dennis Moran topped the try-scoring list in Super League VII, in only his second season at the Broncos since joining them from the top Australian club Parrakatta Eels. He scored only eight tries in three seasons with the Eels, but in his first two seasons with the Broncos scored 33.

Racquet Sports

TOP 10 TABLE TENNIS WORLD CHAMPIONSHIP GOLD MEDAL WINNERS

	COUNTRY	MEN'S	WOMEN'S	TOTAL*
1	China	41.5	48	89.5
2	Hungary	42	26	68
3	Japan	23.5	23.5	47
4	Czech Republic	17.5	10.5	28
5	Romania	–	17	17
6 =	England	8	6	14
=	Sweden	14	–	14
8	USA	5	5	10
9	Austria	3	3	6
10	Germany	1	4	5
	All countries	161	154	315

* Includes team events, singles, doubles, and mixed; 0.5 golds were possible when doubles pairs could be of different nationalities – today, only players of the same nationality can play in pairs

Source: *International Table Tennis Federation (ITTF)*

TOP 10 MALE SQUASH PLAYERS

	PLAYER/COUNTRY	AVERAGE POINTS*
1	Peter Nicol, England	1,312.500
2	Jonathon Power, Canada	1,213.844
3	David Palmer, Australia	1,034.375
4	John White, Scotland	634.444
5	Stewart Boswell, Australia	624.219
6	Thierry Lincou, France	474.219
7	Anthony Ricketts, Australia	371.094
8	Ong Beng Hee, Malaysia	354.688
9	Lee Beachill, England	350.781
10	Martin Heath, Scotland	294.444

* As at January 2003

Source: *Dunlop PSA World Rankings*

The players' rankings have been decided by taking the total points they have scored and dividing this figure by the number of tournaments in which they have competed. Peter Nicol confirmed his pre-eminent position by winning the England National Squash Championship in February 2003.

TOP 10 FEMALE SQUASH PLAYERS

	PLAYER/COUNTRY	AVERAGE POINTS*
1	Sarah Fitz-Gerald, Australia	1,956.471
2	Carol Owens, New Zealand	1,745.278
3	Natalie Pohrer, England	1,322.905
4	Linda Charman-Smith, England	915.471
5	Vanessa Atkinson, Netherlands	876.750
6	Tania Bailey, England	860.342
7	Cassie Campion, England	848,750
8	Rachael Grinham, Australia	833,368
9	Rebecca Macree, England	565.095
10	Fiona Geaves, England	542.158

* As at January 2003

Source: *WISPA World Rankings*

Women's squash has been played at an international level since the 1920s. British players dominated the sport until Australian player Heather McKay played undefeated from 1962 to 1980. Fellow Australian Sarah Fitz-Gerald has been World Open Champion on five occasions (1996–98 and 2001–02).

TABLE TENNIS FIRSTS

"INDOOR TENNIS" WAS FIRST PLAYED in the early 1880s by British army officers in India and South Africa, using lids from cigar boxes as bats and the rounded part of champagne corks as balls. English athlete James Gibb introduced the use of celluloid balls after 1900, developing the game he called "Ping Pong", echoing the sound of the ball in play. This was registered in 1901 as a trade name by croquet pioneers John Jacques and by Parker Brothers in the USA. The studded rubber bat surface was invented by E. C. Goode in 1902. The Fédération Internationale de Tennis de Table (International Table Tennis Federation) was founded in 1926, and table tennis first became an Olympic sport in 1988.

TOP 10 COUNTRIES WITH THE MOST WIMBLEDON SINGLES TITLES

		SINGLES TITLES		
	COUNTRY	WOMEN'S	MEN'S	TOTAL
1	USA	46	33	79
2	UK	36	35	71
3	Australia	5	20	25
4	France	6	7	13
5	Germany	8	4	12
6	Sweden	–	7	7
7	Czechoslovakia/ Czech Republic	3	2	5
8	New Zealand	–	4	4
9	Brazil	3	–	3
10	Spain	1	1	2

Men's singles championships have been held – with breaks during both World Wars – since 1877 and women's since 1884.

TOP 10 FEMALE TENNIS PLAYERS*

	PLAYER/COUNTRY	WEEKS AT NO. 1
1	Steffi Graf, Germany	377
2	Martina Navratilova, Czechoslovakia/USA	331
3	Chris Evert, USA	262
4	Martina Hingis, Switzerland	209
5	Monica Seles, Yugoslavia/USA	178
6	Serena Williams, USA	48
7	Lindsay Davenport, USA	38
8	Tracy Austin, USA	22
9	Jennifer Capriati, USA	17
10	Arantxa Sanchez-Vicario, Spain	12

* Based on weeks at No. 1 in WTA rankings (1973 to 25 February 2003)

As well as the most weeks, Steffi Graf achieved the longest unbroken run at No. 1, with 186 weeks (17 August 1987–10 March 1991).

TOP 10 | MALE TENNIS PLAYERS*

	PLAYER/COUNTRY	WEEKS AT NO. 1
1	**Pete Sampras,** USA	286
2	**Ivan Lendl,** Czechoslovakia/USA	270
3	**Jimmy Connors,** USA	268
4	**John McEnroe,** USA	170
5	**Björn Borg,** Sweden	109
6	**Andre Agassi,** USA	87
7	**Stefan Edberg,** Sweden	72
8	**Lleyton Hewitt,** Australia	65
9	**Jim Courier,** USA	58
10	**Gustavo Kuerton,** Brazil	43

* Based on weeks at No. 1 in ATP rankings (1973 to 13 January 2003)

Jimmy Connors had the longest unbroken run at No. 1, a total of 160 weeks, from 29 July 1974 to 22 August 1977. Pete Sampras's longest run was 102 weeks, from 14 April 1996 to 29 March 1998.

◀ **For Pete's sake**
Pete Sampras holds more Grand Slam singles titles than any other man in the history of the sport.

Water Sports

TOP 10 OLYMPIC ROWING COUNTRIES

	COUNTRY	GOLD	MEDALS SILVER	BRONZE	TOTAL
1	USA	29	29	21	79
2 =	East Germany	33	7	8	48
=	Germany*	21	13	14	48
4	Great Britain	21	16	7	44
5	Soviet Union#	12	20	11	43
6	Italy	14	13	10	37
7 =	Canada	8	12	13	33
=	France	6	14	13	33
9	Romania	15	10	7	32
10	Australia	7	8	10	25

* Not including West/East Germany 1968–88

Includes Unified Team of 1992; excludes Russia since then

Olympic rowing dates from 1900 for men, but as recently as 1976 for women. The total includes several discontinued events. Britain's Steve Redgrave has won five Gold medals at five consecutive Olympic Games, 1984–2000, a unique feat in an endurance sport for which he received a knighthood.

TOP 10 FASTEST WINNING TIMES OF THE OXFORD & CAMBRIDGE BOAT RACE

	WINNER	YEAR	TIME (MIN:SEC)
1	Cambridge	1998	16:19
2	Cambridge	1999	16:41
3	Oxford	1984	16:45
4	Oxford	2002	16:54
5	Cambridge	1996	16:58
6	Oxford	1991	16:59
7	Cambridge	1993	17:00
8	Oxford	1985	17:11
9	Oxford	1990	17:15
10 =	Oxford	1974	17:35
=	Oxford	1988	17:35

The Boat Race's course from Putney to Mortlake (6.78 km/4 miles 374 yards) in southwest London has been used since 1843 – although the race was rowed in the opposite direction in 1846, 1856, and 1863.

TOP 10 OLYMPIC CANOEING COUNTRIES

	COUNTRY	GOLD	MEDALS SILVER	BRONZE	TOTAL
1	Hungary	14	25	21	60
2 =	Germany*	22	16	15	53
=	Soviet Union#	30	14	9	53
4	Romania	10	10	14	34
5	East Germany	14	7	9	30
6	Sweden	14	11	4	29
7	France	3	7	16	26
8	Bulgaria	4	5	8	17
9	Canada	3	8	5	16
10 =	Poland	0	5	10	15
=	USA	5	4	6	15
	Great Britain	–	2	1	3

* Not including West/East Germany 1968–88

Includes Unified Team of 1992; excludes Russia since then

Canoeing has been an official Olympic sport since 1936, although it was first seen as a demonstration sport at the 1924 Paris Olympics.

ACROSS THE CHANNEL

ALTHOUGH CHANNEL CROSSINGS had previously been made using flotation aids, the first swimmer to do so unaided was a British sailor, Captain Matthew Webb (1848–83), on 24–25 August 1875. Sustained by beef-tea, beer, coffee, and an omelette, and despite being stung by a starfish, he landed at Calais after 21 hours, 44 minutes, and 55 seconds in the water. It was not until 6 September 1911 that Thomas William Burgess (UK) became the second man to swim the Channel. The first woman to make the crossing was Gertrude Ederle (USA), on 6 August 1926, and in 1934 Edward Temme (UK) became the first person to swim the Channel in both directions.

TOP 10 FASTEST CROSS-CHANNEL SWIMMERS

	SWIMMER/COUNTRY	YEAR	TIME (HR:MIN)
1	Chad Hundeby, USA	1994	7:17
2	Penny Lee Dean, USA	1978	7:40
3	Tamara Bruce, Australia	1994	7:53
4	Philip Rush, New Zealand	1987	7:55
5	Hans Van Goor, Netherlands	1995	8:02
6	Richard Davey, UK	1988	8:05
7	Irene van der Laan, Netherlands	1982	8:06
8 =	Paul Asmuth, USA	1985	8:12
=	Gail Rice, USA	1999	8:12
10	Anita Sood, India	1987	8:15

Source: Channel Swimming Association

An earlier record, of 9 hours 36 minutes, was set in 1973 by Lynne Cox (USA), aged 16 – the minimum permitted age for solo swimmers – while the current female record has been held since 1978 by another American, Penny Dean, who was aged 23 at the time.

TOP 10 MEN'S OLYMPIC 100M FREESTYLE TIMES

	SWIMMER/COUNTRY	YEAR	TIME (SEC)
1	Pieter van den Hoogenband, Netherlands	2000	47.84
2	Pieter van den Hoogenband	2000	48.30
3	Matt Biondi, USA	1988	48.63
4	Pieter van den Hoogenband	2000	48.64
5	Alexander Popov, Russia	2000	48.69
6	Gary Hall Jr., USA	2000	48.73
7 =	Alexander Popov	1996	48.74
=	Michael Klim, USA	2000	48.74
9	Michael Klim	2000	48.80
10	Gary Hall Jr., USA	1996	48.81

Gary Hall Jr. is a member of a family of swimmers: his grandfather Charles Keating was an All-America swimmer at the University of Cincinnati, his uncle a member of the 1976 US Olympics team, while his father, Gary Hall Sr., won silver medals at the 1968 and 1972 Olympics and a bronze in 1976.

TOP 10 WATERSKIERS WITH THE MOST WORLD CUP WINS

	WATERSKIER/COUNTRY	M/F*	SLALOM	JUMP	TOTAL
1	Andy Mapple, UK	M	29	–	29
2	Emma Sheers, Australia	F	2	15	17
3	Jaret Llewellyn, Canada	M	–	16	16
4	Toni Neville, Australia	F	4	7	11
5	Wade Cox, USA	M	10	–	10
6 =	Bruce Neville, Australia	M	–	9	9
=	Kristi Overton-Johnson (née Overton), USA	F	9	–	9
8	Freddy Krueger, USA	M	–	8	8
9	Scot Ellis, USA	M	–	7	7
10 =	Susi Graham, Canada	F	6	–	6
=	Carl Roberge, USA	M	1	5	6

* Male/female

Waterskiing was invented in 1922 by 18-year-old Ralph W. Samuelson of Lake City, Minnesota, USA, using two 2.4-m (8-ft) planks and 30 m (100 ft) of sash cord. The first international governing body, the World Water Ski Union, was established in 1946 in Geneva, Switzerland.

THE 10 LATEST WINNERS OF THE AMERICA'S CUP

	WINNING BOAT/SKIPPER/COUNTRY	CHALLENGER/COUNTRY	SCORE
2003	Alinghi, Russell Coutts, Switzerland	Team New Zealand, New Zealand	5–0
2000	Team New Zealand, Russell Coutts, New Zealand	Prada Luna Rossa, Italy	5–0
1995	Black Magic, Russell Coutts, New Zealand	Young America, USA	5–0
1992	America³, Bill Koch, USA	Il Moro di Venezia, Italy	4–1
1988	Stars and Stripes, Dennis Conner, USA	KZ1, New Zealand	2–0
1987	Stars and Stripes, Dennis Conner, USA	Kookaburra III, Australia	4–0
1983	Australia II, John Bertrand, Australia	Liberty, USA	4–3
1980	Freedom, Dennis Conner, USA	Australia, Australia	4–1
1977	Courageous, Ted Turner, USA	Australia, Australia	4–0
1974	Courageous, Ted Hood, USA	Southern Cross, Australia	4–0

One of the costliest and most prestigious of all sporting events, the America's Cup has also been among the most one-sided, with the New York Yacht Club competitor winning every event from 1851 to 1980.

▼ America's Cup winners
Team New Zealand crosses the finishing line off its home country to take the 2000 America's Cup.

Horsing Around

TOP 10 | HORSE RACING BETTING COUNTRIES

	COUNTRY	VALUE (£)*
1	Japan	22,900,000,000
2	USA	11,180,000,000
3	China (Hong Kong)	6,860,000,000
4	UK	5,160,000,000
5	Australia	3,780,000,000
6	France	3,690,000,000
7	South Korea	2,220,000,000
8	Italy	1,460,000,000
9	Malaysia	920,000,000
10	Canada	790,000,000

* Value of indigenous betting

◀ **Horse racing**
With some 14,000 horses in training, the British horse racing industry employs an estimated 60,000 people directly, and many more in the allied betting industry.

TOP 10 | FASTEST WINNING TIMES OF THE GRAND NATIONAL

	HORSE	YEAR	TIME (MIN:SEC)
1	Mr. Frisk	1990	8:47.8
2	Rough Quest	1996	9:00.8
3	Red Rum	1973	9:01.9
4	Royal Athlete	1995	9:04.6
5	Lord Gwyllene	1997	9:05.8
6	Party Politics	1992	9:06.3
7	Bin Daree	2002	9:09.0
8	Papillon	2000	9:09.7
9	Grittar	1982	9:12.6
10	Bobbyjo	1999	9:14.0

Raced at Aintree since 1839, the present distance of 4 miles 856 yards was established in 1890. The times of the substitute races held at Gatwick in the years 1916–18 are not included.

TOP 10 TRAINERS WITH THE MOST FLAT RACE WINS, 2002

	TRAINER	TOTAL PRIZE MONEY (£)*	WINS
1	Mark Johnston	2,299,831.37	134
2	Mick Channon	1,544,354.93	123
3	Richard Hannon	1,724,799.28	121
4	Sir Michael Stoute	2,410,886,96	105
5	Barry Hills	1,701,228.68	90
6	John Gosden	1,305,968.18	85
7	Tim Easterby	1,461,472.25	81
8 =	John Dunlop	1,440,551.15	79
=	Nick Littmoden	624,615.84	79
10	Ian Balding	795,405.52	67

* Including money won for coming 2nd or 3rd
Source: Racing Post

Mark Johnston received the Flat Trainer of the Year Award for 2002. He and Henry Cecil are the only trainers ever to have trained more than 100 winners in nine consecutive seasons.

TOP 10 NATIONAL HUNT JOCKEYS, 2002

	JOCKEY	PERCENTAGE WON	RUNS	WINS
1	Tony McCoy	32	681	219
2	Richard Johnson	22	481	106
3	Tony Dobbin	23	323	76
4	Mick Fitzgerald	18	298	56
5	Graham Lee	13	378	51
6	Ruby Walsh	28	163	46
7	Warren Marston	13	330	45
8	Ben Fenton	17	239	41
9	Jim Culloty	15	251	39
10	Leighton Aspell	11	324	37

Source: Racing Post

National Hunt jockeys compete for significantly less money than flat-racing jockeys. The top jockey here, Tony McCoy, won £1,371,317 in the 2002–03 season (more than double his nearest rival). On 27 August 2002, riding Mighty Montefalco at Uttoxeter, McCoy broke Richard Dunwoody's previous record total of 1,699 to become the leading British jump jockey.

TOP 10 JOCKEYS OF ALL TIME IN THE UK

	JOCKEY	CHAMPION JOCKEY TITLES	BEST SEASON TOTAL	CAREER FLAT WINNERS*
1	Gordon Richards	26	269	4,870
2	Pat Eddery	11	209	4,575
3	Lester Piggott	11	191	4,513
4	Willie Carson	5	182	3,828
5	Doug Smith	5	173	3,111
6	Joe Mercer	1	164	2,810
7	Fred Archer	13	246	2,748
8	Edward Hide	0	137	2,591
9	George Fordham	14	166	2,587
10	Eph Smith	0	144	2,313

* As at end 2002 season

Gordon Richards' career spanned the period 1921–54, with a record 269 wins in his best season, 1947. Pat Eddery's win on *Silver Patriarch* in the St. Leger at Doncaster on 13 September 1997 elevated him to the position of third member of the exclusive three-member club of jockeys with 4,000 career wins.

TOP 10 SHOW JUMPING HORSE AND RIDER COMBINATIONS, 2002

	HORSE/RIDER	COUNTRY	POINTS
1	Gladdys S, Ludger Beerbaum	Germany	1,531
2	Dobel's Cento, Otto Becker	Germany	1,478
3	Tinka's Boy, Markus Fuchs	Switzerland	1,411
4	For Pleasure, Marcus Ehning	Germany	1,300
5	Goldfever 3, Ludger Beerbaum	Germany	1,263
6	Baloubet De Rouet, Rodrigo Pessoa	Brazil	1,243
7	Dollar du Murier HTS de Seine, Eric Navet	France	1,184
8	De Sjiern, Jeroen Dubbeldam	Netherlands	1,112
9	Loro Piana Havinia, Gianni Govoni	Italy	1,070
10	Shutterfly, Meredith Michaels-Beerbaum	Germany	1,068

Source: *Fédération Equestre Internationale*

The FEI Gandini Show Jumping Riders' World Ranking list ranks riders according to the points they are awarded at competitions throughout the year. Where Games or Championships are held less frequently, a proportion of any points obtained in previous years is retained on the list. For instance, if an event is held every two years, 50 per cent of the points are dropped after one year and the rest after two years.

TOP 10 OLYMPIC EQUESTRIAN COUNTRIES

	COUNTRY	MEDALS GOLD	SILVER	BRONZE	TOTAL
1	Germany*	22	13	12	47
2	USA	9	17	15	41
3	Sweden	17	8	14	39
4	France	11	12	11	34
5	West Germany	11	5	9	25
6	Italy	6	10	7	23
7	Great Britain	5	8	9	22
8	Switzerland	4	10	7	21
9	Netherlands	8	9	2	19
10	Soviet Union#	6	5	4	15

* Not including West Germany or East Germany 1968–88
 # Includes Unified Team of 1992; excludes Russia since then

These figures include the medal totals for both individual and team disciplines: Show Jumping, Three-Day Event, and Dressage. German rider Reiner Klimke won eight medals – six gold and two bronze – in Olympic events during the period 1964–88.

Motor Racing

TOP 10 CART MONEY WINNERS

	DRIVER/COUNTRY	TOTAL PRIZES* ($)
1	**Al Unser Jr.,** USA	18,828,406
2	**Michael Andretti#,** USA	17,928,118
3	**Bobby Rahal,** USA	16,344,008
4	**Emerson Fittipaldi,** Brazil	14,293,625
5	**Mario Andretti,** USA	11,552,154
6	**Rick Mears,** USA	11,050,807
7	**Jimmy Vasser#,** USA	10,627,244
8	**Danny Sullivan,** USA	8,884,126
9	**Paul Tracy#,** Canada	8,825,270
10	**Arie Luyendyk,** Netherlands	7,732,188

* As at 1 January 2003

Still active at end 2002 season

Source: *Championship Auto Racing Teams*

◄ CART success
Michael Andretti, one of the most successful CART riders of all time, races towards the finish at the Milwaukee Mile in 1999.

TOP 10 CONSTRUCTORS WITH THE MOST FORMULA ONE GRAND PRIX WINS

	CONSTRUCTOR/COUNTRY	YEARS	WINS*
1	**Ferrari,** Italy	1951–2002	169
2	**McLaren,** UK	1968–2002	135
3	**Williams,** UK	1979–2002	105
4	**Lotus,** UK	1960–87	79
5	**Brabham,** UK	1964–85	35
6	**Benetton,** Italy	1986–97	27
7	**Tyrrell,** UK	1971–83	23
8	**BRM,** UK	1959–72	17
9	**Cooper,** UK	1958–67	16
10	**Renault,** France	1979–83	15

* To the end of 2002 season

Having finished second in two races (Monaco GP and Italian GP) in the inaugural World Championship season, Ferrari eventually registered their first win in the fifth race of the 1951 season, the British Grand Prix at Silverstone on 14 July, with José Froilan Gonzalez of Argentina as the driver. The only race McLaren did not win in the 1988 season was the Italian Grand Prix at Monza, which was won by Gerhard Berger of Austria in a Ferrari.

TOP 10 FASTEST GRAND PRIX RACES, 2002

	GRAND PRIX	CIRCUIT	WINNER'S SPEED (KM/H)	(MPH)
1	**Italy**	Monza	241.090	149.807
2	**Belgium**	Spa-Francorchamps	225.970	140.412
3	**Japan**	Suzuka	212.645	132.123
4	**Germany**	Hockenheim	209.263	130.031
5	**San Marino**	Enzo e Dino Ferrari	205.613	127.763
6	**Spain**	Catalunya	203.753	126.607
7	**Great Britain**	Silverstone	201.649	125.300
8	**USA-Indianapolis**	Indianapolis	201.476	125.192
9	**Brazil**	Interlagos	200.098	124.336
10	**France**	Magny-Cours	199.136	123.738

Grand Prix racing is European in origin. Since the late 19th century, car races took place on public roads, which is reflected in the construction of today's circuits, which incorporate chicanes and bends that test drivers' skills to the limit. Formula One began after World War II, when a distinction was made between these and less powerful Formula Two cars.

TOP 10 FASTEST WINNING SPEEDS OF THE INDIANAPOLIS 500

	DRIVER/COUNTRY	CAR	YEAR	SPEED (KM/H)	(MPH)
1	**Arie Luyendyk,** Netherlands	Lola-Chevrolet	1990	299.307	185.981
2	**Rick Mears,** USA	Chevrolet-Lumina	1991	283.980	176.457
3	**Bobby Rahal,** USA	March-Cosworth	1986	274.750	170.722
4	**Juan Pablo Montoya,** Colombia	G Force-Aurora	2000	269.730	167.607
5	**Emerson Fittipaldi,** Brazil	Penske-Chevrolet	1989	269.695	167.581
6	**Helio Castroneves,** Brazil	Dallara-Chevrolet	2002	267.954	166.499
7	**Rick Mears,** USA	March-Cosworth	1984	263.308	163.612
8	**Mark Donohue,** USA	McLaren-Offenhauser	1972	262.619	162.962
9	**Al Unser,** USA	March-Cosworth	1987	260.995	162.175
10	**Tom Sneva,** USA	March-Cosworth	1983	260.902	162.117

Because American drivers start on the run and race round oval circuits, consistently higher average lap speeds are achieved than in Formula One. Car racing in the USA on purpose-built circuits dates back to 1909, when Indianapolis Speedway opened. CART (Championship Auto Racing Teams, Inc.) was formed in 1978, and in 1996 the Indy Racing League was established in response to disputes over regulations governing the Indy 500. Indy 500 races have counted for CART points in 1979, 1980, and 1983–95.

TOP 10 FORMULA ONE DRIVERS WITH THE MOST GRAND PRIX WINS

	DRIVER/COUNTRY	CAREER	WINS*
1	**Michael Schumacher,** Germany	1991–	64
2	**Alain Prost,** France	1980–93	51
3	**Ayrton Senna,** Brazil	1984–94	41
4	**Nigel Mansell,** UK	1980–95	31
5	**Jackie Stewart,** UK	1965–73	27
6 =	**Jim Clark,** UK	1960–68	25
=	**Niki Lauda,** Austria	1971–85	25
8	**Juan Manuel Fangio,** Argentina	1950–58	24
9	**Nelson Piquet,** Brazil	1978–91	23
10	**Damon Hill,** UK	1992–99	22

* To the end of 2002 season

Michael Schumacher started his Formula One career with Jordan in 1991, but after just one race moved to Benetton. He took his first Grand Prix win, the Belgian, in 1992, his first full racing season. He overtook Alain Prost's career points record by winning the 2001 Japanese Grand Prix.

▼ **"The Maestro"**
King of the race track during the 1950s, Juan Manuel Fangio (1911–95) won 24 Grand Prix races and secured a record five world titles.

Sports Media

TOP 10 SPORTS PROGRAMMES WITH THE LARGEST TV AUDIENCES IN THE UK, 2002

	COMPETITION OR MATCH	DATE	CHANNEL	AVERAGE AUDIENCE
1	World Cup 2002: England v Denmark	15 June	BBC1	12,468,000
2	World Cup 2002: England v Brazil	21 June	BBC1	12,461,000
3	World Cup 2002: England v Nigeria	12 June	BBC1	12,224,000
4	World Cup 2002: England v Sweden	2 June	ITV1	12,209,000
5	World Cup 2002: Argentina v England	7 June	BBC1	11,999,000
6	World Cup 2002: Post-match	7 June	BBC1	10,495,000
7	World Cup 2002: Germany v Brazil	30 June	BBC1	10,076,000
8	Match of the Day Live: European Championship Qualifier: England v Macedonia	16 Oct	BBC1	9,321,000
9	Grand National	6 Apr	BBC1	8,542,000
10	Commonwealth Games 2002: Closing Ceremony	4 Aug	BBC1	8,504,000

Source: *BARB/SPC*

While all England's earlier 2002 World Cup matches attracted 10 million-plus viewers, the largest TV sports audience of the year was not for the one in which they were knocked out by losing 1–0 to Brazil, but for the preceding game in which they were victorious, defeating Denmark 3–0, with goals scored by Ferdinand, Owen, and Heskey. Respectable though these audience figures are by contemporary standards, the multiplicity of channels now available and the use of video enabling viewers to record and view outside real time, mean that they are little more than a third of the estimated 32.5 million who watched the 1970 World Cup, when England lost to Brazil, or the 32 million who in 1966 saw England's World Cup defeat of West Germany.

TOP 10 SPORTS BIOGRAPHIES IN THE UK, 2002

	TITLE/AUTHOR(S)	SALES
1	Keane: The Autobiography, Roy Keane and Eamon Dunphy	214,293
2	Murray Walker: Unless I'm Very Much Mistaken, Murray Walker	205,476
3	Taking on the World, Ellen MacArthur	135,779
4	Blessed: The Autobiography, George Best	118,039
5	Cloughie: Walking on Water – The Autobiography, Brian Clough	67,589
6	Serious, John McEnroe	65,361
7	Opening Up: My Autobiography, Mike Atherton	61,326
8	Real Monty: The Autobiography of Colin Montgomerie, Colin Montgomerie and Lew Mair	48,118
9	It's Not About the Bike: My Journey Back to Life, Lance Armstrong	31,904
10	King of the World, David Remnick	28,964

Source: *Nielsen BookScan*

TOP 10 SPORT FILMS

	FILM	YEAR	SPORT
1	Rocky IV	1985	Boxing
2	Space Jam	1996	Basketball
3	The Waterboy	1998	American football
4	Days of Thunder	1990	Stock car racing
5	Cool Runnings	1993	Bobsleighing
6	A League of Their Own	1992	Baseball
7	Remember the Titans	2000	American football
8	Rocky III	1982	Boxing
9	Rocky V	1990	Boxing
10	Rocky	1976	Boxing

The boxing ring dominates Hollywood's most successful sports-based epics (based on worldwide box-office income), with all those in the Top 10 having made at least $120 million.

TOP 10 BESTSELLING SPORTS VIDEOS IN THE UK, 2002

	VIDEO	SPORT
1	Roy Keane – As I See It	Football
2	The Premiership – Own Goals and Gaffs	Football
3	Liverpool FC – The Official History	Football
4	Arsene Wenger's Magic Hat	Football
5	Bill McLaren – Rugby at Its Best	Rugby
6	WWE – Wrestlemania X8	Wrestling
7	Germany 1 England 5	Football
8	Manchester United – The Official History	Football
9	Liverpool FC – No Heart as Big	Football
10	Murray Walker's F1 Greats	Formula 1

Source: *British Video Association*

TOP 10 LATEST BBC "SPORTS PERSONALITY OF THE YEAR" WINNERS

YEAR	WINNER	SPORT
2002	Paula Radcliffe	Athletics
2001	David Beckham	Football
2000	Steve Redgrave	Rowing
1999	Lennox Lewis	Boxing
1998	Michael Owen	Football
1997	Greg Rusedski	Tennis
1996	Damon Hill	Motor racing
1995	Jonathan Edwards	Athletics
1994	Damon Hill	Motor racing
1993	Linford Christie	Athletics

First presented in 1954, when it was won by athlete Chris Chataway, this award is based on a poll of BBC television viewers. At the end of 1999, Muhammad Ali was voted Sports Personality of the Century.

TOP 10 SINGLES BY SPORTS TEAMS IN THE UK

	TITLE	TEAM	YEAR
1	Back Home	England World Cup Squad	1970
2	World in Motion	England World Cup Squad with New Order	1990
3	This Time We'll Get It Right	England World Cup Squad	1982
4	Anfield Rap (Red Machine in Full Effect)	Liverpool FC	1988
5	We Have a Dream	Scotland World Cup Squad	1982
6	Ole Ola (Muhler Brasileira)	Rod Stewart with Scotland World Cup Squad	1978
7	Ossie's Dream (Spurs are on Their Way to Wembley)	Tottenham Hotspur FC	1981
8	Blue is the Colour	Chelsea FC	1972
9	Snooker Loopy	Matchroom Mob with Chas & Dave	1986
10	Leeds United	Leeds United FC	1972

All these singles made the UK Top 10, and the first two were chart-topping hits. Some of the sportsmen (none of the records features women) received professional help from the likes of New Order and Rod Stewart, while Chas & Dave, who bolstered the only non-football entry (by the Matchroom Mob of snooker professionals), also had an uncredited appearance on the Spurs single at No. 7.

TOP 10 MOST EXPENSIVE OLYMPIC GAMES TV RIGHTS

	VENUE	YEAR	RIGHTS ($)
1	Athens	2004	394,000,000
2	Sydney	2000	363,000,000
3	Atlanta	1996	240,000,000
4	Turin*	2006	135,000,000
5	Salt Lake City*	2002	120,000,000
6	Barcelona	1994	90,000,000
7	Nagano*	1998	72,000,000
8	Seoul	1988	26,000,000
9	Lillehammer*	1994	24,000,000
10	Los Angeles	1984	19,800,000

Winter Games

▼ A run for their money

As the Olympic Games attract ever-larger international TV audiences, so the costs, levels of sponsorship, and TV rights have escalated to multi-million dollar levels.

Leisure Pursuits

PARTICIPATION ACTIVITIES IN THE UK

	ACTIVITY	PERCENTAGE MEN*	ACTIVITY	PERCENTAGE WOMEN*
1	Walking/hiking	19	Walking/hiking	23
2	Snooker	15	Keep fit	18
3	Swimming	13	Swimming	17
4	Cycling	12	Cycling	7
5	Football	10	Racket sports	4
6	Golf	9	Snooker	4
7	Keep fit	8	Weights	4
8	Weights	8	Running/athletics	3
9	Running/athletics	7	Bowls	2
10	Racket sports	6	Darts	2

* Based on the percentage of people over age 16 participating in each activity in the four weeks before interview

Source: *Office for National Statistics*, UK 2000 Time Use Survey

In recent years, walking, keep fit/yoga, cycling, and weight training have become much more popular, while activities such as snooker and darts have declined in popularity.

▼ In the swim
Swimming is one of the UK's most popular leisure activities, while competitive swimming and diving attract more lottery funding than any other sport.

SPORTS WITH THE MOST LOTTERY FUNDING IN THE UK

	SPORT	LOTTERY FUNDING* (£)
1	Swimming and diving	263,218,876
2	Association football	191,872,718
3	Athletics	164,242,095
4	Lawn tennis	84,946,960
5	Cricket	71,538,169
6	Hockey	61,763,185
7	Basketball	42,292,674
8	Rugby (union and league)	37,699,365
9	Bowls	37,414,798
10	Ice skating	35,400,811

* Total capital awards to date, February 2003

Source: *Sport England*

If funding for multiple activities was included, multi-sports would come third in the list with £169,917,743 allocated in 204 awards.

TOP 10 MOST POPULAR TYPES OF TOY

	TYPE OF TOY	MARKET SHARE PERCENTAGE (2000)
1	Video games	23.2
2	Infant/pre-school toys	11.6
3 =	Activity toys	10.8
=	Other toys	10.8
5	Games/puzzles	10.5
6	Dolls	9.7
7	Toy vehicles	8.2
8	Soft toys	6.5
9	Action figures	4.4
10	Ride-on toys	4.2

Source: *Eurotoys/The NPD Group Worldwide*

This list is based on a survey of toy consumption in the European Union, and can be taken as a reliable guide to the most popular types of toy in the developed world.

TOP 10 TOY-BUYING COUNTRIES

	COUNTRY*	SPENDING ON TOYS PER CAPITA (2000) ($)
1	USA	126.1
2	UK	90.1
3	Canada	87.9
4	Belgium	73.7
5	Japan	72.4
6	Denmark	58.8
7	France	57.4
8	Ireland	56.1
9	Sweden	51.3
10	Switzerland	50.5

* Of those covered by survey

Source: *Euromonitor*

FIRST COMPUTER GAMES

THE FIRST ARCADE GAME, the precursor of all modern computer games, was invented by Nolan Bushnell and Ted Dabney and given the name "Computer Space". Described as "a cosmic dogfight between a spaceship and a flying saucer", it went on sale in 1971, but proved too complicated to achieve wide appeal. Its creators, along with Al Alcorn, then designed Pong, a game launched in 1972 that achieved enormous success, selling about 100,000 units. Nolan formed a company called Syzygy, later renamed Atari, and in 1975 sold a version of Pong to be played on a TV set, beginning the era of the home computer games console.

FIRST FACT

THE 10 MOST DANGEROUS SPORTS IN THE UK

	ACTIVITY	DEATHS OVER FIVE-YEAR PERIOD	TOTAL PARTICIPATIONS PER YEAR	RISK OF DEATH PER 100 MILLION PARTICIPATIONS*
1	Air sports	51	1,000,000	1,000
2	Caving	11	350,000	600
3	Mountaineering	51	4–8,000,000	100–200
4	Motor sports	65	11,000,000	120
5	Boating and sailing	69	23,000,000	60
6 =	Fishing	50	37,000,000	30
=	Horse riding	62	39,000,000	30
8	Swimming and diving	191	370,000,000	10
9	Hockey	2	9,000,000	4
10	Rugby	2	12,000,000	3

* Ranked by number of times a sport is participated in, not by number of adults taking part

Source: *Professor David Ball*, Sports Exercise and Injury

TOP 10 COUNTRIES SPENDING THE MOST ON CONSOLE AND COMPUTER GAMES

	COUNTRY	SALES (2000) ($) TOTAL	PER CAPITA
1	Canada	1,724,000,000	56.1
2	USA	14,348,000,000	52.1
3	UK	2,648,000,000	44.6
4	Japan	4,155,000,000	32.7
5	Germany	2,648,000,000	21.1
6	South Korea	1,724,000,000	20.9
7	Italy	990,000,000	16.5
8	Sweden	113,000,000	12.7
9	Australia	219,000,000	11.4
10	France	639,000,000	9.7

Source: *Euromonitor*

Acknowledgments

Special US research: Dafydd Rees
Sport consultant: Ian Morrison

Alexander Ash; Caroline Ash; Nicholas Ash; Professor David Ball; David B. Barrett; Richard Braddish; Thomas Brinkoff; Tina Cardy; Pete Compton; Joanna Corcoran-Wunsch; Kaylee Coxall; Luke Crampton; Adrian Crookes; Sidney S. Culbert; Alain P. Dornic; Philip Eden; Raymond Fletcher; Christopher Forbes; Cullen Geiselman; Russell E. Gough; Monica Grady; Andrew Grantham; Stan Greenberg; Andrew Hemming; Duncan Hislop; Doug Hopper; Andreas Hörstemeier; Richard Hurley; Alan Jeffreys; Todd M. Johnson; Tessa Kale; Larry Kilman; Rex King; Robert Lamb; Dr. Benjamin Lucas; John Malam; Roberto Mamrud; Dr. Gregg Marland; Chris Mead; Roberto Ortiz de Zarate; Sarah Owen; Tony Pattison; Adrian Room; Bill Rudman; Robert Senior; Karel Stockkermans; Mitchell Symons; Thomas Tranter; Alexis Tregenza; Lucy T. Verma; Tony Waltham; Dickon White; Nigel Wilcockson; Peter Wynne-Thomas

Academy of Motion Picture Arts and Sciences (AMPAS) – Oscar statuette is the registered trademark and copyrighted property of the Academy of Motion Picture Arts and Sciences; ACNielsen MMS; *Ad Age Global*; The Advertising Association; Aintree Racecourse; *Airline Business*; Air Transport Intelligence; American Library Association; America's Cup; Amnesty International; *Amusement Business*; *The Art Newspaper*; Art Sales Index; Association of Tennis Professionals (ATP); Audit Bureau of Circulations Ltd; Bat Conservation International; BBC Radio 1; BBC Radio 4; Booker Prize; *BP Statistical Review of World Energy 2002*; British Academy of Film and Television Arts (BAFTA); British Broadcasting Corporation (BBC); British Cave Research Association; *British Crime Survey*; British Museum; British Phonographic Industry (BPI); British Record Industry Trust (BRIT Trust); British Video Association (BVA); Broadcasters Audience Research Board Ltd (BARB); *Business Week*; Cameron Mackintosh Ltd; Cannes Film Festival; Central Intelligence Agency (CIA); Centre for Environmental Initiatives; Championship Auto Racing Teams (CART); Channel Swimming Association; *Checkout*; Christian Research; Christie's;

Classical Music; *The Columbia Granger's Index to Poetry in Anthologies*; Columbia University (Pulitzer Prizes); Commission for Distilled Spirits; CricInfo; *Criminal Statistics England & Wales*; CyberAtlas; Deloitte & Touche Sports; Department of Environment, Food and Rural Affairs (DEFRA); Department of Health; *The Economist*; Electoral Reform Society; Elephant Trade Information System (ETIS); Energy Information Administration (EIA); English Tourism Council; Environmental Technology Center; Euromonitor; European Film Academy; Eurotoys; *Evening Standard*; Fédération Equestre Internationale (FEI); Fédération Internationale de Football Association (FIFA); The Financial Times Ltd; Florida Museum of Natural History; Food and Agriculture Organization of the United Nations (FAO); *Forbes*; Forestry Commission; *Fortune*; Fund for the Replacement of Animals in Medical Experiments (FRAME); Gemstone Publishing, Inc; General Register Office for Scotland; Global Reach; Health and Safety Executive (HSE); Higher Education Statistics Agency (HESA); Home Accident Surveillance System (HASS); Home Office; Imperial War Museum; Indianapolis Motor Speedway; InsideHoops.com; Interbrand; International Agency for Research on Cancer; International Association of Athletics Federations (IAAF); International Atomic Energy Agency; International Coffee Organisation; International Intellectual Property Alliance (IIPA); International Labour Organization (ILO); International Olympic Committee (IOC); International Paralympic Committee; International Shark Attack File; International Skating Union (ISU); International Ski Federation (FIS); International Table Tennis Federation (ITTF); International Tea Committee Ltd; International Telecommunication Union (ITU); International Union for the Conservation of Nature (IUCN); International Water Ski Federation (IWSF); International Weightlifting Federation (IWF); Inter-Parliamentary Union; Interpol; Kennel Club; Lloyds Register-Fairplay Ltd; Lycos; McDonald's; *Melody Maker*; MRIB; MTV; Museum of Rugby; Music Control UK; Music Information Database; National Academy of Recording Arts and Sciences, USA (NARAS); National Aeronautics and Space Administration, USA (NASA); National Basketball Association, USA (NBA); National

Football League, USA (NFL); National Fraud Information Center, National Consumers League, USA; Natural History Museum; NetRatings; *New Musical Express (NME)*; Nielsen; Nielsen BookScan; Nielsen Media Research; Nobel Foundation; The NPD Group Worldwide; Office for National Statistics (ONS); Official UK Charts Company; *OperaGlass*; Organisation Internationale des Constructeurs d'Automobiles (OICA); *The Overstreet Comic Book Price Guide*; Penguin Books; Performing Right Society; Pet Food Manufacturers' Association (PFMA); Petplan; Phobics Society; The Poetry Poll; Pollstar; Professional Golfers' Association (PGA); Professional Squash Association (PSA); *Racing Post*; Radio Joint Audience Research Ltd (RAJAR); *Railway Gazette International*; Royal Brompton National Heart and Lung Hospital; Royal Opera House, Covent Garden; RSSSF; Russell Reynolds Associates; Ryder Cup; *Screen Digest*; SearchEngineWatch.com; Shakespeare Centre; Society of London Theatre (SOLT) (Olivier Awards); Society of Motor Manufacturers and Traders Ltd; Sony Radio Academy Awards; Sotheby's; S. P. Consultants; Sport England; Star UK; *Stores*; Students for the Exploration and Development of Space (SEDS); *The Sunday Times*; Swiss Re; Tate Britain; Tate Modern; TeleGeography; TNS; Tour de France; Union Cycliste Internationale (UCI); United Nations (UN); United Nations Educational, Scientific and Cultural Organization (UNESCO); United Nations Environment Programme (UNEP); United Nations Population Division (UNPD); United Nations System-wide Earthwatch; Universal Postal Union (UPU); US Census Bureau; *Variety*; Verifone; VH1, USA; Victoria & Albert Museum; WebElements; Whitbread Book Awards; Women's International Squash Players Association (WISPA); Women's Tennis Association (WTA); World Association of Newspapers (WAN); *World Atlas of Coral Reefs*; World Bank; *World Christian Trends*; World Conservation Monitoring Centre (WCMC); World Health Organization (WHO); World Intellectual Property Organization (WIPO); World Motocross Championships; *World of Learning*; World Snowboarding Federation (WSF); World's Strongest Man Contest; World Tourism Organization (WTO); Zurich World Rankings;

Acknowledgments

Publisher's acknowledgments

Dorling Kindersley would like to thank the following for their contributions: Editorial Sharon Lucas; Design Marianne Markham; Picture Research Franziska Marking, Cynthia Frazer, Marie Osborn; Picture Library Hayley Smith, Richard Dabb, Claire Bowers; Design Revolution

Index

Ursula Caffrey

Packager's acknowledgments

The Bridgewater Book Company would like to thank Susie Behar, Alison Bolus, Stephanie Horner, and Tom Kitch for editorial assistance, and Richard Constable, Chris Morris, Warrick Sears, and Barbara Theisen for their design work.

Picture Credits

The publisher would like to thank the following for their kind permission to reproduce their images: (Position key: c=centre, b=bottom, r=right, l=left, t=top)

1: Getty Images/Alan Klehr (b); Getty Images/Alan Thornton (t); 2–3: Corbis/Alan Schein Photography (t), 2–3: Image Quest 3-D/Scott Tuason (b); 4: Pa Photos (b); 5: Getty Images/Sylvaine Achernar; 6–7: Corbis/Rick Doyle; 8–9: Corbis/Paul Hudson; 10: NASA; 11: NASA; 12: NASA; 13: Science Photo Library/NASA; 14–15: Corbis/Brandon D. Cole; 17: Getty Images/Sylvaine Achernar; 18–19: Corbis/Galen Rowell; 23: Science Photo Library/ArSciMed; 24–25: Popperfoto/Reuters; 27: Rex Features/El Tiempo; 28–29: Image Quest 3-D/Scott Tuason; 43: Corbis/Yann Arthus-Bertrand; 44: Photodisc; 45: Photodisc; 47: Photodisc; 48–49: Corbis/Gavriel Jecan; 50: Foodpix; 52: Corbis/Peter Turnley; 54: Corbis/Wolfgang Kaehler; 55: Corbis/Lindsay Hebberd; 57: Getty Images/Luc Beziat; 60–61: ImageState/Pictor/Jurgen Magg Photography; 63: Press Association Picture Library/EPA; 64: Getty Images/Tony Garcia; 67: Getty Images/Paul Edmondson; 69: Hulton Archive/Getty Images; 70: Corbis/Steve Kaufman; 71: Corbis/Galen Rowell; 74–75: Getty Images/Austin Brown; 82: Panos Pictures/Jean-Léo Dugast; 84: Press Association Picture Library/EPA; 85: Corbis/Bettmann; 86–87: Axiom/Jim Holmes; 88–89: Getty Images/Ron Chapple; 90: Getty Images/China Tourism Press; 94: Panos Pictures/Jeremy Hartley; 97: Camera Press/Tom Wargacki; 98: P A Photos/Matthew Fearn; 101: Getty Images/Derek P. Redfearn; 102–103: DK Picture Library/Alistair Duncan; 105: Courtesy of Sotheby's Picture Library, London; 106: Retna Pictures Ltd/ Michael Putland; 108–109: Getty Images/Darrell Gulin; 110: P A Photos/EPA; 112: Kobal Collection/Paramount; 113: Redferns/Michael Ochs Archives; 114: Redferns/Nicky J. Sims; 115: Redferns/George Chin; 117: Redferns/James Dittiger; 119: Redferns/John Gumon; 120: Redferns/David Redfern; 122: Corbis/Lynn Goldsmith; 123: Redferns; 124: Rex Features/Alex Oliveira; 125: Rex Features/Matt Baron/BEI; 127: Pa Photos; 128: Redferns/Martin Philbey; 129: Redferns/John Gunion; 130: Kobal Collection/Paramount; 132–133: Corbis/Alan Schein photography; 134: Pa Photos/Jordan Peter Jordan; 135: Rex Features/Donald Cooper; 136: Album/Lucus Films LTD & TM/Keith Hamshere; 138: Dinodia Picture Agency; 139: Aquarius Library/Miramax; 140: Kobal Collection/Columbia/ Marvel; 141: Kobal Collection/Wing Nut Films/Pierre Vinet.; 143: Rex Features/Dreanworks/Everett (EVT); 145: Kobal Collection/ Miramax/David James; 146: Rex Features/Miramax/Everett (EVT); 148: Kobal Collection/Paramount/Miramax/Clive Coote; 150: Kobal Collection/Focus Features/Studio Canal/Guy Ferrandis; 152: Kobal Collection/Universal/Vivian Zink; 154: Kobal Collection/Paramount; 156: Kobal Collection/20th Century Fox; 157: Rex Features/Warner Br/Everett (EVT); 159: Kobal Collection/Warner Bros/Bob Marshak; 160: DK Picture Library/Magnus Rew; 162: Getty Images/Don Smetzer; 164–165: Getty Images/Alan Klehr; 166: Corbis/SABA/ Keith Dannemiller; 169: Corbis/David Samuel Robbins; 170: Getty Images/David Seed Photography; 172: Getty Images/Bruce Hands; 174–175: Corbis/David Samuel Robbins; 176: Corbis/SABA/Mark Peterson; 177: Rex Features; 178: Corbis/Mark E. Gibson; 179: Corbis/Francesca Muntada; 180–181: Getty Images/Yellow Dog Productions; 182: Rex Features; 184: NASA; 192–193: Getty Images; 195: Getty Images/VCL (tr); 196: Pa Photos/EPA; 198: Corbis; 200: Hulton Archive/Getty Images/American Stock/Archive Photos; 201: Hulton Archive/Getty Images; 202–203: alamy.com/ Charlie Newham; 203: Getty Images/VCL (tr); 204: Rex Features; 206–207: Getty Images/Alan Thornton; 208: Empics Ltd/Aubrey Washington; 210: Empics Ltd/Tony Marshall; 211: Empics Ltd/Tony Marshall; 212: Getty Images/Al Bello/Allsport; 213: Getty Images/ Agence Zoom; 214: Empics Ltd/Adam Davy; 215: Empics Ltd/Tony Marshall; 216: Action Plus; 217: Action Plus; 218: P A Photos/EPA; 225: Topham Picturepoint/John Babb/Pro Sport; 229: Empics Ltd/Tony Marshall; 230: Empics Ltd; 231: Getty Images/David Cannon; 233: Empics Ltd/Fotopress Photographer Phil Walter; 234: Empics Ltd/Forum Press; 235: Corbis/Rick Doyle; 236: Getty Images/David Norton; 238: Empics Ltd/DPA Photographer Gero Breloer; 239: Empics Ltd/Sport and General; 240: Empics Ltd/John Marsh; 241: Empics Ltd/Steve Etherington; 243: Corbis/Wally McNamee; 256: Album /Lucus Films LTD & TM/ Keith Hamshere.

All other images © Dorling Kindersley. For further information see: www.dkimages.com